Copywriting for the Electronic Media

From the Wadsworth Series in Mass Communication

GENERAL

BROADCAST AND CABLE

Copywriting for the Electronic Media

A Practical Guide

Milan D. Meeske
University of Central Florida

R. C. Norris
Texas Christian University

Wadsworth Publishing Company
Belmont, California
A Division of Wadsworth, Inc.

Senior Editor: **Rebecca Hayden**

Editorial Associate: **Naomi Brown**

Production Editor: **Deborah Oren McDaniel**

Designer: **Merle Sanderson**

Print Buyer: **Barbara Britton**

Copy Editor: **Steven W. Hiatt**

Indexer: **D. Eugene Evans**

Cover: **Merle Sanderson**

Printed in the United States of America

1 2 3 4 5 6 7 8 9 10—91 90 89 88 87   49

ISBN 0-534-06636-4

Library of Congress Cataloging in Publication Data
Meeske, Milan D.
   Copywriting for the electronic media.

   (Wadsworth series in mass communication)
   Bibliography: p.
   Includes index.
   1. Advertising copy.   2. Broadcast advertising.
I. Norris, R. C.   II. Title.   III. Series.
HF5825.M38   1987   659.14   86-5674
ISBN 0-534-06636-4

To Margaret and Marylee

Contents

Preface

Two major premises guided our planning of this book. The first is that students need plenty of practice if they are to become effective copywriters. Student copywriters are of course accustomed to seeing and hearing slick, high-budget commercials for national advertisers. They typically want to imitate such commercials right away in class. Our second premise, however, is that it's preferable to learn to write for the local station—Little Rock, Omaha, Albany—where budgets are smaller and production facilities less sophisticated. That's where the beginning jobs are, not in New York, Chicago, Los Angeles, or even Atlanta. This book thus seeks to prepare students for the real world of beginning copywriting—the small or medium market—from which they can move on when they gain experience.

This text thus emphasizes exercises that can teach and sharpen specific copywriting skills, using realistic situations typical of copywriting in small- and medium-market stations. Our experience as commercial broadcast copywriters forms the basis of the text and the exercises. The exercises have been tested in the classroom and examined by commercial broadcasters and agency writers.

This approach combines the information of a textbook with the practicality of a workbook. Over seventy exercises are included, more than enough for a normal fifteen-week semester. We believe that this is a reasonable and practical approach to teaching what is considered by many an art. We have sought to include the usual copywriting materials, along with materials not always found in texts. This material includes a chapter on copywriting style and another on the legal concerns of copywriting. To help students understand our points, we've included examples of storyboards and actual copy that aired. The examples vary from ads used by the smallest stations to spots prepared by national agencies. This variety strengthens the real-world copywriting orientation that we've sought to convey.

An Overview of Contents

The first six chapters deal with writing for both radio and television. We open with a discussion of the copywriter's role in broadcasting and cable operations. A day in the life of a copywriter is described to give students an idea of actual working conditions at different types of stations. Then we discuss the role of creativity along with the qualifications needed by a copywriter. Chapter 3 presents the basic mechanics of copywriting and format, the importance of neatness, methods of making corrections in copy, and a brief grammar review. Chapter 4 introduces the student to organizing material in preparation for writing a broadcast spot. Then we look at consumer motivation, followed by the anatomy of a commercial, station promo, or PSA.

The next two chapters deal exclusively with copywriting for radio, while chapters 9 and 10 parallel the previous two with a focus on television and cable operations. The final three chapters deal in turn with the writer as an image maker, the legal restrictions facing the copywriter, and the copywriter's role in an advertising campaign.

Following each chapter are exercises so that students can practice the skills taught in that chapter. Because each chapter builds on the previous ones, material learned in doing earlier exercises helps in doing later assignments.

A Word of Thanks

The following are friends and colleagues who went out of their way to help: James C. Alexander, formerly of Central Advertising Agency, Tandy Corporation; William Cavness, WGBH, Boston; Twyla Cole of TCU, who pored over the Fort Worth end of the manuscript; Keith Fowles, University of Central Florida, who read much of the Orlando portion; Jim Gober, owner and station manager, KWYK and KNDN, Farmington, New Mexico; and Marina Long, Alice Moulton, and Walter McDowell of WFTV, Orlando, Florida. We owe special thanks to these reviewers, whose anonymous responses provided by the publisher gave us vital feedback: Graeme A. Bond, Florida International University; E. Scott Bryce, St. Cloud State University; Don Dick, Southern College; David Eshelman, Central Missouri State University; Robert E. Eubanks, Sam Houston State University; Sharon A. Evans, Western Illinois University; Charles T. Lynch, California State University, Northridge; Peter E. Mayeux, University of Nebraska—Lincoln; Paul Prince, Kansas State University; Robert L. Snyder, University of Wisconsin—Oshkosh.

We appreciate the help of the many professionals in broadcasting, cable, and advertising who provided an abundance of scripts and other illustrative materials. Many of their names appear in the credits to identify the creative material they so graciously supplied. We also acknowledge our editor, Rebecca Hayden, for her assistance and encouragement.

Broadcasting is a business, and at or near the center of this business is the copywriter, the creative person who writes those compelling words about the sponsor's product. This person might as well be you. No broadcast station in this country can operate without one or more copywriters. The announcer's plea to visit John's Used Car Lot is based on what you write. The station's salesperson who pounds the pavement selling air time will be unsuccessful unless you convert the efforts into copy that sells. The station's accounting department has no invoices to process until you have provided copy that helps bring buyers into the sponsor's place of business. And while cable TV operations rely less on advertising revenue than do broadcast operations, cable still offers opportunities for copywriters.

Unfortunately, the radio and television public knows little or nothing of your creative work. Radio listeners tend to relate to their favorite disc jockey. Television viewers feel a kinship to their local news, weather, and sports reporters. But you, the copywriter, work behind the scenes. All that you do helps meet the payroll of those on mic or on camera.

When one of the authors of this book took over as chief copywriter at station KNOW, Austin, Texas, he found the following poem in his typewriter, left there by his predecessor:

> *I hope the salesman drops down dead*
> *And starts to roast in hell*
> *Who says when bringing copy in*
> *Now this time, really sell.*

Yes—now really sell. That's what it's all about, and that's what the role of the writer of broadcast copy is all about. Really sell. It makes no difference if you are selling used cars for John, fine furs for Koslow's, or selling listeners on staying tuned to your station.

Our goal is to help you become a broadcast copywriter who can write copy that sells. Your job may be busy and demanding, and it may give you far less time for creative reflection than you had thought. If you can add as much creativity as possible to this fast-paced occupation, you'll be considered a professional.

In small-to-medium market stations where the majority of jobs are available, the copywriter, sometimes called the continuity writer, may be handling up to fifty accounts a week. You have to react rapidly. Your copy has to flow without long periods of cogitation. How do you accomplish this task? You do it with dedication, humor, and what Winston Churchill termed blood, sweat, and tears. You are entering the field of the unsung heroes of broadcasting. You will not get display credits on a television program. You will not hear your name proclaimed by the local disc jockey as the one who wrote the commercial just presented. All you will get is a paycheck and the pleasure of knowing that your station or agency could not continue without those persuasive words that came from your typewriter.

Yours is a world that is characterized by persuasion, creativity, ethics, and anonymity. It's a good world. It's an honorable world. It's a world in which the opportunity to grow and expand is entirely up to you. It's the world at the center of broadcasting.

The purpose of this book is to help you become a copywriter. Like so many things, you need to know everything at once, but that isn't the way learning takes place. This book takes you through a building-block process—you learn one skill at a time and build on it. What you learn in Chapter 3, for example, needs to remain with you for the remainder of the semester. Don't master motivation in Chapter 5 and then ignore it as you write the exercises in future chapters. Be bold enough to read ahead. Be secure enough to review past chapters. And don't be surprised if your particular instructor assigns chapters out of sequence. Different teachers have different methodologies—all valid. This is, after all, a workbook as well as a textbook, and it needs to work for your instructor as well as for you.

Keep in mind that there are few absolutes for copywriters; practices at various stations, cable operations, and agencies vary. While there are conventions—practices common to nearly all good broadcast copy—arguments abound over whether to type in all caps and lowercase, and there is less than common agreement over whether to time the length of copy by word count or by reading aloud against a stopwatch. The methodology given in this book is based on experience and general use in the industry. But be prepared to be flexible.

As you use this text, you will find repetition. Repetition is at the heart of learning. In music, sports, and other endeavors, it's called rehearsal and practice. Lewis Carroll said, "If I tell you a thing three times, it's true." Discount that as you may, being told an important point more than once helps reinforce the point.

Functioning well in any field is related in large part to knowing the vocabulary, the jargon of that field. Broadcast copywriting is no exception. Chapter 1 starts with definitions of basic terms. Chapters 7 and 9 give you definitions for radio and television production writing. But you should turn quite soon to the extended glossary in the back of the book. If you don't know a *bed* from a *break,* you may have trouble at your first station.

Your attention is also called to the bibliography at the back of the book. It isn't extensive, but it is intended to help broaden your copywriting horizons. Finally, copywriting is much like swimming—you learn it by doing it. Do the exercises. You'll swim much better.

1

The Broadcast Copywriter

Broadcasting in the United States is a free-enterprise business and the financial underpinning of that business is advertising. It's true that there are commercial-free educational stations, and while individual TV set owners may pay a monthly rent or subscription fee for cable programs, most radio and television programs come into our homes at no cost to the set owner. This is possible because the cost—and profit—of operating a broadcast station is borne by advertising.

Advertising: those sixty-second radio announcements that tell you about product benefits and services available in the community. Advertising: those thirty-second commercials that advise you via television and cable TV of products and services that are locally available.

You hear these commercials on your radio, you see them on your television set, but someone wrote those compelling words and visualized the pictures before you received them on your set. That someone was the broadcast copywriter.

He or she was a person like you who sat at a typewriter and worried over choosing precise words that would motivate a listener or viewer to visit the sponsor's advertised location and purchase the product or use the service. This copywriter might be employed by one of a number of agencies responsible for preparing broadcast advertising copy, or by a broadcast station or cable TV operation.

Basic Definitions

Virtually every line of work has its own vocabulary, and the field of broadcast copywriting is no exception. You'll find it easier to follow what comes next in this chapter if you take a moment to go over the definitions given here.

copywriter. The person who writes broadcast commercials. May also write public service announcements (PSAs) and station promotion copy (defined below).

continuity writer. Same as copywriter. The term *continuity* is a hold-over from the 1930s, when nearly everything said on the air was written first, even the announcer's remarks between pieces of music: thus the term continuity. The copy that the copywriter provides is sometimes called continuity.

commercial. The sponsor's message promoting its products or services, as written by the copywriter.

copy. Usually same as commercial, but may also be a PSA or a station promo.

public-service announcement. A noncommercial announcement carried without charge by a station or cable operation for nonprofit organizations and causes such as Boy Scouts, Girl Scouts, drug abuse programs, Fire Prevention Week, and so on. May be written by a station copywriter, an agency writer, or by someone involved with the organization itself. Some local stations often rewrite PSAs obtained from outside sources to fit the station's particular broadcasting style.

salesperson. The person who calls on the client, makes the sale, and generally collects information about what the client wants stressed in the commercial. May sell for a station, cable operation, or agency. Other titles for this function include sales executive, an account executive, and time salesperson. May also write his or her own copy.

spot. May be a commercial, a PSA, or a station promo.

station promo. A promotional message about some feature of the station or one of its programs designed to recruit listeners or viewers for the station. May be written by a member of the station's copy department or, in larger stations, by a writer in the promotions department.

traffic. The department within a sta-tion that schedules when a commercial, PSA, or station promo is to be read or played on the air. Sponsors may purchase commercials for specific times and the traffic department is responsible for scheduling according to how the spot was sold.

You're urged now to develop the habit of turning regularly to the glossary at the back of the book to learn additional terms.

Stations, Agencies, and Cable Operations

The United States has over 4,775 AM radio stations, more than 3,700 FM stations, and at least 900 television stations including both VHF and UHF.[1] *Broadcasting Yearbook* lists over two hundred advertising agencies that handle major broadcasting advertising accounts. Each week, *Broadcasting* magazine lists the number of stations on the air at that time. Look for the listing headed "Summary of Broadcasting."

Cable operations reach over 44 percent of all television homes and the number is growing.[2] Then there are national and many local advertising agencies. While some agencies may specialize in billboards, direct mail, or print media only, many do handle local broadcast advertising accounts.

Additionally, there are "in-house" agencies. A number of large corporations own their own advertising agencies. An example is the Central Advertising Agency, which is a part of the Tandy Corporation and handles all advertising for Tandy's Radio Shack Division.

You should realize at the outset that writing for cable is no different from writing for television. Both use TV cameras and other electronic picture-making devices to help sell products and services. All three—stations, agencies, and cable operations—offer jobs for copywriters.

The Broadcast Station

The size of the station largely determines the nature of your work as a copywriter. Chapman and Associates, an organization that buys and sells broadcast stations, uses a four-tier system to classify station markets. Stations serving a population of 15,000 or under are considered to be in a small market. A medium market ranges in population from 15,000 to 50,000, while a large market includes populations of 50,000 to 500,000. The fourth category, major markets, comprises those stations in the top fifty markets such as New York, Dallas, and Miami.[3] Figure 1.1 shows how a medium-market radio station is organized, while Figure 1.2 outlines the functions of a TV station in a large market.

1. *Broadcasting Magazine* 108 (12):86 (March 25, 1985).
2. *Ibid.,* 10.
3. Conversation with William Whitley, Chapman and Associates, Irving, Texas, February 1985.

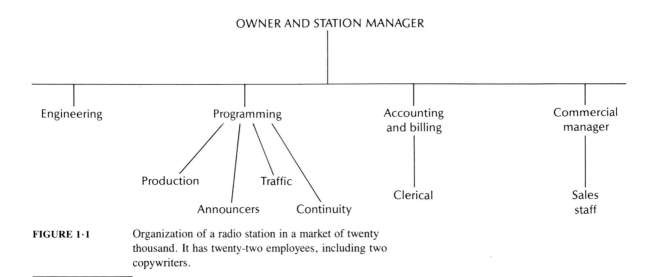

FIGURE 1·1   Organization of a radio station in a market of twenty thousand. It has twenty-two employees, including two copywriters.

You would expect to find small stations in small markets, but it is also not unusual to find small stations in large markets. Station size, as opposed to market size, depends on the station's transmitted power and the size of its staff.

Some radio stations have a total staff of seven full-time employees, and some have over one hundred workers. A small television station might have no more than fifteen full-time employees, and there are giants with almost four hundred on the staff. Your initial employment as a copywriter will most likely be in one of the small stations or agencies or with a local cable operation.

A check of both radio and television stations in the Dallas/Fort Worth metroplex, in Spokane, Washington, in Omaha, Nebraska, and in Orlando, Florida, showed that a number of stations do not use full-time copywriters—that is, people who just write copy. Practices vary, but you should be prepared to both write and sell, write and produce your copy on either audiotape or videotape, or perhaps write and announce.[4] Station or agency size will most often determine your copywriting job description.

In the two accounts that follow—small station writing, and medium-to-large station writing—you should keep in mind that practices differ from station to station. Don't expect your station to follow precisely the outlines given here.

Writing for the Small Station   Let's say that your first job is with a 250-watt AM radio station in a market of 15,000—a small-market station. Your duties include both writing and selling, but writing is your major responsibility. The station has one full-time salesperson and the station manager also helps with sales.

It would not be unusual for you to be responsible for twenty or more accounts. The manager and the salesperson do some copywriting also. But you must write for three competing automobile dealers who sell both new and used cars, two drug stores, a number of supermarkets, three farm implement dealers, and competing department stores. One of your concerns is to make competing stores, products, services sound different from one another.

---

4. Telephone poll conducted by the authors during November 1984.

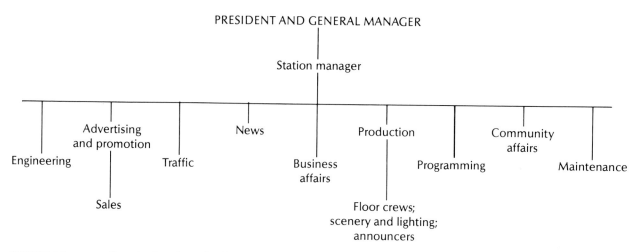

PRESIDENT AND GENERAL MANAGER

Station manager

Engineering · Advertising and promotion · Traffic · News · Business affairs · Production · Floor crews; scenery and lighting; announcers · Programming · Community affairs · Maintenance · Sales

FIGURE 1·2   Organization chart of a TV station in a market of five hundred thousand. The station has 169 employees and no advertising copywriter. All advertising comes through agencies.

Your first job, and you're already up against the problem of *positioning*—that is, making similar products or services stand apart from each other. The experience you gain in solving the problem several times a day in the small market will stand you in good stead as you move to larger markets.

In class, you may have had a week to write and rewrite an assignment. Here you must pound out each spot as quickly as possible. You started learning your craft in college, but it's here that you polish it.

Mentally, you take your work home with you. You go to sleep writing tomorrow's spots for Al's Lumber, Deason's Used Cars, and Jacob's department store.

You are back at work at nine the next morning. The day begins with a sales meeting. The manager assigns you to the new farm implement store in town. Your job: sell the owner air-time. You make a call on the new store and are back at the typewriter shortly before eleven. You have three commercials that must be rewritten by noon.

From one until five, you freshen some copy written last week, write four new spots that the salesperson brought you around two o'clock, write a PSA for the high-school band's new uniform drive, spend an entire fifteen minutes polishing the opening sentence—the lead—for Huggens Pharmacy, and finish the day with copy for a new account that the station manager just sold. You put the cover on your typewriter and console yourself about not selling time to the new farm implement store by saying, "After all, I'm a copywriter, not a salesperson." Wrong. Writing commercial copy is an important part of selling.

You've been busy, you've been creative, you've been productive. You go to sleep knowing that tomorrow will be much like today—with one big exception: It will be different. You'll call on different accounts; you'll write different copy; you'll encounter different problems in copywriting and in selling; and you'll solve them. You're gaining valuable experience.

Much of what you write goes on the air live, so you learn to give the announcer clean, easy-to-read copy. You learn the importance of accuracy. Live copy doesn't go through the rehearsal process of taped copy; you don't have the chance to correct errors.

You learn firsthand how traffic interacts with sales; how billing deals with both departments when charging the advertisers for commercials that were aired; and how you, the copywriter, are part of the station's overall operation.

Writing for Medium and Large Stations   In time, you move to a larger station, either radio or television. Now you're a full-time copywriter in a department with one other full-time writer, one part-time writer, and perhaps an intern from the local university. Two of the station's staff of eight salespeople specialize in co-op sales. This is a system by which a national company reimburses the local retailer for advertising the national product. Through these sales and through copy sent by advertising agencies you learn about *local tags, beds,* and *donuts*. If you don't know what these terms mean, don't worry. You'll know by the end of the semester, or you may wish to look them up in the glossary now.

You still work against a deadline. You still write for a variety of accounts. But now it's possible that you no longer write station promo copy, as this task may be done by the station's promotions department. It's also possible that you may now handle fewer accounts because of the larger number of writers and because more accounts are handled by agencies. As a result, you're expected to turn out better copy than you did in the smaller market station because you have more time to polish your copy.

Now, most of your copy is put on tape—audio or video—before it goes on the air. Some directors will want you in the control room with them to make necessary changes in the copy, while others don't want a writer near them while they produce the tape; practices and people vary. Don't be surprised if the salesperson and the client are present when your copy is produced on tape.

You're making more money now. You're putting into practice everything you learned in the smaller station. You still take problems home with you at night, but your experience helps you solve them. You are indeed a broadcast copywriter, and your thoughts may even turn to heading your own agency someday.

The Advertising Agency

The large agency approach, with fifty or more employees, is usually "one writer, one product." In fact, a team of writers may be assigned to a new account, along with a staff of other creative experts. While the very large agencies are concentrated in New York with branch offices in other major cities, agencies with over a hundred employees exist in Philadelphia, Houston, Miami, St. Louis, Dallas, and other major cities.

But the total number of these agencies is small in comparison with the number of local agencies in cities all over the nation. You need only check the phone book to find the agencies serving your area.

Organization   Regardless of size, agency services tend to fall into one of four categories. As agency size increases, you'll find that these services become departmentalized as follows: administration, account services, media services, and creative services. An agency that provides all of them is known as a full-service agency.

An advertising agency is a business that performs a service for its clients by handling advertising, along with public relations, in all media. Like broadcast stations, agencies have a top administrator and account executives who serve as the link between the agency and the client. They represent the first two departments mentioned. These people must know as much about the client's business as possible. They understand the client's advertising objectives and marketing goals. What happens in the next two departments—media services and creative services—begins with the account executive, but certainly does not end with this person.

People in the media services department research and make recommendations regarding whether to buy time on radio or television; newspaper, magazine, or billboard space; or a mix of the various media. The media services people guide the client not only in what to buy, but where—for instance, network saturation, selected cities across the nation, concentration in one geographical region only.

Creative services is the department in which you, the copywriter, work. Among your coworkers are commercial artists who execute the TV storyboards you create, layout specialists for print advertising, and others.

While listed last, this department is the heart of the agency. The work done by creative services largely determines whether the agency flounders or flourishes. Traffic—scheduling the flow of creative work—may be a part of this department.

Don't expect all agencies to be organized as outlined here, but do expect these various duties to be performed. Some agencies, for example, will have a separate department charged with handling public relations accounts. Some one-person agencies also exist, and this person is kept busy changing the four or five different hats he or she must wear.

Writing for the Small or Medium Agency You're now employed by an advertising agency with fifteen people on staff. It's a full-service agency involved in media service, broadcast accounts, print and public relations accounts, outdoor advertising, and some direct mail.

You've been assigned four accounts: one for radio, two for television, and one for newspaper. The radio account is a campaign for a new auto parts store. You've written a fifteen-second jingle to open each of the four different radio commercials. At ten that morning, you and the account executive concerned are due at Sound Services Studio to hear its musical production of the jingle.

Between nine and ten o'clock you polish newspaper copy for a two o'clock deadline. On the way back from approving the jingle, you and the account executive discuss recording the radio spot with the jingle on audiotape tomorrow; production time has been set for 9:30 the following morning at a local radio station. You, the client, and the account executive will be on hand. Your job will be to make last-minute copy changes if required. .

You have the newspaper copy ready at two o'clock. Then you turn to the first of the two television commercials facing you. It's a local account for a large jewelry store. That afternoon you and the account executive for this account visit the jewelry store to get the feel of the place. You and the store manager discuss the model who is to appear in the TV commercial. You ask questions and begin to form ideas for the spot. Back at your desk, you rough out the approach you wish to use. You have three more days to polish.

Just before five, you take a look at the second television commercial. It's for an old, established restaurant that for years has been open only for dinner, but is now serving lunch. Your job is to get downtown business executives to drive an extra six blocks for lunch. How do you sell this extra six blocks . . . atmosphere? good service? excellent food at reasonable prices? plenty of parking? Is it one of these or all of them? You'll confer with the account executive right after tomorrow morning's radio production.

Next week you start to work on a leather goods brochure.

You're working now with a team composed of the account executive, a commercial artist, a layout specialist, people from production studios, and talent. The team will vary from one account to another. You write more than just radio and television copy. You're also involved in original music, photography, print . . . the full gamut of full-service advertising. While you don't personally do it all, the work of the team depends largely on you. You have really arrived in creative services.

Cable TV

Cable TV operations, unlike broadcast stations, receive most of their income from fees paid by home subscribers. Local advertising, while welcomed by cable companies, does not finance them to the extent it does broadcasters.

Depending on the nature of the local franchise, a cable system may also provide a number of public-access channels. These channels carry city council meetings, school board meetings, county commissioner court hearings, and other civic occasions and public meetings, though they do not generate revenue.

The cable system may also provide some of its own programming as well as offer programs from cable networks such as Home Box Office, ESPN, and Cinemax. Cable systems may insert commercials in open time slots in the programs supplied by the cable program networks, or they may insert them in slots in the public access programming. Commercials may come from local or national advertisers. If the advertising comes from local sources, the cable system might write and produce the commercial as a TV station would. As in broadcast TV, local commercials may also be prepared by ad agencies.

The Freelance Copywriter

In time you may wish to become a freelance copywriter. Opinions differ over whether this approach is best for the beginning copywriter or for the more experienced. It's an argument that will probably never be fully settled because copywriters and abilities differ—though you can tell from the opening sentence of this paragraph that we favor gaining some work experience before turning to freelancing.

Volunteering to write PSAs for the Y, the Boy Scouts or Girl Scouts, or local youth clubs while still in school is a form of freelancing that helps build a portfolio to show future employers. Part-time employment for either a station or agency while still in school or even after graduation constitutes freelance activity. Both volunteer work and part-time work offer the opportunity to gain valuable experience and a chance to work in the "real world" of copywriting.

On the other hand, a station, agency, or client will require a record of known ability if it is to seek you out to be the specific writer for a specific product or service. You most often build this reputation by having worked as a staff writer at a station or agency.

The Copywriter's Background

You must be able to type. Accuracy and a speed of at least sixty words per minute will be expected of you. Learn to think at the typewriter; copywriters don't have time to compose in longhand. Don't expect a word processor, and don't be surprised if you're given a manual typewriter.

Broadcasting is a people business, and a good copywriter likes and understands people. You particularly need to understand why people buy certain products and why they use a given service. Cameras, character generators, microphones, and all the other electronic niceties are each a means toward an end, not an end in themselves. They are there only to help you communicate with people.

People are not only your listeners and viewers but also your coworkers. In the stress of meeting constant deadlines, you must still be able to get along with those around you who are also racing against the clock. You may personally dislike a certain announcer, but you cannot let personal feelings interfere with professional performance. As a copywriter, you are a professional.

You must have a firm grasp of the English language, including grammar, punctuation, and spelling. It is certainly true that broadcast writing follows a conversational style, but that does not imply that bad usage is acceptable. It does mean that you should develop an ear for the way people talk. Chapter 3 deals with writing natural-sounding, grammatical copy.

Learn to meet deadlines. Copy that is late is worthless. Discipline yourself now to get things done on time. Learn to work under pressure, since broadcasting lives by the stopwatch.

A knowledge of music can be helpful to the copywriter. Don't limit your listening to one type of music, since the client's product may not fit your personal preference. Music used to open a commercial for a farm tractor should differ from music used to advertise a fur salon. Music helps develop a sense of rhythm, and this can be important to a copywriter. Then, of course, there are jingles. While you may not compose the music for the jingle, what you write must fit someone's music.

Learn as much as you can about the business of broadcasting. In addition to the course in copywriting you're now taking, sign up for courses such as survey of broadcasting, sales and advertising, and marketing—not all of which may be offered by your school's radio-television department. Consider courses in psychology, perhaps sociology, and in English. You need a liberal arts education as broad as you can get.

On the production side, courses in radio and television production would be valuable. Your job in some stations and with some agencies may require you to help produce what you've written. It also follows that what you write must be producible.

Does getting a job as a copywriter require a college education? No. But it helps. You may compete with a bright high-school graduate for your first job. And, as many stations require an audition tape for announcers seeking employment, you may be asked for a portfolio of what you've written. Start as soon as possible to build a portfolio of effective commercials written in class.

Finally, if you don't believe that advertising helps people, if you don't believe in the free-enterprise system, change your major to underwater basket weaving.

POINTS TO REMEMBER

- Broadcasting in the United States is a free-enterprise business financed by advertising. Broadcast and cable commercials are either written by a copywriter at the station or cable operation, or by an agency writer.

- Copywriters today may be expected to do double duty—that is both write and sell time, write and produce, or perhaps write and announce.

- When writing for an agency, you may be required to not only write radio and television copy but also to write advertisements for print, design brochures, or perhaps serve as an account executive.

- Don't hesitate to begin your career with a small organization—a small station, a small agency, a small local cable operation. These jobs will allow you to polish the skills you learned in college. Your background skills must include:

  a. the ability to type carefully

  b. a willingness to strive for accuracy

   c. a knowledge of and feel for language

   d. a working knowledge of broadcast and cable production

▪ You must be able to get along with people. Broadcasting and cable are pressure-packed, deadline-filled situations, and a person at odds with fellow employees does not do well in such situations.

▪ Strive for as broad an education as possible.

Using the local yellow pages or *Broadcasting Yearbook,* check for the number of radio stations, television stations, cable operations, and advertising agencies in your area. Based on these numbers, where do you think you are most likely to find initial employment?

Assume that you are the advertising manager for a local department store. Who would you be most likely to retain to write broadcast commercials for your store: a freelance student who has just graduated from college with no experience, or a freelance copywriter with ten years of experience? Be prepared to discuss your answer in class.

Begin now to listen to radio commercials and watch television commercials. Choose a radio commercial that appeals to you and analyze it as follows:

1. Was music or a sound effect used?

2. How many voices were involved?

3. If more than one voice, was the commercial dramatized—that is, did it employ actors as opposed to announcers?

4. What was the length of the spot?

5. Was the product or service advertised for a local business or for a national corporation?

6. Do you think the commercial was written and presented by the local radio station, or do you think it probably originated with a larger organization with full product facilities?

Watch for a television commercial that catches your attention and analyze it as you did the radio commercial in Exercise 3.

2 The Nature of Copywriting

T he key to the advertising process is this: Someone has to come up with ideas that will sell products. This process may involve more than one person, of course. The advertiser may have an idea he or she wishes to use; the salesperson may also have a suggestion. In the final analysis, however, it is up to you, the copywriter, to take someone else's idea or generate one of your own and make it sell the product. That is the nature of the copywriting process in a broadcast station, and it can be difficult when you are responsible to several salespeople with long lists of clients.

We think of the person who comes up with a new idea for an advertiser's product as being creative. Certainly, that is part of the advertising process, since new products require new ideas. But it's important to remember that advertising involves much more than the creation of new ideas. These ideas must be communicated to listeners and viewers in such a way that they gain attention, are remembered, and stimulate a decision to buy. That doesn't always happen. Some commercials have used highly creative ideas that attracted audience attention and even won awards—but failed to increase sales. Selling the client's product or service, after all, is the copywriter's job, and creative ideas alone won't be sufficient. They must be placed in a structure that will reinforce buying patterns or create new ones.

We'll look at how you might structure a creative commercial idea in subsequent chapters, but first let's look further at this process we call creativity. As a copywriter, you'll have to create new ideas every working day. How are new ideas created? Where do they come from? How does a copywriter remain creative despite the need to generate new ideas for a variety of clients? A closer examination of the creative process will provide some of the answers.

Creativity and Copywriting

The word *creativity* is mysterious and often confusing. As a result, it's important to define the term. In its simplest form, creativity is just another name for finding new combinations of ideas. That is exactly what you'll do when you prepare a commercial. You may occasionally come up with a completely original idea, but more often you'll take some elements of the client's sales data and combine them in a new way. That's what the creative people did for 7 Up when they wanted to stress its difference from cola drinks. They called 7 Up the UnCola, a new idea combination designed to tell people that the ingredients in the product did not include cola.

The marketing and creative teams for Sears also used a new idea combination. They called a new line of low-maintenance batteries the Incredicell. Though smaller than other batteries, the Incredicell is supposed to generate as much power as larger batteries without requiring maintenance. The battery is an incredible cell, so the copywriters used a new word combining these ideas to describe it. Another new idea combination was created for a manufacturer of vitamin supplements. The vitamins, according to a commercial, include everything from "A to zinc."

Finding new idea combinations may be a simple definition for creativity, but the act of creation is not so simple. For one thing, creative thinking doesn't just happen. It requires hard work and discipline, especially when the ideas don't come quickly. Further, there is a common belief that either you are creative or you are not. In fact, all people have some degree of creative ability. Your task as a broadcast copywriter will be to maximize that ability.

A story is told about a copywriter who struggled to find an idea for a new product. That night as the writer slept, he suddenly awoke when a solution seemed to pop into his mind. It's unlikely that the incident was as simple as it sounds. While the writer searched for an acceptable idea, information was being stored in his mind. Instead of having the idea appear out of the blue, his mind probably continued to work at the problem subconsciously, which resulted in his getting an idea in the middle of the night.

This incident does suggest the sort of mental discipline you need to use if you are to generate new idea combinations. Some people may come up with better ideas than others, but it's probably because they work harder. Here's a four-step process you can use to discipline your mind before you write a commercial so that you can generate new idea combinations. Notice how these steps cater to appeals—personal needs a spot can aim to satisfy. We'll focus on appeals in Chapter 5.

- *Step one*. After you've gathered as much information as possible about the product, store, or service, fix it firmly in your mind. Study the information, think about how this client relates to its competitors and to other, noncompeting businesses. Think about the major elements of the client's business.

- *Step two*. Visualize a satisfied consumer reacting favorably to the product, store, or service. Be sure this is a "post-purchase" impression.

- *Step three*. Evaluate the benefits and rewards that caused the customer's favorable response. Ask yourself, "What factors about this product, store, or service caused the customer's satisfaction?" Consider three possibilities.

    a. Was the customer satisfied because he or she received *tangible benefits* from the advertiser's product? Was the person able to complete a job easier, quicker, or more economically after using it?

    b. Was the customer satisfied because he or she received *personal gratification* from using the advertiser's product? Did the person feel personal pride, satisfaction, or pleasure after using the product?

    c. Was the customer satisfied because he or she received a *desirable response from others* after using the product? Did people display envy or admiration, or did they praise the customer because of the product or service?

- *Step four*. After you've gone through the first three steps, ask yourself a final question: What strong points of the advertiser's product lead to its benefits? You should stress these strong points in your commercial.

Let's see how this process might work. Suppose that a discount jeweler wants to advertise on your station. The jeweler has made a special purchase of men's and women's brand name watches. All styles, including dress and sport watches, are included. All the watches are priced at $48.88 and include a manufacturer's warranty. The watches are to be advertised two weeks before Christmas.

First, you study the information: the brand names being sold, the styles, the price. Second, you envision a shopper who has completed her Christmas shopping at the sale. She has purchased a sport watch for her son, dress watches for her husband and daughter and also for herself. Third, you evaluate the reason for this hypothetical shopper's satisfaction. Did this special sale enable her to do a job with more ease, was she pleased with herself, or did others admire her because of her bargains? While these choices might overlap, the primary reason for the shopper's happiness could be self-satisfaction. She's pleased with herself because she completed her shopping, found gifts her family will really use, and saved money doing so. In the final step, you summarize the main points in your scenario that caused the shopper to be satisfied. They are brand name watches in a variety of styles, with warranties, all at one low price, all at one convenient location. These are the points you should stress in your commercial.

Use this process to guide your creative thinking before you write a message, whether it's a commercial, a public-service announcement, or a promotional announcement. If your time is very limited, use the four steps as a quick guide to planning your message. If you have a day or two to do the work, go through the first three steps and then let the information simmer in your mind. Even without conscious effort, your mind will react to the input, and you'll find it easier to write a spot when your deadline is near.

Qualifications of the Copywriter

Many broadcast sales orders are rush jobs. The salesperson has convinced the client to advertise on your station, and now the commercials must be written and produced quickly. It's difficult in this setting to create new combinations of ideas. You should be as creative as possible, but getting the job done efficiently is often what your employer will expect of you. Here are some additional qualifications that you will need to survive in this fast-paced environment.

A Sense of Inquiry

A creative and effective copywriter is likely to be someone who is interested in trying novel approaches. He or she has an inquiring mind that thinks, "Why not try this . . ." rather than staying with the tried-and-true. The key word is *why*. Why this? Why not that?

Use the "Why not . . ." approach when searching for an idea. It can help you develop new idea combinations, especially if you're willing to give your mind free rein. Begin a sentence with "Why not . . ." and finish it with whatever pops into your mind. Don't be too critical of your initial ideas. Generate as many ideas as you can and evaluate them later. Even ideas that initially seem outlandish can be worthwhile.

Here are some examples of "Why not . . ." thinking. A copywriter who grew tired of writing spokesperson scripts for automobile dealers wondered, "Why not use someone to play the car dealer's wife and do a parody of the spokesperson approach?" The commercial was written, approved, and has been interspersed in the car dealer's broadcast advertising schedule ever since. In another instance, a furniture store wanted to run a weekend sale even though the exterior of the building was being remodeled. "Why not call it a remodeling sale?" the copywriter asked. The novel twist provided much more to work with. A restaurant decided to sell two pizzas for the price of one on Tuesday nights, normally a slow night. "Why not call it 'Two for Tuesday'?" wondered the copywriter, coining a clever description for a merchandising effort.

Discipline

Little more needs to be said. You will go through times when the orders pile up and the ideas just aren't there. Broadcasting doesn't allow the luxury of waiting for *the* idea. You must write copy and prepare it for broadcast. As a copywriter, you must produce the best spot that you can and then move on to the next order.

Knowledge of the Language

Simplicity is the key to broadcast writing. Avoid complex sentences and overblown vocabularies. Unfortunately, poor sentence structure and incorrect grammar do appear. Occasionally, they may be part of a deliberate attempt to be creative. More often the writer simply doesn't know the rules of good language. Commercials should be written in acceptable English that is accessible to the average person. Your job will be easier and the public will have a better appreciation of the media if you use accepted rules of grammar and usage. We'll discuss this point further in Chapter 3.

Knowledge of the Media

As a broadcast copywriter you must understand the capabilities of the station for which you work. Many commercial ideas are only producible in a sophisticated studio with adequate time and a large budget. They can't be done in a small-market station. Thus, you must understand two things. First, what can radio or television best accomplish in selling a product? Second, what level of production capability exists at my station?

Ability to Deal with Matters of Taste

As a copywriter, you will face some personal decisions. You will be asked to write for advertisers that sell products you don't like, and you'll be asked to take approaches with which you don't feel comfortable. This will undoubtedly cause some dissonance on your part, but it's an element of copywriting that you must be prepared to handle professionally.

Consider some of these possibilities. If you don't drink alcoholic beverages, you might feel uncomfortable writing a commercial for a night spot that encourages listeners to drink and have a good time. Agency writers are now asked to write commercials for feminine hygiene products or for rashes attributed to athletic endeavors. Finally, commercials for and against abortion are on the air. How would you respond if you were asked to write for advertisers representing products or positions like these?

You must first recognize the nature of broadcasting. It is a business, and stations sell airtime to make money. You can hope that your station won't sell airtime to clients with questionable products or advertising approaches, but some stations will do so just to pay the bills. Keep in mind that stations do not choose advertisers to please their copywriters—they choose advertisers that can pay the advertising rates.

When asked to write for an advertiser you don't like, such as a car dealer who wants to make his own inane pitches, you have no choice but to adopt a professional attitude and write a positive commercial. If you are asked to take an approach you don't find comfortable, professionalism again comes into play. Check with the salesperson to see if another approach is possible (don't go directly to the advertiser unless you have permission). If no compromise can be worked out, you have no choice but to write a positive spot.

POINTS TO REMEMBER

- Creativity involves disciplining your mind to create new idea combinations.
- An inquiring mind that asks "Why this? Why not this . . ." can help a copywriter develop new ideas.

- To create new idea combinations, a copywriter should envision a satisfied customer enjoying the benefits offered by the client's product or service.

- Avoid complex sentences and overblown vocabularies in writing commercials.

- A knowledge of the broadcast media is essential for a broadcast copywriter.

- A copywriter must respond professionally when asked to write spots for clients or products that are of questionable taste.

Identify an object in your classroom: an eraser, a pencil sharpener, or a chair. Write about the object in free-form style. Describe the object in terms of a new idea combination. (In other words, don't confine yourself to accepted meanings for the object. Strive for new meanings, new uses.)

Upon completion, read your essay aloud. Compare other essays that merely describe the object and those that place it in a new idea framework.

This is an exercise in using the four-step process to develop new idea combinations. You're planning a commercial for Valu-Stores, a discount department store with locations throughout Yourtown. The stores carry the following items: clothing, sporting goods, jewelry, automotive supplies, notions, health and cosmetic items, and electronic goods—TV sets, radios, and home computers. This spot is aimed at housewives. Its emphasis should be on back-to-school shopping.

1. Identify the major points of this business.

2. Visualize and describe a satisfied Valu-Stores customer.

3. What caused the shopper's favorable response? Explain.

    a. Tangible benefits

    b. Personal gratification

    c. Favorable responses from others

4. Summarize the strong points of the advertiser's business that provided these benefits.

This is an exercise in using the four-step process to develop new idea combinations. You're planning a commercial for Import Motors of Yourtown. The dealership has been in business since 1962. It sells Audi, Porsche, and Mercedes cars. Its address is 4403 Main Street. The service department is noted for high-quality work. New and used cars are available. Stress the nature of these imported cars, not prices or colors.

1. Identify the major points of this client.

2. Visualize and describe a satisfied Import Motors customer.

3. What caused the shopper's favorable response? Explain.

    a. Tangible benefits

    b. Personal gratification

    c. Favorable responses from others

4. Summarize the strong points of the advertiser's business that provided these benefits.

This is an exercise in developing "Why not . . ." ideas. For each of the products, services, or businesses listed below, write down both a conventional and an unconventional "Why not . . ." idea. Begin each idea with the words "Why not . . ." Develop your best ideas into partial commercials. Write only an introduction and body for each idea. Expand the list with items you see around your home, city, or school.

1. A Chinese restaurant

2. A chimney-sweep service

3. A waterbed

4. Popcorn that is available in twelve different flavors, including peanut butter, chocolate, mint, and others

Listen to the radio or watch TV as much as you can for one day. Note the commercials that you feel have the best new idea combinations. Compare notes in class.

Drawing on the material from Exercise 3, write a commercial for Import Motors. Don't worry about length or form. You may wish to write the spot for a single voice. Write the commercial using as much of the four-step planning data as possible.

Student Name _____   Advertiser _____

Date Submitted _____

Broadcasting is a matter of one-to-one communication. Although radio, television, and cable TV are classified as mass media, people consume them as individuals. Arthur Godfrey, a noted broadcast performer, once remarked that he formed a mental picture of an individual and then talked directly to that person. If you're to communicate effectively, you should write, talk, or perform for an audience of one.

Throughout the book, your writing efforts will be directed toward this more intimate form of broadcast communication through emphasis on a conversational style. This chapter will give you guidelines for this approach to writing, along with an introduction to the form to use in presenting your copy on paper. But first, the announcer or performer has to be able to read your copy, and here are guidelines to help you accomplish that.

Copy Appearance

The physical appearance of your copy on paper can make a difference in its effectiveness. The announcer, the TV performer, or the director who may be producing your spot must be able to read and understand what you've written. In Chapters 7 and 9 you'll find detailed instructions for the more complicated formats such as sound and music entries and multiple voice spots. First, we'll focus on the basics of putting a simple, single-voice format on paper.

Copy Paper

Most stations or agencies provide copy paper with the station's call letters or the agency logo at the top. It will have spaces for indicating the advertiser's name, your name as writer, the date the copy was written, and the date the spot is to run on the air. The length of the spot is often asked for also. Stations and agencies differ somewhat in the information they want on their copy paper: The examples will illustrate some of these differences.

For use in class, paper of the weight used for office copying machines is acceptable. What you should avoid is lightweight paper that crackles when handled by the announcer near the microphone. Don't use colored paper because the lack of contrast between it and the typewriter ribbon could make reading difficult. For the same reason, don't use a red ribbon in your typewriter.

Radio Note that the copy paper (Figure 3.1) for WBAP, 50,000 watts, does not ask for the writer's name, but does want the name of the salesperson. This example is headed *production*, indicating that the commercial is to be a studio production. Also, the writer is provided with a blank for instructions—for example, "Closing jingle #435 provided by Jenkin's agency." Finally, the copy paper provides space at the bottom of the page for noting the music to be used. This space appears for legal purposes to help the station insure that clearance is obtained for any music used in the commercial.

Radio station KXOL wants to know the names of both the writer and the salesperson. Note also that its copy paper (Figure 3.2) provides the writer with numbered lines down the left-hand side. These lines can be a rough guide for timing the spot as a whole or timing cuts

PRODUCTION

Client:_____

Start: _____

End: _____

Salesman: _____

Length _____ :30 _____ :60 _____ other

Instructions:_____

_____

:30

:60

Music used:_____

FIGURE 3·1   *Courtesy WBAP.*

and additions to the copy. Even though fifteen lines do not always time out at sixty seconds, that is a frequent guideline. Note also that KXOL uses the term *continuity.*

KNDN's copy paper (Figure 3.3) contains an admonition at the bottom of the page that applies to both the writer and the announcer: "Sell this message. This client pays your salary." The best announcer will have trouble selling from poorly written copy. KNDN is unusual because it programs in both English and Navajo. Copy is written first in English and then

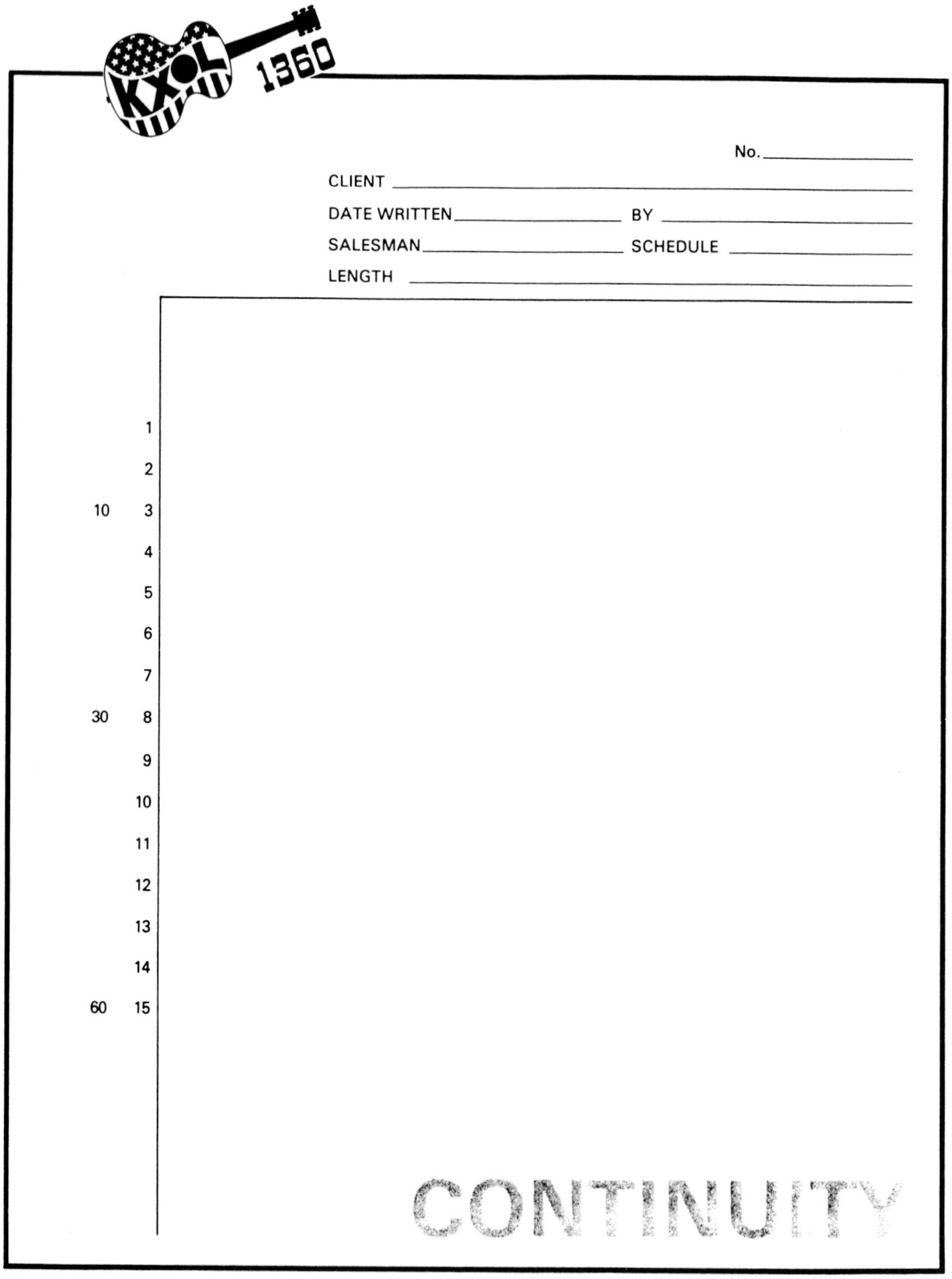
KXOL 1360

No. ______

CLIENT ______

DATE WRITTEN ______ BY ______

SALESMAN ______ SCHEDULE ______

LENGTH ______

1
2
10 3
4
5
6
7
30 8
9
10
11
12
13
14
60 15

CONTINUITY

FIGURE 3·2 *Courtesy KXOL.*

translated for air delivery. The English copy for a one-minute spot is written to time out to forty seconds because it will take the full sixty seconds when translated into Navajo.

Television Television copy paper differs from radio in its two-column approach. The narrower left column is used for **video** and the wider right column is for **audio.** Figure 3.4 shows one example from station WSOC-TV, while the second (Figure 3.5) is used for television copy at an agency, Goodman & Associates.

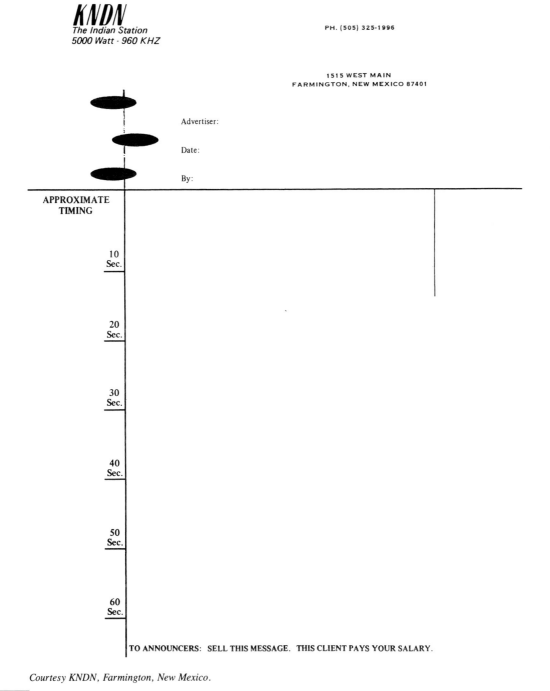

KNDN
The Indian Station
5000 Watt · 960 KHZ

PH. (505) 325-1996

1515 WEST MAIN
FARMINGTON, NEW MEXICO 87401

Advertiser:

Date:

By:

APPROXIMATE
TIMING

10
Sec.

20
Sec.

30
Sec.

40
Sec.

50
Sec.

60
Sec.

TO ANNOUNCERS: SELL THIS MESSAGE. THIS CLIENT PAYS YOUR SALARY.

FIGURE 3·3   *Courtesy KNDN, Farmington, New Mexico.*

Typing Format

All radio commercial, PSA, and station promo copy should be typed double-spaced. Single-spaced copy is too cramped to be read aloud easily. (Throughout this book, however, radio scripts have been typeset single-spaced to save space.) Double-spacing also leaves room for simple corrections to be made. Television copy is frequently single-spaced, but this copy is generally memorized or read from a teleprompter.

WSOC-TV
RETAIL SERVICES
P.O. Box 34665, Charlotte, NC 28234

JOB NO. _____   CLIENT _____   AGENCY _____
WRITER _____   PRODUCT/SERVICE _____
SPOT NO. _____   LENGTH _____ APPROVALS: RSD _____ CLIENT/AGENCY _____
MUSIC _____
TALENT: VO _____
            OC _____

VIDEO	AUDIO

© WSOC-TV Retail Services

FIGURE 3·4   *Courtesy Alan Batten and WSOC-TV.*

It's preferable to type copy that's to be delivered orally in upper- and lowercase letters because that's the style we're accustomed to seeing, and it is easier to read. However, some stations and agencies do prefer that copy be typed in all capital letters, and if that's the policy, you should follow it. But the general rule is to type what's said in caps and lowercase and to type instructions in all caps. Here is a radio spot example:

TELEVISION CONTINUITY

CHANNEL_____ DATE_____

SPONSOR_____ LENGTH 10″____ 30″____ 60″____

SUBJECT_____ CODE_____ SCHEDULE_____

GOODMAN & ASSOCIATES, INC., ADVERTISING/PUBLIC RELATIONS
601 Penn Street, Fort Worth, Texas 76102 817 332-2261

VIDEO	AUDIO

FIGURE 3·5   *Courtesy Goodman & Associates, Inc.*

Client _____

Date Written _____

Written by _____

ANNOUNCER   All that goes up must come down, and Homestead Lumber is proving it by bringing prices down. (PAUSE) Yep, prices are coming down . . . way down at Homestead Lumber.

Note that the identification of the speaker, in this case the announcer, is in all caps because this is an instruction. The instruction for the announcer to pause is also in all caps. What the announcer says is in caps and lowercase.

Here's an abbreviated television example:

Client _____

Date Written _____

Written by _____

VIDEO	AUDIO
BOY ON CREEK BANK, CANE POLE IN RIGHT HAND, SANDWICH IN LEFT HAND. HE TAKES A BITE OF SANDWICH.	ANCR (VO) A good fisherman should never go hungry, and Joe's mom knows that.
MS JOE AS HE TAKES ANOTHER BITE OF SANDWICH	JOE LOOKING INTO CAMERA. My mom really knows how to make a sandwich . . . she always uses Richman Ham. I like to bite into this sandwich . . . but boy, would I like a bite on my hook!

Observe that the camera instructions are in all caps. In the audio column, the instructions are again in all caps, while what is said is single-spaced in caps and lowercase. The term *MS* in the video column means *medium shot,* while the audio instruction *VO* means *voice over.*

Neatness Counts

Typos, strikeovers, and numerous corrections are blocks to good delivery. The spot you write must be legible. If you have a small number of errors—generally not more than three—you can correct them without confusing the announcer or performer. If there are a number of errors, it's always best to retype.

Type on one side of the page only. If the announcer has to reverse the paper to read what you've written on the back, an unwanted break in delivery could result—or the announcer could simply think that the end of the page was the end of the commercial and not read all of it. In addition, remember that if your copy runs more than one page, it is probably too long. If your spot is especially complicated and requires more than one page, observe the following rules:

1. Never split a sentence between two pages.
2. Centered, near the bottom of the first page, type MORE.
3. Begin the second page with the same copy data used on the first page, following the client's name with PAGE TWO.

Client's Name __Smith's Dept. Store__   PAGE TWO

Date Written: __4/23/86__

Written by: __Ima G. Copywriter__

Length: __60 seconds__

Making Corrections You should use a sharp, soft lead pencil to make corrections. A large, blunt lead will produce corrections that are difficult to read. You should not use copyediting marks to correct errors. A sign for transposing words or letters is likely to confuse the announcer. For example, instead of marking a typing error like this: people, retype the word correctly. Whiteout paint works well for retyping corrections. Remember, copyediting symbols are used by editors to tell printers which changes should be made in print copy. A typesetter is trained to understand these marks and has time to interpret them, but an announcer does not. When you do need to make corrections, you should observe the following rules:

1. Correct misspelled words by blacking out the entire word and clearly printing in the correct word. The following examples are acceptable.

   celebrating
   Smith's is ▮▮▮▮▮▮▮▮ its sixtieth year.

   or

   celebrating
   Smith's is ▮▮▮▮▮▮▮▮ its sixtieth year.

   Note that individual letters should be corrected:

   i
   Poor: You are invęted to the grand opening. . . .

   invited
   Better: You are ▮▮▮▮▮▮ to the grand opening. . . .

2. Add small amounts of new material by clearly inserting it above the sentence to be altered.

   in stock,
   Every new car has been marked down.

3. Avoid making corrections in longhand. Print your corrections clearly.

   Poor: *this week only*

   Better: this week only

4. You can eliminate small amounts of material in your copy.

   The doors open at 9 o'clock Tuesday morning.

   This could be corrected to read:

   The doors open at 9 ▮▮▮▮▮▮ Tuesday morning.

You should limit your corrections to the four types illustrated above and retype if any corrections are more extensive.

Abbreviations You should generally avoid abbreviations in broadcast copy. They force the announcer to translate a symbol into a word and may easily cause confusion. For example:

Poor: The sale runs through Mon., Sept. 3.
Better: The sale runs through Monday, September 3.

As with many aspects of copywriting, there are exceptions to the rule. Some words are so commonly abbreviated that announcers are accustomed to seeing them that way.

1. You may use the abbreviations Mr., Mrs., Ms., and Dr. These titles will probably be followed by a name that will help clarify the meaning. For example:

   Mr. Jones, Dr. Smith

2. Some city and local addresses are so commonly abbreviated that they may be written that way. City names such as Ft. Worth, St. Louis, and Ft. Smith are commonly abbreviated. Local addresses may also be commonly abbreviated.

   I-80 for Interstate 80
   S-O-B-T for South Orange Blossom Trail

   Accepted practices in your area will help you determine the suitability of such abbreviations.

3. The names of certain organizations, businesses, and government agencies may also be abbreviated if they're well known by their initials.

   Organizations: Y-W-C-A, Y-M-C-A
   Businesses: I-B-M, A-T-&-T
   Government: I-R-S, F-S-L-I-C

If you want abbreviations read as initials, type them in capital letters separated with hyphens, as in the examples above. Don't use periods to separate the initials because a period is generally used to complete a sentence.

If you want the abbreviated content read as an acronym, write the initials in a solid combination of capital letters.

   MADD, Mothers Against Drunk Driving . . .

Don't use typewriter symbols such as %, @, and $\frac{1}{2}$. You should spell these terms out to help the announcer. The dollar sign ($) is an exception because it is easily understood. You might write either $25.95 or twenty-five dollars and ninety-five cents. The latter form lets the announcer know exactly how you want it read.

Time of Day   Don't use A.M. or P.M. on the air; they sound too similar. Write out the time of day to avoid confusion. For example:

   Poor: "The sale begins tomorrow at 9 A.M."
   Better: "The sale begins tomorrow morning at 9."

Keep in mind that abbreviations affect two important links in broadcast communication: the announcer and the listener/viewer. If you don't think the announcer can automatically translate the abbreviation into a word correctly, spell it out. By the same token, don't use an abbreviation if you're not certain the listener will immediately recognize what it stands for.

Keep It Conversational

Broadcast commercials, PSAs, and station promos should be written in a conversational style, easy for the announcer to read and easy for the audience to understand. To accomplish this, you should follow the copywriter's basic rule: Write each spot so that it can be read and understood the first time through.

It's true that commercials and other spots enjoy repetitive exposure, but it's equally true that a listener or viewer doesn't stay tuned to the station just to get a second chance to comprehend your spot. Let these repeat airings of your copy serve to reinforce, rather than to clarify.

Another factor enters in as well. People are bombarded with advertising messages from all the media. As a copywriter, you must be aware that each spot competes with many other messages for the attention of the listener or viewer. If your commercial can't be easily understood, the potential consumer may not pay attention to it. Keeping your copy conversational is one way to make the listener feel, "Hey, he's talking to me."

Avoid stilted language and awkward wording: Your broadcast copy should be both conversational and grammatically acceptable. The following guidelines will help you achieve a conversational style.

Contractions

Contractions are commonly used in your daily conversation, and they're just as appropriate on the air. For example, we seldom say, "It is not warm today." We more naturally say either "It isn't warm today," or "It's not warm today." Contractions help you write copy that follows natural speaking patterns and that is comfortable for the announcer.

Here are some contractions used frequently on the air:

Aren't for *are not*	*He'll* for *he will*
Doesn't for *does not*	*It's* for *it is*
Don't for *do not*	*They'll* for *they will*
He's for *he is*	*Won't* for *will not*

Some copywriters question the use of the contraction *it'll* for *it will*. It's not easy to say, and it will confuse the announcer at times.

Contractions should be avoided if the advertiser wants to place special emphasis on certain words. Hard sell commercials, for example, use more formal wording to achieve emphasis. You might want to write such a commercial as follows:

ANNOUNCER   Smith's are not kidding! They will not refuse an acceptable offer during their clearance sale. Do not miss this fantastic opportunity!

Clichés

Copywriters often fall into the habit of using overworked words and phrases that are easy to use and may even sound conversational, but lack strong sales appeal. The clichés listed in Table 3.1 should be avoided in your copy.

TABLE 3·1

---

31 CLICHÉS TO ELIMINATE FROM YOUR COPY

Conveniently located . . .	The friendly folks at . . .
Now that (season) is in the air . . .	Everyday low, low prices . . .
All the names you know and love . . .	How about . . .
Don't forget . . .	For all your _____ needs . . .
Stop in soon . . .	Friendly, qualified personnel . . .
The next time you're in the mood for . . .	Serving you for over _____ years . . .
Doesn't it make sense to . . .	Lowest possible prices . . .
Remember . . .	We refuse to be undersold . . .
It's sale time at . . .	We'll meet or beat any reasonable offer . . .
Stretch your budget with these values . . .	Huge selection . . .
Super savings . . .	People who care about you . . .
Savings throughout the store . . .	But wait, there's more . . .
And while you're there . . .	Fantastic
Check out . . .	Unbelievable
A select group of _____ is 25% off . . .	Don't miss out . . .
You'll save big . . .	

Courtesy Chris Lytle, Chris Lytle and Associates.

Overworked superlatives are as much a danger as clichés. If you describe all sales as "outstanding," all bargains as "tremendous," or all shoes as the "cutest you can find," the listener/viewer is apt to discount your claims. Trite, overworked words have a doubtful place in advertising.

Yes, superlatives can be advantageous in your copy if chosen with care. Look for fresh ways to extol the virtues of your product or service. Try words like *active, alive, brimming, captivating, electrifying, hefty, ingenious, lively, merry, prominent, secluded, striking, tingling, understated,* and *vivid.*

Consult your dictionary or thesaurus for variations of tired words. If you can't find the right word, create your own. It takes inspiration to describe a hamburger as an "incred-a-burg-able," but it's fresh, catchy, and stimulating.

Question Lead-Ins

You should generally avoid question lead-ins. A positive statement such as "Cool your house the inexpensive way" invites attention, but "Are you looking for an inexpensive way to cool your house?" invites an answer. The listener who pauses to answer the question mentally may miss your sales key. If the listener answers no to the question, he or she will probably tune out the rest of the message. And in this example, at least, the statement took only about one-half the words used in the question. In broadcasting, time is money.

Be just as careful using questions in concluding statements. "Save dollars at Jones Automotive" is better than "Why not save dollars at Jones Automotive?"

Point of View

Use pronouns and identifying phrases carefully so that they identify the sponsor and not the station. It's misleading to have a staff announcer say, "Come by and see our selection." That wording is appropriate only when a spokesperson from the store reads the commercial. If one of the station's announcers is to read the spot, write: "Go by Smith's and see their selection."

To expand on this point, consider the following example. As you read the commercial, keep in mind that the staff announcer is at the station. You're listening to your radio and you know where the announcer is.

ANNOUNCER   Mother's Day is only 2 days away, and you can't put off getting that special present for that special person. Come in today and make your selection from our complete line of Mother's Day gifts. We've got gifts for the kitchen, bathroom, bedroom, and den. All at prices you can afford. When you visit us, you know you'll find the special gift for that special mother. Mother's Day gifts . . . a specialty at Goodson's Department Store. Open until 9 this evening in Bastrop Mall.

Two things are wrong with this commercial. First, the point of view actually invites you to visit the radio station, because that's where the announcer is. Second, this point of view robs the commercial of the opportunity to sell the sponsor's name—an important ingredient in any selling message. Let's rewrite the spot.

ANNOUNCER   Mother's Day is only 2 days away and you can't put off getting that special present for that special person. Visit Goodson's Department Store and make your selection from Goodson's complete line of Mother's Day gifts. At Goodson's, you'll find gifts for the kitchen, bathroom, bedroom, or den. All at prices you can afford. When you shop at Goodson's, you know you'll find the special gift for that special mother. Mother's Day gifts . . . a specialty at Goodson's Department Store. Open until 9 this evening in Bastrop Mall.

This spot keeps the announcer in the station and sends the listener to Goodson's, where we wanted that person to go all along. Don't underestimate the value of plugging the sponsor's name.

Punctuation

You should punctuate broadcast copy more extensively than other types of writing. Your punctuation marks help the announcer deliver the written copy as intended. Punctuation acts as a guide for pauses, emphasis, and oral interpretation in general.

The period, comma, dash, and ellipsis are the most commonly used punctuation marks, followed by the question mark and the exclamation point. The colon and semicolon have virtually no place in writing broadcast copy.

The Period

The Period   The period is used to indicate the end of a declarative sentence or thought. It calls for a pause and/or a change of pace. Periods are widely used in broadcast copy. Shorter sentences are often more effective. You may even use the period in incomplete sentences, as follows:

ANNOUNCER   Ice. Snow. Bad roads. These are the signs of winter.

In broadcast copy, however, you might also write the message in this manner:

ANNOUNCER   Ice . . . Snow . . . Bad roads. These are the signs of winter.

In either instance, you, as the writer, want the announcer to pause for emphasis after *ice,* after *snow,* and after *bad roads.* As you write, try to "hear" your copy the way you want it to sound on the air. When you have finished writing, read it aloud.

The Question Mark

The Question Mark   Use the question mark in broadcast copy as it would normally be used. If you omit a question mark at the end of a question, you may set up a stumbling block for the announcer. The omission of the question mark is often the result of carelessness in the haste of meeting a deadline.

While not a broadcast commercial example, the following three sentences help illustrate the importance of terminal punctuation in conveying meaning.

> Are you ever going.
> Are you ever going!
> Are you ever going?

The first is an understatement describing someone who is winning. The second is an exclamation of admiration for someone who is winning. The third refers to someone who has worn out his or her welcome. Clearly, the careless omission of a required question mark can change meaning.

The Exclamation Point

The Exclamation Point   Exclamation points appeared in a hard sell commercial earlier in this chapter; a further discussion of hard sell copy appears in Chapter 8. For now, remember to use the exclamation point when you want the announcer to emphasize a statement.

ANNOUNCER   Williams's opens its doors at 8 tomorrow morning! That's right
                              . . . one hour early! One hour early so you can start early for
                              the big midwinter sale!

If you replace the exclamation points in this copy with periods, the announcer's delivery would probably be much quieter and more sedate.

The Comma When you use a comma, you are usually indicating a pause shorter than a period calls for. Remember "Ice . . . Snow . . . Bad Roads"? Let's repunctuate the copy using commas.

ANNOUNCER	Ice, snow, and bad roads. These are the signs of winter.

Now the announcer is apt to read the series of words in a more connected fashion. It all depends on how you want your copy to sound on the air.

The comma doesn't always signal a pause, but it is a convention of punctuation. Such is the case of the comma in direct address. When one person directly addresses another by either name or title, as in a dialog spot, a comma is necessary before and after the name or title. A period can eliminate the need for the comma after the name or title. Note the punctuation in the following dialog spot.

MARK	Hey, Joe, where'd you get those wheels?
JOE	Same old wheels, Mark. Had 'em for years.
MARK	Yeah, but, Joe, I never saw that shine before.
JOE	Like I said, Mark. Same old wheels, new auto polish.

The Dash The dash (—) calls for a complete break in thought. You use it for a pause longer than that called for by the comma. Its pause length is about the same as a period's, but you use it to indicate a thought grouping, not to mark the end of a sentence. The copywriter's dash is typed as a double hyphen--a mark brought about with the advent of the typewriter. Use the dash to punctuate parenthetical expressions and to guide oral interpretation.

ANNOUNCER	John Jones—Yourtown's largest volume car dealer—has done it again.

The Ellipsis The ellipsis—three periods (. . .)—may be used for a more complete break than a dash to indicate a shift in thought within a sentence or to separate phrases.

ANNOUNCER	William Florez (FLOOR ess) is an electronics technician, but don't look for him at your local repair shop . . . he's working in the Navy.

The Hyphen The hyphen is used to help the announcer read word or letter groups that go together. Use it to make combination words easier to read. For example:

> end-of-month party
> once-a-year event

Use hyphens to indicate that alphabetical combinations are to be read as groups.

A-T-&-T

One word of caution: Don't hyphenate words at the end of a line. Doing so causes the announcer to look to the next line to complete the word and increases the chances of error. Complete the word, even if the margins aren't as precise as you might like.

Underlining   While strictly speaking not a form of punctuation, underlining can be used to let the announcer know which words you want given special stress. Example:

ANNOUNCER   These Moonlight Madness prices are in effect only this <u>Friday night</u>.

                                          or

ANNOUNCER   These Moonlight Madness prices are in effect <u>only</u> this Friday night.

The use of underlining depends on the effect you want. As with all copy marks, underline only when you want special emphasis. Underlining too many words may undercut the effect you're seeking to create.

Using Numbers

Numbers should be written with care, since they may be difficult for the announcer to read and for the listener/viewer to comprehend. Use complicated figures sparingly—and simplify them if possible by making them meaningful for the listener or viewer.

Write numbers as the announcer is accustomed to seeing them, usually as figures; here broadcast copywriting practice differs somewhat from other types of writing. For example: 50 cents, 12 o'clock, 5 thousand. It is best to spell out all fractions: one-third, one-half, three-fourths. If a decimal point is used, it is best to write it out: 8-point-8 percent financing.

As a general rule, use figures for numbers one through 999 except for one and eleven. These numbers should be spelled out when they stand alone to help the announcer avoid confusing them with other symbols on the typewriter.

Round off large and detailed numbers if possible. Listeners probably won't remember that a house is priced at $67,975. Unless the advertiser requests the exact number, round it off with terms like *under, almost* and *just over.* You could well refer to the cost of the above house as "under $68,000."

Telephone Numbers   You should not use telephone numbers in a spot unless the sponsor requests that you do so. They're difficult to read and even more difficult to remember. An advertising agency spokesperson told of this experience. In a national television campaign aired in forty-two markets, one-half of the commercials displayed the local retailer's phone number while the others said, "See your local retail dealer" and did not display a phone number. Results from the two approaches were the same.

If the client wants the telephone number used, repeat it at least twice. The most common way of writing a telephone number in your copy is to use the form we're accustomed to seeing in the telephone book: For example, 292-2808.

Some stations prefer that you hyphenate the figures to give added emphasis: 2-9-2—2-8-0-8. You may find that some telephone numbers lend themselves to an even clearer presentation. The number 123-4000 might be written as 123-4 thousand. Follow local preferences in writing telephone numbers. If a telephone number is used in a TV spot, it's best to superimpose the number on the screen.

Street Addresses Street addresses may also be difficult to read, and often they provide no meaningful frame of reference for the audience. For example, where is 6894 East Main Street? You could help orient the listener by writing "Smith's on East Main . . . just 2 blocks south of City Park." Of course, this approach only works if you know your community well enough to identify commonly known reference points. If there is no good reference point, you must use the address.

Pronunciation

Words or names that are difficult to pronounce should be avoided, but that isn't always possible. When they must be used—for example, when you need to identify an important ingredient in a product or when the advertiser's name is difficult to pronounce—provide a pronunciation guide.

One approach is to put the guide in capital letters several spaces above the opening lines of the copy. The guide thus becomes a copy instruction and need not be repeated in the text. This approach is especially appropriate when the spot is to be recorded and the announcer will have a chance to rehearse. Example:

Client: __Gaggenau__

Date Written: __8/13/86__

Written by: __Joan Withers__

NOTE: PRONOUNCE SPONSOR AS   GAG-ah-no

ANNOUNCER	Collyville Electric introduces the state of the art in kitchen appliances from Gaggenau.

A second approach is to type the pronunciation guide in parentheses after the word in question, as was done in the example on page 45. The advantage of the second approach is that you can include the guide in the text each time the word or name is used. This method is likely to get better results when—as often happens—the announcer doesn't have a chance to rehearse the copy.

Also, don't assume that your station's announcer knows the pronunciation of local place-names. These voices are often from out of state. Help them: Accuracy begins with you, the writer.

You may find it possible to turn a hard-to-pronounce name into a humorous commercial. Such is the case in the following example.

Y106 . . 10617FM

Client: ___INTER-FLORIDANA/JEVER_____

Length: ___:30_____

MALE I	Hey, great party . . . This beer really makes it . . . Jever, huh?
MALE II	Uh, no, it's pronounced Yayver . . .
MALE I	It says right here . . . J-E-V-E-R . . . Jever.
MALE II	No, you see, that's German, which means you pronounce the J like a Y . . . Yayver.
MALE I	What's the matter with you? This is America . . . we pronounce a J like a J . . . But what I like about Jever is the taste . . . This is a beer that gets noticed.
MALE II	Yeah, it's the hops—you know from the first taste that you're enjoying a superior pilsner.
FEMALE I	Hey, great party. This beer really makes it . . . Jever, huh?
MALE I	No, it's Yayver . . . You pronounce the J like a Y . . . Yayver.
FEMALE I	No, it says right here . . . J-E-V-E-R . . . but what I really like . . .
MALE II	Oh, I give up . . .
ANNOUNCER	Jever, the German pilsner supreme, distributed by Old Dutch Imports, Orlando.

Courtesy Inter-Floridana Inc., Orlando, Florida. Jever Beer, West Germany.

A Brief Grammar Review

Writing in a conversational style doesn't mean playing havoc with the English language. You do have to sell the product or service, but you aren't called upon to offend the educated members of your audience. Language is mainly a matter of habit, something we learn by example. The following review notes some of the bad examples heard on the air so that you can avoid making these errors in your own copy.

The Reflexive Pronoun

The term *reflexive* simply means to refer to a previous noun or pronoun in the sentence. Any pronoun that ends in *self* is reflexive and must have a previous noun or pronoun for reference. Take the sentence "I did it myself." Here you're on safe ground. At the head of the sentence is the pronoun *I* for the reflexive *myself* to refer back to.

Unfortunately, when the president of the United States appears on national television and says, "Nancy and myself will attend," or when a national network news commentator says, "David and myself will be there," we have national exposure to bad examples.

Listen to the way those around you tend to misuse reflexive pronouns. How often do we hear a conversation that goes:

"How are you?"

"Fine. And yourself?" This sentence has no noun or pronoun for the "self" in "yourself" to refer to. Grammatically, the exchange should go:

"How are you?"

"Fine. And you?" Unfortunately, many people seem afraid to use the straightforward, nonreflexive personal pronoun.

Pronouns—Case

The grammatical term *case* simply refers to the function of the pronoun in the sentence. Is it the subject of the sentence, is it a direct or indirect object, or does it express possession? Examples of errors in indicating case relationships do occur on the air. Here's one from a station promo spot.

ANNOUNCER   Here at _____ we're changing to the music you like best . . . country music. Willie and me will be with you every night from . . .

Why not "Willie and I"? As with the reflexive pronoun, we seem to go out of our way to avoid the personal pronoun *I* even when usage calls for it.

On the other hand, take this off-the-air example. In this spot, the announcer was a spokesperson for the sponsor, but his copy was written by the station's continuity department.

ANNOUNCER   Hi, I'm back to tell you more about Sanders Home Repair. Bill Sanders invited Jack and I to visit his shop last week, and . . .

Invited Jack and I? Would you say, "He invited I to visit"? Invited Jack and me. Objective case. Case closed.

Adverbs

Most English adverbs end in *ly. Slowly, rapidly, quickly,* and *freshly* are all adverbs—words that modify a verb, an adjective, or another adverb. A television commercial advertising cat food contained the line "made of fresh caught fish." You could have fresh catfish, fresh redfish, but fresh caught fish? The construction requires an adverb, so that the line should read "made of freshly caught fish." To repeat: Why offend the many listeners/viewers who know better when it is so easy to use the correct form?

Subject-Verb Agreement

When the verb fails to agree with the subject, it is usually because you have failed to identify the subject correctly. Take the correct example "A group of scientists is studying the problem." The singular subject *group* is followed by the singular verb *is*. But it is easy to note the plural *scientists* and throw in the plural verb *are*. Here's an example from a commercial broadcast in the Northeast:

ANNOUNCER   This fine selection of dresses are going on sale tomorrow.

This selection are going on sale? No, "This selection is . . ." Of course, you could rewrite to say, "All of these fine dresses are going on sale . . ."

Modifiers

English is a language that depends on word order. We make sense in a sentence by the order in which we string words together. For example, adjectives such as *good, fine, lovely,* and *handsome* tend to modify the word they immediately precede. Take the following line from a radio commercial:

ANNOUNCER   These are good boys's suits and are going for half price.

This raises the question: If these are good boys suits, what is available for bad boys?
    Or take this example heard in the St. Louis area:

ANNOUNCER   Tomorrow's sale features handsome gentlemen's Panama hats.

Does this line mean that the store does not have hats for those who are not handsome? Perhaps we are being picky—but some listeners tend to be that way. Be accurate: Make your modifier modify what it's supposed to modify.
    Then some adjectives just cannot be modified. These words are considered absolutes; chief among them are the words *unique* and *round*. There are others, but we'll focus on *unique* because it seems to be a favorite among copywriters.
    Quite simply, you cannot say "very unique," "most unique," or "quite unique." A thing is either unique, or it isn't. From off the air, these incorrect examples:

ANNOUNCER   You know your dress will be most unique when you get it at Dawn's.

Strike out *most* and the statement is all right.

ANNOUNCER   This very unique table setting . . .

Strike out *very* and the statement is acceptable.

Troublesome Verbs

Lie and *lay* and *sit* and *set* tend to be the main sets of troublesome verbs. In each set, the first verb is intransitive while the second is transitive. A commercial prepared by a large agency began this way:

ANNOUNCER   When you lay down for your afternoon nap . . .

You may lay a book on the table, but you lie down for a nap. You sit in a chair, but you set the dishes on the table. You may wish to check any standard grammar text for a discussion of transitive and intransitive verbs. Here are some additional correct examples taken from commercial copy.

ANNOUNCER   Don't just sit there, phone Hollaway's Garden Service.

                                          or:

ANNOUNCER   After lying around on the beach, you'll find nothing is more soothing than Skintex Lotion.

Spelling Problems

Discussion here is limited to those words that sound alike but are spelled differently. Carelessness is frequently the cause of misspelling these words.

its (possessive adjective)	*it's* (contraction of *it is*)
your (possessive adjective)	*you're* (contraction of *you are*)
whose (possessive adjective)	*who's* (contraction of *who is*)
to (preposition)	*too* (adverb)
their (possessive adjective)	*there* (never shows possession)

POINTS TO REMEMBER

▪ To communicate effectively in broadcast commercials, public-service announcements, and station promos, write in a conversational style. Write for an audience of one. Don't depend on repeated broadcasts of your copy to get your message across. Write so that your message is understood the first time it is heard or seen.

▪ Keep in mind that accuracy begins with the writer. This means not only getting the price of the product right or being sure you have the sponsor's name and address correct, but also using acceptable grammar, spelling, and punctuation.

▪ Begin the good habit now of proofreading your copy. The best way is to read it aloud. Test how it sounds to you. Act out your television commercials, and be sure that the visual material your copy calls for can be presented in the time allotted.

▪ Keep the spot's point of view in mind as you write. Is the announcer inviting the audience to visit the station or go to the store? Remember that misused point of view can rob you of the opportunity to plug the sponsor's name.

▪ Your desk should contain a good dictionary, a thesaurus, a grammar text or stylebook, a sharp pencil with a number two lead, and a spare typewriter ribbon.

Copywriting Style Test

In the blank at the left of each series below, write the letter that designates the style form preferred for ease of reading on the air.

_____ 1. a.   Once in a lifetime values.

b.   Once-in-a-lifetime values.

_____ 2. a.   Here are a few examples of the bargains.

b.   Here are a few ~~examples~~ of the bargains.

_____ 3. a.   Located at 1231 W. Major Blvd., next to Red Bird Mall.

b.   Located at 1231 West Major Boulevard, next to Red Bird Mall.

_____ 4. a.   This special sale begins TONIGHT at 6.

b.   This special sale begins <u>tonight</u> at 6.

_____ 5. a.   You pay only 5 percent down!

b.   You pay only 5% down!

_____ 6. a.   Come and see how luxurious condominium living can be.

b.   Come and see how luxurious condominium
living can be.

_____ 7. a.   Smith's is open from 10:00 A.M. to 6:00 P.M. Monday through Saturday.

b.   Smith's is open from 10 to 6 Monday through Saturday.

_____ 8. a.   These prices will not last long!

b.   These prices won't last long!

_____ 9. a.   These special prices begin this evening at 6.

b.   These special prices begin this evening at 6 P.M.

_____ 10. a.   Here's what Kissimmee Hardware offers you.

b.   Here's what Kissimmee (Kih-SIM-ee) Hardware offers you.

_____ 11. a.   If you like pizza that's made the Italian way, but is still affordable, the Pizza Place is for you.

b.   If you like pizza that's made the Italian way . . . but is still affordable . . . the Pizza Place is for you.

_____ 12. a.   MAN: Grumbling. Another rainy day . . . will the sun ever come out?

b.   MAN: (GRUMBLING) Another rainy day . . . will the sun ever come out?

_____ 13. a.   Prices start at just $49,939.

b.   Prices start at under 50 thousand dollars.

_____ 14. a.   You pay one-half off the original price!

b.   You pay ½ off the original price!

_____ 15. a.   Smith's is having a 99¢ sale.

b.   Smith's is having a 99 cent sale.

_____ 16. a.   Deposits insured by the F-D-I-C.

b.   Deposits insured by the FDIC.

_____ 17. a. Low 9-point-9 percent financing.

        b. Low 9.9% financing.

_____ 18. a. Smith's, 2 blocks east of Yourtown Mall on Central Avenue.

        b. Smith's, at 1240 Central Avenue.

_____ 19. a. You need not be emplyed.

        b. You need not be employed.

_____ 20. a. Drive the Brand X 4 x 4 pickup.

        b. Drive the Brand X 4-by-4 pickup.

Write a single-voice, 60-second radio spot to be read by a staff announcer for the Hometown Sewing Center, 1984 S. W. Main Street. Do not use music or sound effects. The phone number is 123-9854. The Sew Well sewing machine by the Master Corporation is on sale for $169.99. The price is $40 below list. The Sew Well has 12 different stitches, including a zigzag stitch. It has built-in buttonholer, blind hem, and will sew stretch fabrics. The store is two blocks southwest of City Hall on Main Street.

Write a single-voice, 60-second radio spot for Italian Grocery and Deli, 231 Park Ave., in Yourtown. Phone number: 123-6681. Write the spot so that it can be delivered by Mr. Victor Venturini, owner of the store.

Facts: Boiled Ham, $1.89 Lb., Genoa Salami, $5.39 Lb., Domestic Provolone, $3.69 Lb., Polly-O-Mozzarella, $3.19 Lb. Stress that the Italian Grocery and Deli is the only true Italian grocery in Yourtown. They prepare special party platters. Store hours, M–F 9 A.M.– 6:30 P.M., Sat. 9 A.M.–6 P.M.

Write a 30-second, single-voice radio commercial for Valu-Mart's 99-cent sale. Include items you think might reasonably sell for 99 cents. In writing the spot, use at least six common commercial clichés. When you've finished, rewrite the spot to eliminate the clichés. Use only hard facts and fresh, specific phrases. Hand in both versions of the commercial.

Write a single-voice, 60-second radio commercial for your favorite sports car. Describe its appearance, its accessories, and its fuel economy. Use as many superlatives as you can. When you've finished, exchange papers with a classmate and read the spots aloud. Discuss the impact of the superlatives on the selling power of the commercial.

Once you've discussed the commercials, edit out most or all of the superlatives from the spot you've written. Read the spot aloud again. Which approach has more selling power?

This is an exercise in reading edited copy. Edit the 60-second spot you wrote for Hometown Sewing Center in Exercise 2 to a 30-second spot. Eliminate words and sentences as necessary. Keep your editing as legible as possible but don't retype the spot. When you've finished, exchange papers with a classmate. Read the revision aloud, but *don't* rehearse it! Try to read the spot as well as you can, following the revisions as you read.

Juan Jiménez processes frozen Mexican food that is distributed over a four-state area. He has picked your agency to write radio copy for him. He is particularly insistent on correct Spanish pronunciation for the following words that will appear in the copy: Jiménez, jalapeño, frijoles, pecan.

Go to an authority for assistance. Be sure you can guide the announcer with the word jalapeño. What word or words do we have in English that contain the "ñ"sound?

The following radio dialog may or may not need editing for grammar, punctuation, or spelling. You be the judge and make such editorial changes as you see fit.

TOM	Wow. Julie where'd you and Sue go last night.
JULIE	It's this way Tom. Sue wanted to try that new Chinese restaurant . . .
TOM	The one out on highway 30.
JULIE	Right. Its only fifteen minutes from downtown, and once you get their, boy is the food tremendous.
TOM	Whats the name of the place.
JULIE	The Panda. They got a big, stuffed Panda out front. And like I say, there food is tremendous.
ANNOUNCER	It's just like Julie said . . . The Panda . . . tremendous Chinese food . . . only five miles out highway 30 north, next to the Raceway.

Student Name _____   Advertiser _____

Date Submitted _____   Commercial Length _____

Student Name _____ Advertiser _____

Date Submitted _____ Commercial Length _____

Student Name _____   Advertiser _____

Date Submitted _____   Commercial Length _____

Student Name _____   Advertiser _____

Date Submitted _____   Commercial Length _____

4

Broadcast Copy Preparation

The amount of time you spend planning a spot will vary. Hopefully, you will have sufficient time to think about the structure of the commercial and the manner in which you organize it. But, as we've already noted, the amount of time you can spend on a given spot will be limited at stations with a large volume of retail advertising. Still, you should *always* plan every spot. Even a few minutes, if they are well spent, can determine whether your spot will motivate people to respond.

Another comment about planning: All too often copywriters think first about technique—how the spot will look or sound when produced. Planning the sales message becomes a secondary concern. The resulting commercial may look or sound clever, but it may not sell the product. It is your job as a copywriter to motivate listeners or viewers to buy the product. Therefore, it is essential that you plan to sell the product first and concern yourself with technique second.

The Copy Platform

An important aid in planning a commercial is a *copy platform,* a checklist that helps you prepare a successful sales strategy. A copy platform helps focus planning by drawing your attention to the key elements of the sales data. It helps you work more efficiently to prepare a sales message that really works.

The copy platform we'll present here can be used for a radio, television, or cable TV spot. It's primarily designed for the copywriter working at a station or cable system; however, it can be expanded for use with higher budget accounts at advertising agencies.

Many variations of the copy platform are in use, but the following example has been devised for its logic and ease of use. It consists of seven items.

1. *Client and product, service, or store.* This item is a simple recognition of the client and specific commodity being advertised. For example:

   Federated Tire Stores, Five Locations in Yourtown

2. *Objective.* With this item you ask an important question: What objective do you want the commercial to accomplish? Do you wish to introduce a new product, reinforce a favorable image among present users, announce a change in an existing product, or generate store traffic for the client?

   There is no approved list of advertising objectives, so you'll have to generate your own objectives with each advertising order. Since advertising is the communication of ideas, advertising objectives should deal with a specific communications activity—for instance, demonstrating a product benefit. Don't say that your goal is to sell the product or increase sales by a given percentage. Those are marketing goals.

   The sales order will tell you what is desired of the advertising purchase. For example: Write two thirty-second spots for the client from the enclosed data. But the wording of the sales order probably won't be precise enough to tell you what the commercial should accomplish. Examine the sales data. Then state your objectives specifically and thoroughly. Complete the following sentence and you'll be off to a good start in stating your advertising objective: "The purpose of this commercial is to . . ." Use standard communication terminology to describe what you want to accomplish—for instance, to introduce, to persuade, to change, and so forth. If a furniture store has a special purchase of recliners, for example, your objective is to promote that special merchandise.

3. *Target audience.* It's a waste of time to try to reach all of the available audience. It can't be done. As a result, your goal is to define the portion of the audience that you wish to reach. Think in terms of the customer. Who uses this product? Who will buy it? Prepare a clear statement that specifically indicates the audience to whom your advertising is directed.

You can define your audience by using the standard demographic categories of sex, age, educational level, income, race, and so on. For example, a typical demographic might be males aged 18–34.

Major advertisers often supplement demographic data with psychographic research data. Psychographics help pinpoint the psychological characteristics of the audience, including such aspects as value systems and lifestyle patterns (see Chapter 5).

4. *Sales theme.* Now that you've decided who you want to reach and what you want to accomplish, it's time to move to the heart of the copy platform and develop the major selling point you hope the spot will convey.

The sales theme or central selling point is the focal point of your commercial. It consists of (1) a major sales point, tied to (2) a strong consumer benefit. The benefit should be a relevant, believable effect of the sales idea.

Let's look at a nationally advertised product with which you may be familiar to see how the sales theme works. Figure 4.1 shows a commercial built on the slogan "Orange you smart." The sales point is that Florida orange juice is good to drink anywhere. The benefit is that it's refreshing and healthful. That point leads back to the slogan "Orange you smart for drinking orange juice."

Remember that the sales theme should be the strongest single thing you can say about the client's product, store, or service. Don't worry about developing it as a slogan in the initial planning stages. That will come later, if at all. State your sales theme as a simple declarative sentence that has broad and meaningful appeal to your target audience. "Wendy's hamburgers have more beef than other burgers" might have been the sales key that led to the famous "Where's the beef?" campaign.

Note, too, that the benefits must be meaningful to the audience. Build benefits for your clients that are so exciting, so believable, so provocative that people can't wait to respond.

A sales theme may sometimes be developed into a memorable slogan that helps gain audience attention. The nature of the sales order will have much to do with your decision. A single spot written for a short schedule probably won't merit the time and thought necessary to develop a catchy phrase. If the spot is part of a campaign, or is scheduled for a long run, the effort has greater justification.

A sales slogan must be planned and nurtured: Its success will depend on the time and effort you devote to it. What is a sales slogan? It's a forceful, imaginative, persuasive idea presented in a striking phrase. A cheese

FLORIDA DEPARTMENT OF CITRUS

PROCESSED ORANGE JUICE

"ORANGE YOU SMART – FISHING"

COMM'L NO.: FCOJ 2336   LENGTH: 30 SECONDS

(MUSIC UNDER THROUGHOUT) | ANNCR: (VO) Isn't that Florida Orange Juice? | SINGERS: (VO) Orange You Smart . . . | (SFX: MUSIC TO ACCENT FINGER TAPPING) for drinking orange juice,

for that clean sunny taste. | Hey, Orange You Smart -- | (SFX: MUSIC TO ACCENT FINGER TAPPING) for drinking orange juice, | pure refreshment any place.

Hey, Orange You Smart for drinking | to your body's content -- the taste only | nature could invent. ANNCR: (VO) 100% pure from Florida. | SINGERS: (VO) Hey Skipper,

Orange You Smart! | (SFX: MUSIC TO ACCENT FINGER TAPPING)

FIGURE 4·1   TV commercial using a sales theme. *(Courtesy Florida Department of Citrus)*

snack is advertised, for example, with the following sales theme: "Combos cheeses your hunger away." You're told the product name and that it *cheeses,* a play on the word *chases,* your hunger away. The slogan is clever and brief, but memorable. Here's another. An automotive dealer's sales theme states, "Seminole Ford . . . where a great deal is happening." This slogan identifies the advertiser, and it tells you that many people shop for cars at this dealer because they get great deals. That's the thrust of a sales slogan. It should be brief, clever, and memorable. The advertiser or product name should be included. Even negatives can be turned to advantage. Retailers located in outlying locations urge customers to "drive a little and save a lot." Major advertisers take a similar approach. For example, the sales slogan for Clorets tells you that "Clorets cost more, but they're worth it."

Remember, the sales theme is the key to a persuasive message. It helps viewers recall the advertiser or product name and the product's selling benefits. On television it can be presented aurally, visually, or both. A carefully developed sales theme can be your best aid in developing audience recall.

To help plan a sales slogan, use the motivational appeals discussed in Chapter 6. Consider the basic need or desire this product or service will appeal to and the need or desire it will satisfy. Motivate people in the audience to use the product or service to satisfy a need they have. Show that the need can be satisfied by the product and its selling features as set forth in your sales theme.

Ben Gay, for example, appeals to the need for physical comfort. Commercials aimed at arthritis sufferers use this sales slogan: "For arthritis pain . . . feel better with Ben Gay." That's what arthritis sufferers want to hear—that a product will relieve their discomfort.

A manufacturer of prepared dinners appeals to status in its sales theme. The product name itself, Dinner Classics, implies that the product is much more than a TV dinner—it's special! The full sales slogan states, "Dinner Classics . . . so good they belong in the dining room."

Every product or service will appeal to one or more basic needs. Analyze the needs and develop a sales slogan that tells viewers how the product and its features will satisfy that need.

5. *Bonus items.* Too many selling points confuse, so it's best to emphasize one *main* sales idea. You may add an extra copy idea or two, but be certain they relate to the main idea of your sales theme.

To help identify your major and optional selling points, make a list of sales items. List anything that comes to your mind. This exercise helps you get to know the product, store, or service better. You may even stumble across a major selling point or benefit that you hadn't thought of.

Once you've completed the list, examine it and arrange the items in order of importance. Delete any items that are too farfetched. Determine the single idea that should be used in your sales theme. Use optional ideas only if they relate to the main idea.

Suppose that you're asked to write a commercial for a men's clothier that is clearing out its fall and winter line of suits from a well-known European manufacturer. Your sales theme is obvious: quality men's suits at reduced prices. Your list might include the name of the designer, the styles available, the prices, other sale items, location of the store, dates of the sale, and the fact that free alterations are available. This latter item could be an important bonus item: quality suits reduced in price, plus free alterations. Other bonus items could include free parking, free delivery, open on Sundays.

Of course, in certain circumstances, any of these items could be the major item stressed in the sales theme. And bonus ideas are not always needed. If bonus points will dilute a strong, clear sales theme, it's best not to include them.

6. *Positioning*. When the client's product, store, or service has a number of competitors, it becomes difficult to make a unique claim for your client. When this happens, you may want to "position" your client against the competition.

Positioning involves the creation of a separate identity for the product, store, or service—an identity that helps consumers distinguish the client from its competitors. Although this separate identity must have substance, it is actually a matter of using a commercial to reorient the consumer's perception of the client's product, store, or service. Burger King, for example, created an identity for itself in the competitive world of fast-food hamburger chains by claiming that its hamburgers were flame broiled and not fried like those of its competitors. Wendy's carved out a niche, too. It offered baked potatoes as well as hamburgers, and consumers loved them. These efforts and others in the "burger wars" involved attempts to establish the advertiser as a separate entity, not one of the crowd. The Ætna spot shown in Figure 4.2 positions the company as one whose agents are involved in helping solve problems.

Local retailers can do the same thing. An appliance dealer with a downtown warehouse turned a potentially negative situation into a positive one by advertising that he could sell for less than competitors because of the "no-frills" showroom. Business boomed. An automobile dealer positioned himself as the "volume dealer" who could sell for less.

A new product, such as push-button toothpaste or nonalcoholic beer, can be positioned against existing products. Likewise, an existing product can be repositioned. This was done with Johnson's Baby Shampoo, which originally was marketed for infants. It was repositioned not only for infants but for adults who wished to wash their hair frequently with a mild shampoo. Whether the product is being positioned or repositioned, the position must be for real. If the product or service doesn't deliver what is promised, the positioning won't work.

7. *Approach*. A suitable approach (tone, mood, or style) must be established for each commercial to match the objective and target audience. A soft, understated, dreamy approach, for instance, would suit an elegant ladies' boutique. On the other hand, a spirited, up-tempo approach would be better for a car dealer's model clearance sale. Mood must always match the audience and the message, so the copywriter must plan for it.

Remember that this copy platform is designed to help you organize the data in a sales order so you can write a commercial that hits its mark. You may not need to follow each step in every commercial, but even a brief copy platform will help you to organize your data and identify your audience.

Ætna

"HURRICANE" :60

ANNOUNCER: When a hurricane this strong hit Houston...

Houston found out you need...

an insurance company...

this strong behind you. Within hours...
AIRLINE CAPTAIN'S VOICE: Houston's got one runway working. So we're gonna take you on in.

ANNOUNCER: An Ætna task force was coming, over a hundred men and women strong...from 'round the country...

ÆTNA CLAIMS ADJUSTOR: Bob Nichols, Atlanta.
CLAIMS MGR.: Bob, keep your coat on, we've got some messy ones down here.

ANNOUNCER: each assigned to the hardest-hit...
SCHOOL SUPT.: Builders are talking months. This school's gotta open in two weeks!

ANNOUNCER: and they plowed ahead, chasing down contractors...

paying a thousand claims a day...
BOY: Is the school gonna stay closed?
BOB NICHOLS: Not if I can help it!

ANNOUNCER: working five A.M. until ten P.M., until Houston was back in business!

THE STANDARD FIRE INSURANCE COMPANY

ANNOUNCER: When there are deadlines to meet, payrolls to meet, challenges to meet...

that's when you're glad you met Ætna!
SCHOOL SUPT: You're not Texas, are you?
BOB NICHOLS: Atlanta.
SCHOOL SUPT.: Atlanta Ætna, we're glad we met ya!

FIGURE 4·2 TV spot that positions a client. *(Courtesy Ætna Life and Casualty)*

It should be noted that this copy platform is for an individual commercial, not a group of spots or a full campaign. (See the exhibits that follow.) A set of spots for a given order may have nothing more in common than a sales slogan. Each spot may have a different target audience and a different objective. As a result, additional spots for the same client require preparation of a separate copy platform. We'll discuss the copy platform again in Chapter 13, which covers broadcast campaigns. You may wish to read Chapter 13 in conjunction with this chapter to gain an appreciation of the use of the copy platform in a full campaign.

EXHIBIT:

EXAMPLE OF A COPY PLATFORM FOR A PRODUCT

1. *Client and product, store, or service:* Natural View Skylights.
2. *Objective:* To introduce and familiarize homeowners with the advantages of skylights as a natural light source in the home.
3. *Target audience:* Homeowners aged 25–54. They are value-conscious people who want to make their homes comfortable without spending a great amount of money.
4. *Sales theme:* Natural View Skylights use free light and save energy all year long.
5. *Bonus item:* The skylights are available in three models.
6. *Positioning:* The product should be positioned as an item that brightens dark rooms while still saving energy costs.
7. *Approach:* Serious, dignified.

EXHIBIT:

EXAMPLE OF A COPY PLATFORM FOR A LOCAL RETAILER

1. *Client and product, store, or service:* Record Mart; three stores in Yourtown.
2. *Objective:* To inform music lovers that Record Mart sells records and tapes by well-known contemporary artists at discount prices.
3. *Target audience:* Males and females, 18–43, who enjoy contemporary hit music and frequently buy records or tapes. They are practical people who want quality but who don't spend their money foolishly.
4. *Sales theme:* The Record Mart lets you enjoy your favorite recording stars and still stay within your budget.
5. *Bonus item:* All tapes are guaranteed for one year.
6. *Positioning:* The Record Mart store will be positioned as a business that appreciates serious music fans and understands their buying and listening habits.
7. *Approach:* The spot will use enthusiastic delivery with excerpts from sample recordings.

Collecting Copy Information

As we noted earlier, you must have sufficient information about the product, service, or place of business before you can write a commercial that will sell. In a small- or medium-market station you will not have the expert assistance that would be available in a large-market station or a large advertising agency. Since you may be writing for thirty or forty clients a week, you must have sufficient information to write a strong commercial each time. You'll be asked to write about a variety of items—from snowblowers to pool supplies, and sewing machines to tires. You don't have to be an expert about each subject, but you do need enough information to be able to write a strong sales message. Let's look at where the copy information should come from and what you should do to supplement the normal information sources.

1. *Salesperson.* The person making the sale is the primary source of information. The salesperson is in direct contact with the advertiser and probably maintains regular contact with the account. The salesperson should present copy instructions in a clear, comprehensive form that provides enough information to enable you to write an acceptable sales message. Generally, data about an advertiser are supplied on a copy information form. A copy information form, such as the one in Figure 4.3, should not only tell you what you need to know to write the spot, but it should also tell you important information about the sales order. When does the spot go on the air? How many spots are to be written? Does the advertiser want to use a specific announcer or production technique?

    The salesperson should supply all such data on a copy information form. But, unfortunately, even the best system doesn't always work. Copy instructions sometimes consist of notes jotted on a scrap of paper or an ad from the newspaper; sometimes they are only verbal. Selling airtime is often more important to the salesperson than servicing the account, and he or she may be thinking ahead to the next commission. When this happens, it is your duty to track down the salesperson and make certain that you get adequate data with which to write a spot. If necessary, you should request permission to contact the sponsor yourself.

2. *Newspaper and magazine ads.* Local newspaper advertisements for the retailer are another source of copy information. In some cases, the salesperson may regularly supply you with such ads. In other cases, it may be necessary for you to look for them and develop a clip file.

    Advertisements from print sources should not be relied upon, but they can be helpful. They often provide sufficient data for a spot—but sometimes too much. More important, print ads are written for the eye, not the ear. The copywriter cannot just copy the wording. It is necessary to rewrite the ad so that it will be appropriate for presentation on the air.

3. *Brochures and pamphlets.* Brochures and pamphlets for products can also be a useful source of copy information. A brochure about a given model of a car or a given brand of lawnmower may provide you with information to write the spot and a fuller understanding of the product. With this background, you can then apply the data to the spot for the local retailer. It is important to note that brochures and pamphlets are also written in print style and must be rewritten for suitable use on the air. More information on the use of brochures appears in Chapter 5.

COMBO_____ FM ONLY_____ AM ONLY_____ FM & AM-AM ONLY_____

CONTINUITY ORDER

CLIENT_____ TODAY'S DATE_____

SALESPERSON_____ CONTRACT NUMBER_____

DUB TO CART_____ PRODUCE SCRIPT_____ START DATE_____END DATE_____

SPEC TAPE ONLY_____ ADD TAGS_____YES NO_____

CLIENT AUDITION_____TAPE____SCRIPT SCHEDULED BY:_____

DUBS_____REELS____CASSETTE_____ NO. CUTS_____30 SECONDS_____

CLIENT PRODUCTION CHARGES-__Y __N NO. CUTS_____60 SECONDS_____

DISPOSITIONS OF TAPES_____HOLD _____RETURN_____DESTROY

CO-OP INFORMATION_____

SCRIPT NUMBERS_____

SPECIAL INSTRUCTIONS:_____

_____

_____

MUSIC - SFX_____

FOR CONTINUITY USE ONLY:_____

_____

_____

_____

_____

_____

_____

_____

_____

JOCK'S INITIALS_____DATE COMPLETED_____

JOCK NOTES:_____

_____

FIGURE 4·3   Radio station copy information form. *(Courtesy BJ105, Orlando, Florida)*

4. *Prepared announcements.* In some instances, the station may have access to broadcast commercials that are already written but do not include the sponsor's name and address. Such commercials may be supplied by the national advertising representative for use in cooperation with a local distributor, as illustrated by the script in Figure 4.4. This use of nationally written co-op advertising is fairly common. When such copy is available, it is a great help to the copywriter.

In other cases, small stations may subscribe to a commercial writing service that provides generic commercials for banks, hardware stores, and the like. In addition, the Radio Advertising Bureau provides generic spots and sample scripts from stations that can be adapted for local use. The generic spots are usually straight-sell commercials that need only be localized with the name and address of the sponsor. Such a service can be a lifesaver to the copywriter in a small station, but remember that the station may have to pay for the service and if a competing station uses the service your spots may sound just like theirs.

5. *The client.* If possible, you should maintain personal contact with clients of the station. But visit the client only if you have the salesperson's permission. If the salesperson wants you to visit the advertiser to inspect a new store, have lunch in a new restaurant, or observe a complicated product firsthand, try to make the visit.

When visiting the client, remember that you are there to gather information. The visit is not to impress the advertiser with your credentials or writing skills. You should let the advertiser do the talking, but if called on for advice, you should be tactful, brief, and positive. A successful visit with the client can clinch the sale and strengthen rapport with the advertiser.

Copy Preparation and Traffic

In addition to the facts you need to prepare the content of a commercial, there are certain items about the scheduling of the commercial that you also need to know. You obviously need to know how long the spot is to be, the number of spots needed for each order, the date and time the spots begin, and when the spot will be aired during the broadcast day. A carefully prepared copy information sheet should supply most of this information. If you don't get the information from the salesperson's copy information sheet, you should consult with the traffic department—the department that receives the sales orders and schedules them on the station log as requested. If you don't coordinate your work with the traffic department, you can't properly date the copy. Several kinds of situations can lead to confused copy.

One concerns the time of the day the spot is scheduled for. If a commercial is to run at given times only—in the late evening newscast or in an early morning disc jockey program, you can safely make certain statements. Others may be totally out of place. For example, it's quite appropriate to urge early morning audiences to "take advantage of Henry's gigantic closeout today." The store will be open during the day, and the morning audience can go to the sale. To make the same statement late in the evening would be inappropriate since the store would probably be closed. You need to know when the spot will be broadcast so that you can properly date the commercial.

You also need to know the specific dates of a special sales promotion of short duration. For example, the copy should not state, "These once-in-a-lifetime values are available Satur-

Criterion
INSURANCE COMPANIES

60-second RADIO SPOT. August 1984

NOTE TO GFR: All you have to do is fill in your phone number and address where indicated on this script. And then give a copy of the script and the music tape to your radio station. They know exactly how to put the music and words together to give you a professional and effective spot. If you need a replacement music tape, call Criterion Marketing at 301-986-3256.

SPOT # __1__   TITLE _Cars and Motorcycles_

JINGLE LYRICS ON TAPE: "Sing it out loud. Criterion. Join the Criterion Crowd."

ANNOUNCER COPY OVER :18 BED:

Criterion no hassle insurance for cars _and_ motorcycles. Either one or both, we've got you covered from the minute of your low down payment. You get countrywide protection and service, with Criterion's famous fast-action 24-hour claim service.

JINGLE LYRICS ON TAPE: "Join the Criterion Crowd."

ANNOUNCER COPY OVER :18 BED:

Yes...for motorcycles _and_ cars. You can stretch your premium payments out with budget terms. You get money-saving deductibles and discounts. If you've had it with hassles, switch now to Criterion no hassle insurance. It's smart, it's easy...to...

JINGLE LYRICS ON TAPE: "Join the Criterion Crowd." (MEDLEY)

AFTER 3 SECONDS OF MEDLEY, FADE FOR TAG COPY:

For cars _or_ motorcycles get your free Criterion rate quote. Just phone ____-____. Call ____-____ today.

FIGURE 4·4   Prepared announcement with local tag. *(Courtesy Robert J. Piwowarczyk, Criterion Insurance Companies)*

day only" when the copy runs on the Saturday of the sale. That line would be appropriate if run on Thursday and Friday. Listeners or viewers on Saturday, however, are likely to ask themselves, "Does that mean the sale is today or a week from today?"

Just as you need to know if spots are to be scheduled at certain times of the day or only on certain dates, you also need to know when there are no stipulations. This may occur when the sales order is for best time available (BTA) or run of schedule (ROS). These terms refer to sales orders that do not specify placement in any specific time period, but instead are scheduled at the station's discretion. Spots written for such orders may be scheduled at any time of the broadcast day, and they may be scheduled every day of the week, including weekends. You need to know if the order is run of schedule so that you keep the copy free of references to time of day and days of the week.

More than one station has embarrassed itself because it ran a spot that was clearly out of date or placed at the wrong time of day. The error is often attributed to the traffic department, and that is where the fault may lie. Nevertheless, the problem may lie with the copywriter. You may have written a spot that didn't fit the time slot requested. Coordination between the sales staff, traffic, and continuity is essential.

POINTS TO REMEMBER

- A spot must be planned if it is to motivate people to respond.

- A copy platform helps the copywriter prepare a successful sales strategy by identifying the (1) objective, (2) target audience, (3) sales theme, (4) bonus items, if any, (5) positioning, and (6) approach.

- The salesperson is the copywriter's primary source of information.

- Newspaper ads, magazine ads, and brochures help the copywriter gather background information but are written for print, not for broadcasting.

- Prepared announcements, with space for the local sponsor's name and address, are sometimes available.

- A copywriter should maintain personal contact with clients, but visit them only with the salesperson's approval.

- The copywriter must consult with the station's traffic director to identify the date and time the spots will begin as well as when the spot will be aired during the broadcast day.

Prepare a copy platform for Smith's Department Store. Assume that you are the copywriter for a contemporary Top 40 radio station.*

Copy Information

Smith's, a well-known department store in your community, is having its seventy-fifth anniversary sale. The store has specially reduced prices on housewares, appliances, and clothing for men, women, and children. The sale runs Wednesday through Sunday. Commercials begin running Monday. Items and prices are too numerous to mention. The audience should see the ad in Tuesday's paper for details. Stress that these are the best prices in Smith's history. Special store hours for the sale: 9 A.M. to 9 P.M. Wednesday through Saturday, and 12 noon to 6 P.M. on Sunday. Shoppers can also register to win a free $500 shopping spree at Smith's.

Write a 60-second radio script for Smith's Anniversary Sale. The spot is to be broadcast only on Monday and Tuesday. Type in caps and lowercase and double-space. Be sure the spot reflects the information in the copy platform.

Prepare a copy platform for Princess Lisa Lamour Cosmetics. Assume that you are the copywriter for a radio station that plays soft, beautiful music.

Copy Information

What: Princess Lisa Lamour Cosmetics introductory offer. Complete eye makeup kit including eight eye mist shadows. Price: $10.75.
Slogan: "Your eyes speak for you."
Offer ends next Sunday. Available at all department stores.

Write a 30-second radio spot for Princess Lisa Lamour Cosmetics. Type in caps and lowercase and double-space. Be certain that the spot reflects the copy platform.

*At the end of these exercises, space is provided for you to write out your assignments.

Prepare a copy platform for Executive Introductions. Assume that you are a copywriter for a contemporary music station.

Copy Information

Client: Executive Introductions, 2130 "A" Street, Yourtown. Phone: 123-1234. This client offers a dignified way for people to meet others. The firm wants to appeal to those who are single, divorced, or widowed, and who are tired of single bars.
Member of Yourtown Chamber of Commerce.
Client does not use computers, but instead provides personalized introductions. This service is available to unattached adults over the age of 21.

Write a 60-second radio commercial for Executive Introductions. Type it double-spaced in caps and lowercase.

1. Client and product, store, or service

2. Objective

3. Target audience

4. Sales theme

5. Bonus items (if any)

6. Positioning

7. Approach

Student Name _____   Advertiser _____

Date Submitted _____   Commercial Length _____

1. Client and product, store, or service

2. Objective

3. Target audience

4. Sales theme

5. Bonus items (if any)

6. Positioning

7. Approach

Student Name _____   Advertiser _____

Date Submitted _____   Commercial Length _____

1. Client and product, store, or service

2. Objective

3. Target audience

4. Sales theme

5. Bonus items (if any)

6. Positioning

7. Approach

EXERCISE 6

Student Name _____   Advertiser _____

Date Submitted _____   Commercial Length _____

5

Motivation

What was your most recent purchase? Was it a stereo, a new car, a complete jogging outfit, a game, a new dress or suit, a fully automatic camera? Whatever it was, something motivated you to buy it. You may honestly say, "Because I wanted it." Certainly we buy goods and services because we need them. And in this world we need affection, and we need the approval of peers. But do we need gourmet food, designer clothing, luxury condominiums, a twelve-cylinder sports car? Many of us do buy these things, and often we rationalize that we need them.

As a copywriter, you need to understand human nature. You need to understand, as Otto Kleppner points out, that "The reason a person *says* he buys a certain product may have nothing to do with his real reason for buying it."[1] The reason you say you took up jogging, spending considerable money to buy running shoes, shorts, sweatbands, other paraphernalia, and a book on the subject, is that jogging will keep you in good health. The real reason may be that you think jogging will give you an opportunity to meet the attractive young man or woman from down the street who jogs by your house every afternoon. To repeat, we always have a reason for making a purchase. As a copywriter, you must be aware of the stated, real, and rationalized reasons that motivate people to buy. You use these reasons to motivate the listener/viewer to buy your product or service. What, then, are the reasons that motivate people to make a purchase? How have researchers categorized human motivations?

Rational and Emotional Motivations

We can classify the reasons for purchasing a product or a service as either rational or emotional. Rational motivations tend to stem from needs, while emotional motivations tend to stem from wants or desires. Rational reasons are linked to basic needs for survival—such as food, clothing, shelter, protection—or to practical needs for products that are dependable, economical, or convenient. For example, people have a rational need to buy dependable products. This factor is the key to the advertising for Maytag clothes washers: "The Maytag repairman is the loneliest man in town."

Listed among our emotional reasons or motives are needs for prestige or status, desires to imitate others or conform to the group, the desire for pleasure, the need for individuality, or a search for creativity. The emotional drive for status or prestige may vary from one individual to another, but it is common to virtually all of us. Rationally, we need clothing, but we often buy designer clothes as a status symbol. J. C. Penney's Plain Pocket jeans were outsold by those with a designer label on the hip pocket.

The urge to have children is considered rational even though we fringe this urge with emotional overtones. Wanting to be loved or admired by others, however, is considered emotional. Parental concern for children somewhat straddles the line between the two categories. Certainly having children and caring for them is necessary to keep humanity from extinction. But purchasing nice things for them—toys, musical instruments, and so on—moves into the emotional. There is no definitive list of rational and emotional motivations, only guidelines.

---

1. Otto Kleppner, Thomas Russell, and Glenn Verrill, *Otto Kleppner's Advertising Procedure,* 8th ed. (Englewood Cliffs, N.J.: Prentice-Hall, 1983), 326.

Self-Interest

It should come as no surprise to you to read that we buy largely from self-interest. We want to comfort ourselves, we need life's essentials for ourselves. Even when we buy for our children or other loved ones, we tend to gratify ourselves as well with the purchase. For the copywriter, this translates into a strong use of the personal pronoun *you*. *You* save money on this purchase; *you'll* have more leisure time through using these services; *your* children will think you're the greatest Santa ever. Let your sales message gratify self-interest and promote self-gratification. Note the following Radio Shack Christmas television spot with its potent use of *your*.

CENTRAL ADVERTISING AGENCY

Client: __Radio Shack__

Copy: __QTAB-0481__

Time: __30 seconds__

VIDEO	AUDIO
SPOKESMAN BACKLIT BY RADIO SHACK LOGO IN LIMBO SET AS HE MOVES CAMERA RIGHT. DISSOLVE TO FAMILY IN LIMBO SETTING	SPOKESMAN: Radio Shack believes a computer for your family is an important investment.
SPOKESMAN STEPS IN FROM CAMERA LEFT, CAMERA PUSHES IN. DISSOLVE TO SHOT OF PRODUCT. SUPER: $159.95	That's why you owe it to them to see the value-priced color computer two.
SPOKESMAN WALKS FROM L TO R DOWN ROW OF PHOTOS OF COLOR COMPUTER IN USE	Widely used in schools and homes, it's expandable with quality peripherals . . .
DISSOLVE TO SPOKESMAN NEAR SOFTWARE LIBRARY. HE INDICATES VARIOUS SOFTWARE ON SHELVES	And supported by a vast library of software for education . . . home management . . . communications . . . and games.
DISSOLVE TO PRODUCT SHOT WITH SUPER: $159.95	The color computer two, at $159.95, is backed by our national service and training.
SPOKESMAN ENTERS FRAME LEFT, LIMBO SET AGAIN. AS HE SAYS "ONLY" SUPER: YOUR ELECTRONIC STORE FOR OVER 60 YEARS	Only at Radio Shack, your electronics store for over 60 years!

Courtesy Central Advertising Agency, Fort Worth, Texas.

Additional analysis of this Radio Shack TV commercial shows the rational appeals of price coupled with quality and the emotional appeal of doing something of value for your family. All of these appeals are directly aimed at self-interest.

Life Cycles and Buying Behavior

You should realize that there is a close relationship between our life cycles and our buying behavior. What we buy relates in large part to the stage of life we are going through. The overview in Table 5.1 illustrates this point.

An understanding of life-cycle buying behavior can help the copywriter select a target audience. Remember, no one appeal is going to attract everyone, and no one product will be wanted by everyone. While many of us tend to spend beyond our means, the copywriter does need to make every effort to make the product or service appeal to buyers who are actually in the market for that product or service. Consider the following radio commercial aimed at the fourth group in the life-cycle chart: Full Nest II, families whose youngest child is six or older.

MUSIC	C SCALE PLAYED HALTINGLY ON PIANO. SEGUE INTO PIANO CONCERTO AND UNDER FOR BED. TAKE BED OUT AT LAST ANNOUNCER LINE AND PICK UP MORE ADVANCED SCALE PLAYING
ANNOUNCER	Six years old is not too young for a musical instrument. Give your child the advantage of musical training with a quality piano from Adcock Music. Easy terms are available from Adcock Music, not only for pianos, but for all musical instruments. Johnny or Suzy may be only in the first grade now, but soon . . . all too soon . . . it will be time for high-school band and orchestra. Give your children the start they need at the time they need it most. Give them music from Adcock Music—quality instruments at prices you can afford. Music is the gift of a lifetime. Give the gift of music to your young ones today. Adcock Music, Sixth and Main, open evenings until 9.
MUSIC	MORE ADVANCED SCALE PLAYING WITH AN APREGGIO

In addition to fitting the spot to the age group and family interest indicated on the life-cycle chart, we may also ask if the appeal in the commercial is rational or emotional. This commercial is both; that is, it contains both rational and emotional appeals: "Easy terms are available from Adcock Music . . ." and ". . . quality instruments at prices you can afford." The theme of saving money while obtaining quality offers a rational approach. Then comes "Give your child the advantage of musical training with a quality piano . . ." This line combines the desire for quality with the emotional appeal of doing something for your child.

How might you write a spot for the same sponsor to reach consumers in the fifth life-cycle category, Full Nest III, whose financial positions are better than those of families in Full Nest II? You'll note that while families in Full Nest III may be harder to influence with advertising, they do have more money to spend and they tend to purchase durables, more tasteful furniture, and non-necessary appliances.

You might suggest to this group that they trade in the old upright piano that Suzy or Johnny learned on for a gracious grand piano with a concert sound that would look impressive in the living room. Appeal to pride of ownership in this group. Ask yourself what music you might want to use with this commercial and what clearance problems might be involved with your selection of music.

TABLE 5·1

AN OVERVIEW OF LIFE CYCLES AND BUYING BEHAVIOR

STAGE IN LIFE CYCLE	BUYING BEHAVIORAL PATTERN
1. Singles: Young, single people not living at home.	Single people have few financial burdens. They are fashion opinion leaders; also recreation oriented. They buy basic kitchen equipment, basic furniture, cars, vacations.
2. Newly Married Couples: Young, no children.	Newly marrieds are better off financially than they will be in the near future. They have the highest total purchase rate and highest purchase rate of durables. Their typical purchases are cars, refrigerators, stoves, sensible and durable furniture, and vacations.
3. Full Nest I: Youngest child under six.	Home purchasing reaches its peak with these families; liquid assets are low. They are dissatisfied with their financial position and amount of money saved. Interested in new products, they buy washers, dryers, TVs, baby food, chest rubs and cough medicines, vitamins, dolls, wagons, sleds, skates.
4. Full Nest II: Youngest child six or over.	The financial position of these families is better. Some wives work. They are less influenced by advertising, and tend to buy products in large packages and multiple units. This group buys many foods, cleaning materials, bicycles, music lessons, pianos.
5. Full Nest III: Older couples with independent children.	The financial position of this group is better still. More wives work and some children have jobs. They are hard to influence with advertising. They have a high average purchase of durables. This group buys new, more tasteful furniture, auto travel, boats, dental services, magazines, and non-necessary appliances.
6. Empty Nest I: Older couples, no children living with them; head is in labor force.	Home ownership is at its peak. Most families are satisfied with their financial position and amount of money saved. They are interested in travel, recreation, self-education, and are likely to make gifts and contributions. They are not interested in new products, but are more likely to buy vacations, luxuries, home improvements.
7. Empty Nest II: Older married couples, no children living at home; head is retired.	This group undergoes a drastic cut in income upon retirement. They are likely to keep their home. Products that appeal to them include medical appliances and medical-care products that aid health, sleep, and digestion.
8. Solitary Survivor (in labor force).	His or her income is still good, but many people in this group are likely to sell their home.
9. Solitary Survivor (retired).	They have the same product needs and buying habits as other retirees. Retirement means a drastic cut in income.

Source: William D. Wells and George Bugar, "Life-Cycle Concept in Marketing Research," *Journal of Marketing Research* (November 1966): 355–63. Reprinted with permission.

Basic Appeals

While we have taken *rational* and *emotional* as the basic categories for motivations, some appeals serve effectively as rational or emotional or both. One of the first questions the copywriter must answer is, "What appeal am I going to use to motivate the consumer?" Whether you employ a rational or an emotional approach will depend largely on the product. In many instances, you will want to use a mix of the two with one or the other predominant.

Cosmetics, for example, are sold almost exclusively on emotion. An ad for a microwave oven is likely to be rational unless an appeal like "keeping up with the Joneses" enters the picture. Your appeal may be a mix. But keep this in mind. Copywriters sometimes wrongly conclude that emotional appeals sell more products than do rational ones. Elizabeth Heighton and Don Cunningham point out that "if consumers were so emotionally suggestible that they bought everything they were told to buy, families would be bankrupt within a week."[2] The promise of gleaming white teeth (emotional) may attract us to a given toothpaste, but the assurance of fewer or no cavities (rational) can help convert the consumer to the product. Attract attention with a tug on the emotions, and clinch the sale with a rational approach.

Appearance

It is a common human desire to want to be attractive, both to the opposite sex and to others around us. Rare are those who really want to be known as the office slob, or who really want to be refused a date because of the way they dress or groom themselves.

While the appeal of appearance products is mainly emotional, rational factors have their place. A pair of shoes can both enhance your appearance and give the benefit of healthful support. They can be, as the expression goes, "sensible shoes." You can stress the durability and the warmth of a wool worsted suit (rational) while also pointing out its stylish cut (emotional).

Love and Family

Love and family appeals tend to focus on the family unit. A camera is one product, for example, that can have a strong family appeal. Capture junior's first birthday or sister's first day at school; record all the family events. And how might you sell an automobile? A family appeal is one way—the car can take you to the beach for a family vacation, to work, or to the supermarket for your groceries.

Love is, of course, not limited to the family, and we must include friendship for purposes of selling appeal. From greeting cards for friends to expensive presents for the special boyfriend or girlfriend, affection helps sell. And don't overlook pets. Hartz reminds us that if we really love our cat or dog, we will buy the Hartz reflecting collar. Note these appeals: "Do you love her enough to provide her with adequate life insurance?" "Give your child the added advantage of a TRS-80 computer." "For those who care enough to send the very best."

---

2. Elizabeth J. Heighton and Don R. Cunningham, *Advertising in the Broadcast and Cable Media,* 2nd ed. (Belmont, Calif.: Wadsworth, 1984), 133.

Convenience

We are creatures who love our comfort, and convenience can be a very comfortable thing. Radios in the 1930s were important pieces of furniture. In the middle 1930s, Philco Radio entered the market with a console radio advertised as the "No stoop, no squat, no squint" model. Philco wanted you to know that you could operate its radio without having to bend your back and get down on your knees, and that the tuning dial and knobs were located so that any one could see and use them comfortably. Today's Seven-Eleven stores sell convenience more than anything else—they are nearby and are open when you need them. What are the convenience options that your client offers? Free and adequate parking? Open evenings? Easy credit? Telephone shopping? Look for the convenience appeal. Keep this appeal in mind and remember it and you may wish to review the discussion on positioning in Chapter 4.

Curiosity

Sometimes we buy just out of curiosity. Why did these tires stand up under the Baja California torture test? Why did this watch keep on telling time after being strapped to the propeller of a speedboat? A belief in the product's quality or dependability may be at the bottom of this, but we remain curious and we want to find out for ourselves. Curiosity alone, however, seldom does the selling job. It is best in grabbing the interest of the listener/viewer—then other motivating factors need to enter.

Star

When Roger Staubach asks, "How do you spell relief?", when Michael Landon demonstrates his Kodak camera, when Bob Lilly tells us that "It was me against the house until I got a Black and Decker Work Mate," we are motivated favorably toward the product largely because we trust these spokesmen. They are our heroes and if one of them trusts a product, so should we. Testimonials—endorsements by those we admire—can have a strong appeal. After all, a former member of America's Team or the man who built the little house on the prairie wouldn't mislead you.

You shouldn't assume from the foregoing that star appeal is for men only. Martha Raye, Jane Russell, Cathy Rigby, and many other outstanding women have been effective in selling a variety of products.

The target audience for a star appeal commercial may be primarily men, primarily women, or both. Michael Landon sells Kodak products to both men and women, and Martha Raye wants both sexes to use Polident.

Ego

We can first look at ego appeals in terms of two classifications: ego-bolstering appeals based on the desire to enhance one's personality or status, and ego-defensive appeals based on the desire to protect one's personality or maintain one's status. Both are closely tied to self-image. Products that fill these needs are generally luxury ones: not just a warm coat, but a full-length mink coat; not just a car but a top-of-the-line luxury automobile with all the options. Our buying behavior tends to reflect our self-image; we buy either as we see ourselves or as we would like to see ourselves.

Five Senses

Sometimes we buy a product simply because it appeals to one or more of our five senses. We buy candy because it tastes good, a recording because we like the sound, a picture because it pleases the eye, popcorn because it smells so good in the theater lobby, a piece of cloth because of the way it feels. You can show a picture on television, you can sample the recording on radio—but how do you communicate taste, feel, and smell in a broadcast spot? By the use of descriptive terms and demonstration. In a TV commercial for a fabric softener, show a woman holding a towel treated with the softener against her cheek. Let the look on her face convey softness, tactile pleasure. Come up with your own fresh phrases that replace the old and worn ones such as "the sweet smell of spring," "the delicious aroma of freshly brewed coffee," "the skin you love to touch."

It is important to note that the appeals and motivating factors discussed in this chapter are not mutually exclusive. A mix of appeals is often needed. Price appeals provide a good example of such a mixture of motivating factors.

Price

Rarely does price alone motivate. An effective ad combines price with quality. The following spot uses price alone to increase sales.

ANNOUNCER   Sam's Supermarket is ready for the weekend with low prices throughout the store. Shop for these budget-wise prices: whole fryers, only $1.15 a pound. Swiss steak, just $1.88 a pound. Chuck roast . . . while it lasts . . . $1.48 a pound. And in the produce department, Sam's Supermarket has apples for 59 cents a pound. Avocados are going for the low price of 4 for one dollar. These and other food values are yours at Sam's Supermarket this weekend. You always save at Sam's Supermarket.

Yes, this ad would attract some customers, but Sam has competition. The store down the block might insist that its copy read this way:

ANNOUNCER   Joe's Supermarket is the store for both quality and money-saving prices. This weekend, Joe is featuring USDA Choice swiss steak, the mouthwatering cut, for only $1.88 a pound. Joe cuts his own meat and you'll watch him trim your chuck roast to your satisfaction. The price? Only $1.48. Joe doesn't believe in prepackaged meat. He wants you to see the rich marbling in the round steak before he trims it for you. The same top quality that you'll find in Joe's meat department extends throughout Joe's Supermarket.

> Yes, garden fresh produce, freshly baked bread, top label canned goods . . . all at low prices. Save money at Joe's Supermarket this weekend.

Listener reaction? It's nice to save money, but it's even better to get top quality for low prices. This is self-interest at work.

Quality

Quality is not last in this list because it is least, but because it permeates and is common to nearly all other appeals. The script above couples price with quality, Hallmark hits quality in its slogan relating to love, our heroes endorse a product because of its quality. We are strongly motivated by quality. Ads for German-built automobiles stress quality, as do ads for Japanese models. But note the pitch of Chrysler Corporation: "We don't want to be the biggest, just the best." Quality, like convenience, emerges as a strong appeal when we position one product against another.

There is no magical formula that will motivate all people all the time. If a foolproof formula did exist, computers could write commercials. Motivational research can provide guidelines but you, the writer, must decide which approach to use for which product for which target audience.

Features—Benefits

When we buy, we want to benefit from the purchase. One of the first things a good copywriter learns to do is to translate a product's features into its benefits.

A feature is a characteristic built into the product by the manufacturer—and it may not always be understood by the consumer. It is your job as a copywriter to translate these features into benefits that will make the buyer want the product. Visit any automobile showroom, appliance dealer, or camera shop and look at the brochures. You will find the product's features in this literature, and it is your job to translate them into customer benefits. Here are some examples taken from brochures.

What the Brochure Says (Feature):	What the Copywriter Says (Benefit):
Has oversize housing of heat and impact-resistant Lexan polycarbonate (Leitz slide projector).	Your Leitz projector will last longer because it resists overheating.
Remarkable McPherson struts (Subaru automobile).	A more comfortable ride.
Active infrared autofocus system (Olympus AFL camera).	Gives you pictures that are always in sharp focus.
Dual-aid filter and water attachment (Stihl Cutquik).	Dust-free cutting, no sawdust to inhale.
Comes complete with Hi-Vac (Snapper Lawnmower).	The Snapper Hi-Vac vacuums grass into an upright position for ease in cutting even damp grass.

POINTS TO REMEMBER

- Copywriters must understand human nature and what motivates consumers to purchase certain products. Rational motivations are based on need for a product, whereas emotional motivations stem from the consumer's wants and desires.

- A rational motivation to purchase a product or service will help the consumer justify an emotionally based purchase decision.

- Life-cycle analysis can help the copywriter define the target audience for an ad's product or service.

- The basic appeals that will attract a consumer to the product include improved personal appearance, love of family, convenience, enhanced self-image, sensory pleasure, the attractiveness of a hero or celebrity, and the desire to save money while obtaining quality.

- As a copywriter, you must convert the features of a product into benefits that will create a desire to purchase on the part of the consumer.

- There is no magic formula that will motivate all people all the time, but we do tend to buy largely from self-interest.

1. Recall your most recent purchase worth $50.00 or more and analyze why you bought the specific item you did.

or

2. Talk with several adults other than your instructor for this class and try to discover why they made a particular choice in a recent purchase. What was their motivation? Avoid talking to someone who teaches advertising.

Visit a camera shop, appliance store, or automobile showroom and obtain product brochures. Select one of the brochures and note the features mentioned in it. Convert these features into benefits that will appeal to consumers. (Use the form at the end of this exercise section.)

Medical science tells us that breakfast is an important meal, important to good health. Watch children's programs on Saturday morning TV and analyze commercials for breakfast cereals in terms of their rational and emotional appeals. How effective would these commercials be for adults?

Analyze the following four commercials and answer these questions.

1. Is the main motivation rational or emotional?
2. What is the target audience for this product?
3. For which family life-cycle does the product have its main appeal?
4. What benefits for the consumer does the commercial offer?
5. To what extent is price alone a motivational factor in the commercial?
6. Which of the nine basic appeals predominates in each commercial?

Note: Not all of the six questions may be appropriate to every commercial.

OTTMANN ADVERTISING AGENCY, INC.

Client: ___Frank Kent Cadillac___

For: ___30-second TV___

___Coupe DeVille___

VIDEO

OPEN: MCU MARY S. GETTING INTO CAR
OUTSIDE DEALERSHIP. ZOOM BACK. 3/4
FRONT AND SIDE AS CAR BACKS FROM IN
FRONT OF SHOW ROOM

DRIVING FOOTAGE: CAR IN FRONT OF
WILL ROGERS BLDGS:
CARTER MUSEUM
AMERICANA HOTEL
WATER GARDENS
FIRST NATIONAL PLAZA
(BY SCULPTURE)
DISSOLVE TO INTERIOR OF CAR. (SLOW
PAN FROM PASSENGER SIDE) DASH, STEER-
ING WHEEL, ETC.; MARY STEPS OUT OF
CAR IN FRONT OF KIMBELL MUSEUM. DIS-
SOLVE TO EXTERIOR SIGN AT DEALERSHIP.
ZOOM IN TO BCU.

AUDIO

You can own a well-equipped FRANK KENT
Cadillac at a very competitive price! It's the
best VALUE on the road today . . . from
FRANK KENT, an authorized factory dealer
52 years. Drive the Cadillac you've always
wanted: Coupe de Ville, Eldorado,
Fleetwood . . . from the dealer that has the
models, colors, options, and price . . . plus
Cadillac's improved fuel economy . . . at
FRANK KENT your total Cadillac Dealer.
Conveniently located corner Lancaster and
Main Streets, Downtown Fort Worth.

Courtesy Ottmann Advertising Agency, Inc., Fort Worth, Texas.

GOODMAN & ASSOCIATES, INC.

Sponsor: ___All Pro Auto Parts, Inc.___

Length: ___30"___

Subject: ___Institutional___

LILLY

(MUSIC UNDER LILLY)   Hi, I'm Bob Lilly here in your local All
Pro store. All Pro has thousands of brand name parts in stock
for both domestic and import cars and trucks.

Their prices are competitive, too. And there's a convenient
location near you where you can get fast service from a real pro.

So, get the parts, the price, and the right advice. Remember,
all you need to know is All Pro.

(JINGLE)   Get the auto parts you need and you get the pro
. . . at the black and yellow sign of All Pro.

LILLY

See the yellow pages for the store nearest you.

Courtesy Goodman & Associates, Inc., Fort Worth, Texas.

CENTRAL ADVERTISING AGENCY

Client: __Radio Shack__

Copy: __TV Antenna__

VIDEO	AUDIO
OPEN: 2 MEN WORKING IN YARD CU FRED	CHUCK—Hey, Fred, the game's about ready to start.
CU CHUCK	FRED—With the reception on my set, I may as well finish the yard work.
SUPER: ARCHER SUPER COLOR SPECIAL 21.88 UHF-VHF-FM MS 2 MEN	CHUCK—You need a Radio Shack Super Color TV Antenna like mine. Got it at a special purchase price . . . only 21.88!
CHUCK ON ROOF INSTALLING MERCH	FRED—What about installation?
CU FRED MS 2 MEN	CHUCK—Did it myself and saved a bundle. It was easy . . . the Shack's got all the cable and hardware, too!
SUPER: ARCHER SUPER COLOR SPECIAL 21.88	FRED—Only 21.88, that's great!
UHF-VHF-FM AT PARTICIPATING STORES	CHUCK—Right, come on in. Let's watch the game on my set.
SUPER: RADIO SHACK TANDY COMPANY	FRED—You kiddin', I'm going to Radio Shack to get my own Super Color Antenna for 21.88.
	CHUCK V/O—Only at Radio Shack . . . a Tandy Company.

Courtesy Central Advertising Agency, Fort Worth, Texas.

KWYK

Advertiser: __Bruce's Sales and Service__

Bruce's Sales and Service 910 San Juan Blvd. is having the greatest giveaway in its history. Now listen closely. Bruce's Sales and Service will be giving away a complete satellite TV system valued at over $3400.00. Just go in and register and you could be the big winner. You can also save on a 19-inch Quasar Color TV Model WT5923UW priced at a low $388.00. Quasar and Bruce's Sales and Service for the quality you deserve at low prices. 910 San Juan Blvd.

Courtesy KWYK, Farmington, New Mexico.

Student Name _____

Product Brochure _____

Features   **Benefits**

Student Name _____

Commercial Analyzed _____

Analysis

Student Name _____

Analysis of Frank Kent Cadillac commercial

Analysis of All Pro commercial with Bob Lilly

Student Name _____

Analysis of Radio Shack commercial

Analysis of KWYK commercial

6 The Anatomy of a Broadcast Commercial

The effectiveness of a broadcast commercial, whether for radio or television, stems from good structure and good organization. Your commercial needs a functional floor plan: an inviting front door through which you entice the listener/viewer; an interest-holding interior in which you inform and create the desire to purchase; and a ready exit through which members of your audience may hurry to the store to take advantage of the benefits you offer.

The A.I.D.A. Formula

The most widely followed formula, or floor plan, for organizing a broadcast commercial is known by the initials A.I.D.A.: A for *attention;* I for *interest;* D for *desire;* and A for *action.* There are other formulas, just as there are varying types of commercials, and we'll examine them later. But for now, we'll examine A.I.D.A.

Attention

People don't buy radio and television sets just to tune to your commercials. They own their sets for entertainment and information. For many, the commercial is an intrusion or at least it offers a break to raid the refrigerator or go to the bathroom. Unless your spot opens with an attention grabber and carries the listener/viewer into the sales message, you've failed.

For radio, you gain attention in three basic ways: with words, with a sound effect, or with music. A possible variation is to use an attention-gaining voice for the words you've written: a Brooklyn cab driver, a Vermont farmer, a deep South secretary, or a Texas rancher.

Using words alone, a radio spot for a hamburger stand might open with "Love at first bite. That's what you'll find when you bite into a juicy hamburger from Tom's Hamburgers."

Here's an example of a radio spot opening with a sound effect.

SOUND	HEAVY TRAFFIC. CAR HORNS.
ANNOUNCER	Stalled in rush-hour traffic again! Day after day you wonder why you put up with this. Well, you don't have to. City Transit makes getting home a pleasure. Air conditioned busses, comfortable seating . . . you can even read the evening paper on your comfortable way home . . .

The sound of rush-hour traffic attracts our attention . . . it's a sound many people relate to.

Or gain attention with opening music—after being sure you have legal clearance to use the music. (Gaining permissions is covered in Chapter 7.)

MUSIC	WILLIE NELSON, ON THE ROAD AGAIN.
ANNOUNCER	No, Willie isn't coming here for a personal appearance, but you can have him in your home every day. It just takes a visit to Tompkin's Music Center . . .

With television, you have the added advantage of both audio and video to attract immediate attention. In a television commercial for the U.S. Postal Service's Express Mail, the opening audio asks: "What does it take to excel?" The accompanying video is a closeup of an American eagle, which immediately soars into flight. Here is a key to attracting video attention—motion.

Note the following two commercials for the way in which they gain attention in their openings—the first for radio, the second for television.

RADIO COMMERCIAL

ANNOUNCER

It took Margie 30 minutes. It took Sally . . . who's never in a hurry . . . 35 minutes. It took Helen all morning. But Helen doesn't have a self-cleaning Kitchen Queen oven. Margie, and yes, even Sally, just closed the oven door, turned on the self-cleaning switch and sat back and waited. Well, Margie didn't merely wait for her Kitchen Queen oven to clean itself. She had coffee, read the paper, and made a couple of phone calls. Sally ran to the store and also drank coffee while her Kitchen Queen oven cleaned itself. But poor Helen. She scrubbed, she scraped, she got ammonia fumes in her eyes, she got worse than dishpan hands, and she didn't really get a clean oven . . . not the clean you get with a self-cleaning Kitchen Queen oven. Your self-cleaning Kitchen Queen oven is available at all quality dealers. Just look for ovens in the Yellow Pages. Look today. Your time is worth it. Kitchen Queen, the one-button self-cleaning oven.

TV COMMERCIAL

VIDEO	AUDIO
LONG SHOT OF MAN ON PSYCHIATRIST COUCH. DR. IS TAKING NOTES.	You don't need a psychiatrist to help you relax.
CLOSEUP OF TROPICAL FISH IN TANK.	You need the Tropical Fish Store.
PULL BACK TO SHOW MAN WHO WAS ON COUCH NOW GAZING CONTENTEDLY INTO TROPICAL FISH TANK.	The Tropical Fish Store can get you started on this fascinating and relaxing hobby with over 100 varieties of tropical fish for your selection.
LONG SHOT OF DEN AT HOME. MAN IN EASY CHAIR, FEET ON OTTOMAN, FISH TANK NEARBY. HE IS COMPLETELY RELAXED.	You can relax with your feet up and enjoy the sight of either fresh or saltwater tropical fish. The Tropical Fish Store has all you need . . . tanks, aerators, and of course, fish.
SAME AS BEFORE. PHONE RINGS. MAN ANSWERS:	Joe? Sam next door. Got a big business deal cooking. Can I come over and relax with your fish?

TROPICAL FISH STORE LOGO WITH ADDRESS	You may want to keep it quiet from your neighbors, but visit the Tropical Fish Store today . . . 113 Jackson Highway. You owe it to your peace of mind. The Tropical Fish Store—113 Jackson Highway, across from the courthouse.

The radio spot seeks to gain attention by making a statement that raises a question in the listener's mind: What did Margie do in thirty minutes? The answer, the listener may reason, could well lie in some timesaving or laborsaving device, something that interests most homemakers. Curiosity holds our attention.

The television commercial gains attention by raising a question: What do you need to relax? On the video side, after a three-second shot of the man on the psychiatrist's couch, we immediately have motion and the varied color of the tropical fish. Again, motion helps gain our attention along with color.

Silence may also be used to attract attention in a television commercial. We are so accustomed to being bombarded with sound that the absence of it can gain our attention: Our curiosity takes over.

There is no absolute formula for gaining attention. Your creativity and insight into human nature are your best guides. Warren Beaman of Beaman Advertising advises, "Keep it simple, keep it honest." Ron Rogers, station manager for KVET, admonishes, "A good opening does attract attention, but it must lead into the sales message." With these two points in mind, analyze the following opening for a radio commercial:

SOUND EFFECT	LOUD EXPLOSION
SOUND EFFECT	FADE IN EMERGENCY VEHICLE SIRENS AND HOLD UNDER FOR:
ANNOUNCER	You'll find an explosion of taste when you visit Jake's Ice Cream Parlor.

This sound-effect opening could certainly gain attention, but who wants the taste of ice cream to feel like an explosion in their mouth? This opening could backfire: It's misleading because it can't be tastefully tied to the product.

Or, try this opening:

ANNOUNCER	Here is a bulletin from our newsroom. A 3-car pileup at Fifth and Main has traffic in a tizzy. And if you're in a tizzy about where to get your new carpet . . .

Both the preceding spots are dishonest and misleading—and they violate the policy of the Federal Communications Commission (FCC) against misleading the radio listener. (This FCC policy is discussed further in Chapter 12.)

In attracting attention for the sales message that is to follow, keep your target audience in mind. A commercial that opens with "Get ready for a truly great beer" could cause people who don't drink beer to tune out. This is all right. You are not out to convert them. Your job is to attract beer drinkers and convert them to your brand. Give thought to the particular audience for your product and gain the attention of this group of listeners/viewers. Watch especially the openings of television commercials for soft drinks, chewing gum, or breakfast cereals during the Saturday morning cartoons. You know from the very opening what the target audience is.

Finally, if you can work a product benefit into your opening, you are on your way to attracting attention. A feature of a certain headache remedy is that it is "buffered with Maalox." This feature translates into the benefit of preventing upset stomachs, so you could open with, "There's no upset stomach when you erase your headache with . . ." Your target audience is people who suffer from headaches but whose stomachs just don't agree with plain aspirin. Here you've gotten their attention with a headache remedy that will not cause stomach upset, and you've already given them a benefit.

The terms *attention getter, lead, lead-in,* and *opening* are interchangeable. It is possible to buy lead services, which send you periodically a list of attention-getting leads to use in your commercials. They are arranged alphabetically by product or service: Automotive, Bakery, Clothing Store, Department Store, and so on. Under Automotive, you might find:

A new car is a safe car.

or:

Save money on gas and maintenance with a car from _____.

Under Laundries and Dry Cleaning:

Put up a good front with a fresh shirt from _____.

While this service may save you some time and thought, it also has disadvantages. One, these canned leads tend to be hackneyed. Second, these services are available to all stations, and you run the risk of your spot for Sam's Laundry opening with the same lead as a competing spot for Karen's Laundry written for another station in town.

An alternative is to keep your own notebook of attention-gaining leads. As ideas come to mind, jot them down. When you're good enough, you can sell your own lead service.

Interest

The crossover from attention to interest is a subtle one and not always clearcut, nor does it have to be. What gains attention may also hold interest. Again, not every commercial is going to hold the interest of every listener/viewer. You aim for the interest of your target audience. Teenagers rarely show interest in life insurance, and elderly drivers show small interest in sports cars.

Look for interest in the two commercials used to illustrate attention-getting leads. The radio spot holds interest primarily for women. This interest is in time- and labor-saving devices. Women can identify with Helen, who had to spend all morning scrubbing her oven, and they are interested in spending their time in better ways. This interest can grow into the desire to buy a product.

The television commercial for the tropical fish store holds interest for a wider number of viewers. The need to relax in this frantic world is common to many of us. And when you can sit back, relax, and lose your tension with something as simple as a tank of tropical fish, interest can well move into desire.

Desire

Desire means, "I want one of those." It means, "I want the yellow lawnmower in that commercial, not the old blue one I now have." Review the previous chapter for the factors that motivate us to purchase. Desires grow out of benefits—for example, the creature comfort desires from ease of operation, low upkeep, and comfortable ride. Remember, when you sell Joe's Steak House, don't sell the steak, sell the sizzle—sell the benefit of the way Joe prepares his steaks just for you. Don't forget the price if it is a selling point of the product, but make it a benefit without forgetting to stress quality.

Action

If the listener/viewer just sits at home and does nothing as a result of your commercial, you have failed. You must move the consumer to action by urging action: "See these values today." "Check the Yellow Pages for the dealer nearest you." "Phone now." "Park free at Thompson's Department Store." This move to action should stress the sponsor's name and address and, if desired, telephone number. Remember, the sale isn't made until *you* get the customer into the store.

A.I.D.A. Summary

In analyzing radio and television commercials for the A.I.D.A. formula, only the opening and closing *A*s will generally stand out clearly; interest and desire frequently merge. Theoretically, you should be able to underline in, say, red those lines that constitute the opening attention-getter (and you frequently can); then underline in blue the interest-gaining portion; in yellow, desire; and in black, the move to action. However, separating interest from desire in a commercial is often not an easy matter. They blend together in a great many spots. As a writer, your concern is to hold interest and create desire for the product. Don't try to be mechanical, taking the approach that after you have written an interest-holding sentence or phrase, you next turn only to creating desire. Instead, feel free to intermix interest with desire if the copy seems to flow better that way.

One of the best summations of the A.I.D.A. formula can be found in the National Association of Broadcasters' publication *Guidelines for Radio: Copywriting*. Here are those guidelines. Note especially the alternatives given for your closing move to action.

A consistently successful formula is the A.I.D.A. approach. This stands for the four elements of a commercial, in their regular order of appearance: attention, interest, desire, action. Grabbing the attention of the listener is the most important function of the commercial, and obviously should come first. The attention-getter can take the form of a sound effect, a statement, a question, a promise, a benefit, or a number of other methods that will leave the audience waiting for more. Interest and desire work from the attention-getter and expand on why the listener should want what you are offering. This can be done in a variety of ways:

- Expand on your attention-getter and work that into part of the selling offer. A sound effect can be used to grab attention, then used throughout the body of the spot to build interest in the product. A comparison between the quiet purr of a PowerPro lawn mower from Lou's Cycle and the clickety-clack of a push-type model can have great appeal.
- Describe one fundamental aspect of the product: "A new PowerPro Lawn Mower from Lou's Cycle comes with a free lawn chair to relax in because it takes you half the time to cut your grass."
- Emphasize the benefits that come from owning the product: "If you get your lawn mowed Saturday morning, you have time to watch it grow all afternoon."
- Explain the selling points that deliver the desired benefits: "The PowerPro Mower comes with a grass catcher lined with disposable garbage bags to make your job easier."

- Demonstrate the economy and enjoyment that come from owning the product: "The PowerPro Mower is so much fun to use that Tom Sawyer would have made a bundle—if he would let anyone else use it."

- Go after prestige or sex appeal: "With a PowerPro Lawn Mower you will experience splendor in the grass."

- Illustrate the disadvantages for not owning a product: "Everyone on the block owns a PowerPro Mower except the Joneses. And you can't see their house because of the grass."

Every spot should be closed with an invitation to act. A reminder like 'get it today' entices the listener to act now, rather than put things off until tomorrow. The more effective the close, the more effective the spot. Because of this, the close should be set up powerfully, progressing logically from one step to the next. There are several varieties of closings:

- Provide good reasons and excuses for buying: "Tired of paying the kid down the street ten bucks for cutting your grass? But a PowerPro and cut it yourself."

- Explain how easy it is to buy and select the product: "Over 50 PowerPro models in stock, from the TX-50 all the way up to the Turbo 9."

- Explain how, where, and when to get it: "Just see Lou's Cycle Shop, 74 Button Street, this weekend. They're going fast."

- Explain prices and terms to make the sale easy: "Just $209 with a trade-in, no matter what your current mower looks like."

- Urge that *now* is the time to buy: "Get yours today, so you can watch the football game tomorrow"[1]

The A.I.D.A. Formula in Action

To help you get a feel for the A.I.D.A. formula, analyze the following commercials and station promotion spots. Yes, a good station promotion or a good PSA spot follows the formula just as faithfully as does a commercial. Here is one written by Janice Gray, director of promotion for WGBH-FM, Boston.

OPERA BOX/   generic spot

WGBH-FM

ANNOUNCER   Everyone knows it's a sin to laugh at the opera. If you really feel that way, there's a program here on WGBH that you'll find . . . enlightening. From The Opera Box, Jim Svejda lets you see up close, behind the operatic performance you witness onstage. To illustrate the point he makes, Jim uses recorded performances . . . some collector's rare 78 RPMs. You're listening now to a 1929 recording of the overture to Rossini's "Barber of Seville". . . For a delightful, sometimes irreverent exploration of the art of opera and the history of singing in the 20th Century, join Jim Svejda for The Opera Box . . . Friday at 10 . . . here on listener-supported WGBH Boston.

And next are the production notes by senior producer Bill Cavness for the station promo.

---

1. Courtesy National Association of Broadcasters.

FIRST SENTENCE LIGHTLY KIDDING . . . REST INFORMATIVE BUT FOR
HEAVEN'S SAKE, <u>NOT</u> HEAVY.

Courtesy WGBH-FM, Boston, Massachusetts.

The opening line of this spot not only gains attention, it gains the attention of the target audience—opera buffs. It has the added possibility of appealing to music lovers who are not devoted to opera but who say, "Hey, this might be for me." Also note that not just words but the delivery of the words is important in this spot. Both interest and desire grow out of (1) knowing that rare, not frequently heard performances will be broadcast, (2) backstage highlights will be offered, and (3) some of the material may even be irreverent. Finally the listener is moved to act and tune in to the program with "name and address' being Friday at 10, WGBH.

Here's an agency-written television commercial, prepared for use in a major metroplex market.

TELEVISION CONTINUITY

Channel _____   Date _____
Sponsor __All Pro Auto Parts__   Length __30"_____
GOODMAN & ASSOCIATES, INC.

VIDEO	AUDIO
CLOSEUP OF MONROE SHOCK HARVEY'S HAND. CLOSEUP OF SHOCK IN OTHER HAND. WIDEN FROM HANDS TO HARVEY.	MUSIC TAKE AND HOLD UNDER Buy one Monroe shock absorber and get the second one half off <u>now</u> during the Monroe Top Shock Sale at All Pro!
DISSOLVE TO HARVEY AS HE WALKS TO THE SIDE OF INDY 500 BANNER.	While you're in, register to win a free trip for two to the Indy 500 . . . May 28th through the 31st.
REVEAL AT BOTTOM OF SCREEN: "MUST BE 18 YEARS OLD TO REGISTER"	The Sweepstakes prize includes round trip fare, hotel accommodations and choice grandstand seating!
DISSOLVE TO HARVEY IN CAR AS HE STARTS ENGINE	So, start your engines. SFX OF ENGINE STARTING
REVEAL BOTTOM OF SCREEN: "DEADLINE . . . MAY 21"	Get those entries in today! No purchase necessary and you don't have to be present to win.
CUT TO ANIMATED LOGO. SCREEN BOTTOM: "ALL YOU NEED TO KNOW IS ALL PRO."	All you need to know is All Pro! MUSIC OUT

Courtesy Goodman & Associates, Inc., Fort Worth, Texas.

This is one of a series of TV commercials produced in the Dallas-Fort Worth metroplex featuring Harvey Martin and Bob Lilly of the Dallas Cowboys. Both had gained all-pro status in football and thus the tie-in to All Pro Auto Parts. Attention is gained in two ways: seeing Harvey Martin and learning about a half-price bargain. Interest perks up with the possibility of a free trip for two to the Indy 500, but interest and desire go hand in hand with the desire to win the trip. Action is urged with the statement "Get those entries in today."

The following radio commercial attracts attention with the statement "It's eleven at night. And you need a refill on that prescription." Many of us have been caught in this situation at one time or another, and we are interested in the answer to the question "What can you do about it?" We are quickly given the answer: "Just call M.D. Pharmacy." Here comes the benefit . . . it is the only drugstore in town that's open until midnight, and it has an answering service for after-midnight calls. What other benefits/desires to use this pharmacy's service do you find in the commercial?

Client: ___M.D. Pharmacy_____

Media: ___Radio 60 sec._____

Date: ___To replace existing copy_____

ANNOUNCER   It's eleven at night, and you need a refill on that prescription. What can you do about it? Wait until morning? No, just call M.D. Pharmacy. You can get it refilled immediately. Because M.D. is Austin's only pharmacy that stays open until midnight. That's right, M.D. is open until midnight every night. What's more, if you call your prescription in after midnight, an answering service will take your order. Then all you have to do is pick it up in the morning. Or, have it delivered . . . that's real convenience. And M.D.'s extra handy location between UT and downtown makes it easy to reach from all parts of Austin. And of course, M.D. takes painstaking care with each prescription they fill. So really now, wouldn't you feel more secure with your prescription at M.D.? Remember, there's only one pharmacy in Austin that stays open until midnight. M.D. Pharmacy, 1701 Lavaca.

Courtesy Beaman Advertising, Austin, Texas.

Additional Formulas

A.I.D.A. isn't the only formula for constructing broadcast commercials. The two additional formulas given here are not in conflict with A.I.D.A., but are variations on the same theme.

The A.I.P.I. Formula

The initials in this formula stand for *attract attention, identify sponsor, present sales message, invite action.* This formula is not really different from A.I.D.A., but it does have the added value of stressing sponsor identification. If the copy doesn't identify who is selling widgets at half price, the spot is pointless. As a general rule, in a 30-second radio spot, mention the sponsor's name three times; in 60 seconds call the sponsor by name five times. Television has the added advantage of keeping sponsor identification visually before the viewer.

The Rush Day Formula

How much time does a writer spend structuring a commercial? Generally, not much. Nevertheless, the proper organization, the proper structuring of a spot, is a key to effective broadcast advertising. But it's something like riding a bicycle: Once you know how, you don't analyze each push of the pedals as you go along—you just ride and pedal. When learning, you had to think about it, but on the job it seems like second nature. This isn't to say that you should become lax in your writing, but it does mean that with experience, good organization in your writing tends to come naturally. The need for structure is always there, of course, it's just that the pressure of time doesn't always allow you to ponder extensively over each step in writing the spot.

On those many days when every salesperson in the station has descended on you with spots that must be on the air immediately (a normal day), you often turn to an abbreviated version of the A.I.D.A. formula: O.S.A.—*O* for *opening* or lead, *S* for *sales message,* and *A* for *action*.

A certain copywriter we know had been grinding out radio spots for twenty-five years and then returned to college for a course in novel writing. She reported, "I wrote my first novel in fifty words and mentioned the hero's name five times." Once the formula gets ingrained, it's hard to break.

National versus Local Commercials

As you watch television commercials or listen to them on the radio, you should quickly note a difference in the structure of national as opposed to local spots. Those commercials written for local businesses tend to follow the A.I.D.A. formula more closely, especially in terms of the closing move to action. Local commercials urge the viewer/listener to go to a specific location for the product advertised—say Mary's Bar-B-Q at 1209 South Drive. This is not practical in national advertising of course. You just can't give the name and address of every Westinghouse or Cadillac dealer in the nation. In many instances, the thrust of a national spot is to put the name of the product before the audience, and to make the product or service desirable. It can be argued that making the viewer/listener want the product is in itself a form of moving to action.

POINTS TO REMEMBER

- While not the only formula for structuring a radio or television commercial, PSA, or station promo, the A.I.D.A. formula is one of the most generally used. The formula of A for *attention,* I for *interest,* D for *desire* and A for *action* can be most helpful for the beginning copywriter, both in structuring spots and in the analysis of commercials heard and seen on the air.

- The A.I.P.I. formula chiefly stresses the use of the sponsor's name. Remember that the first *I* in this formula stands for *identify sponsor.* Identify this important business as often as you can. A review of Point of View in Chapter 3 will assist you in sponsor identification.

▪ The rush day formula of O.S.A.—*opening lead, sales message,* and *action* is one that you move into as you begin to meet the daily deadlines of station operation.

▪ Regardless of what formula you use, you must engage the attention of the listener/viewer, you must create a desire for the product, and you must move the buyer into the store, where the final sale is made.

1. Watch television until you see two commercials that attract your attention immediately—that is, within the first five seconds.

2. Describe what was seen and heard that caught your attention.

3. Did these spots hold your interest? If yes, how? If no, why not? (Perhaps you were not interested in the product.)

4. Do you think these spots would have held the interest of anyone else? If yes, who?

5. If the spots interested you, did you feel a desire for the products or service? Might the commercials create a desire for the products or service in someone else? Who?

6. Did the commercials contain a move to action? Describe how this was done. Were these national or local commercials?

Listen to the radio and analyze any two radio commercials following the outline given in Exercise 1.

Write attention-getting openings for radio spots for the following businesses. After each opening, indicate your target audience and which life-style cycle group your spot is written for.

1. Martha's Maternity Wear

2. Alexander's Handy Man. Alexander's slogan is "Everything for the home repair man."

3. Sounds of the Highway. The store's slogan is "Complete stereo for your car."

Write attention-getting openings for television spots for the businesses listed below. Indicate both the video and audio portions. Do not be concerned about format at this stage in your TV writing. Do, however, indicate your target audience and make clear the life-style cycle group for which you are aiming.

1. Huggens Jewelry. The firm's slogan is "Experts in diamonds for over seventy-five years."
2. Joe Frank's Cadillac.
3. Bon Ton Bakery, which specializes in French pastry.

Write a sixty-second radio commercial for PowerPro lawnmowers in which you gain initial interest by using a sound effect. Follow the A.I.D.A. formula. This lawnmower has electronic push-button starter, is self-propelled, has a nineteen-inch blade, and a centered grass catcher. Height adjustment is the easiest ever. Available at Towbridge Lawn Center, this week only, at 30 percent off. Towbridge Lawn Center is at 919 High Street in the Blue Ridge Shopping Center.

Write a thirty-second television spot for PowerPro lawnmowers using the A.I.D.A. formula. Use the information given in Exercise 5 for the radio spot. The setting must be outdoors. You may use only two performers. They may be of either sex and any age.

MARTHA'S MATERNITY WEAR

ALEXANDER'S HANDYMAN

SOUNDS OF THE HIGHWAY

HUGGENS JEWELRY

JOE FRANK'S CADILLAC

BON TON BAKERY

Student Name _____   Advertiser _____

Date Submitted _____   Commercial Length _____

Student Name _____   Advertiser _____

Date Submitted _____   Commercial Length _____

7 The Radio Commercial: The Mechanics

recent media campaign put it well: Wherever you go, there's radio. Radio is with you at the shore, in a hunting lodge in the mountains, in the bathroom, the kitchen, the bedroom, the den. It's in your car, your plane, your boat, or on your bike. Radio is by far our most portable means of mass communication—and it may be the world's chief medium for communicating entertainment and information and for selling goods and services.

Radio is a theater of the mind. The listener builds the scenery, does the costuming, and decides what the face behind the voice looks like. But you, the writer, provide the materials to build the scenery, the fabric with which to fashion the costume, and the words that suggest the face. You do all this with three elements: sound effects, music, and voice. With a sound effect as simple as crumpling the cellophane from a pack of cigarettes before the microphone, you can suggest a raging forest fire. Well-selected music can put the listener in the Dreamland Ballroom, on the grounds of West Point, at a rock concert, or in Vienna. But it is voice using words that creates most of the selling impact of radio.

It is the words that you write for the station announcer to read, it is the words that you write for the sponsor himself to deliver on mike that move products, that sell services. Music and sound effects are adjuncts. We do not want to underplay the effectiveness of well-selected music or well-executed sound effects in a radio commercial, but instead to put the three elements in perspective. Words come first.

Radio Today

In addition to being a highly portable medium, today's radio tends heavily to specialization in programming. Actually, we don't refer so much to programming in radio as we do to a station's "sound". A given station may be all country and western, or all album rock, or all news and talk. National networks along with wire services do provide national news, and special networks let the local listener hear play-by-play broadcasts of out-of-town sporting events. National spot sales by major agencies expose listeners across the country to the same commercials with the same jingles. All stations have access to the same list of top tunes, so that the music on a given local station often sounds the same as that of any other station with a similar "sound."

The emphasis in radio, however, is much more on local content than it is on network programming. The days of radio network soap operas, dramas, variety programs, and stars such as Jack Benny, Bob Hope, and Fred Allen are gone. Radio stations today do not carry the networks for hours at a time, as many once did. And while any number of stations across the nation may play the same music, they make a special effort to provide local air personalities—locally identified disc jockeys who can bring listeners to the station and keep them loyal.

Your job is to understand the local audience your station attracts and to write accordingly. Pay attention not only to the station's overall programming, but to its geographical location and power. A 250-watt AM station in a metropolitan area is apt to program differently from a 50,000-watt clear-channel station in the same location. The 250-watt station may be after an urban audience, while the 50,000-watt station may be trying to appeal to a more rural audience. You must make your own analysis of your station, but do know the audience for whom you are writing. When in doubt, ask a member of the station's sales force.

The Advantages of Radio

One of the outstanding advantages of radio is its omnipresence. At one time, a radio set was a major piece of furniture in the home. Radio sets were then about the size of today's twenty-one-inch television sets and came housed in finely finished oak or walnut cabinets. Today, a radio receiver can fit in a man's shirt pocket or in a woman's purse. The portability allowed by transistors gives radio the advantage of taking its sales message practically anywhere and everywhere.

Drive-time radio is a favorite for both the station's sales staff and for sponsors. By giving the drivers what they want to hear—weather, news briefs, traffic reports and their favorite music—the station can deliver an audience for your sales message.

Radio is flexible. Radio stations can put a new commercial on the air with amazing speed. It is possible for a salesperson to make a sale at, say, 10 A.M., phone the copy information to the station, and have the advertising message over the air thirty minutes later. No copywriter, no traffic person, and few salespeople like this type of operation, but radio is capable of such rapid work, and this remains one of its strengths.

In radio advertising it is also quick and easy to make changes in broadcast copy. In most small and medium markets, advertisers need only phone the radio station to make changes in copy that can be broadcast an hour later. A weekly newspaper would take a week to make such a change, a daily paper at least twenty-four hours. A local TV station would in all likelihood require a full day's notice. Note that market and station size govern station flexibility; the larger the station, the larger its bureaucracy, and the slower it can make copy changes.

Radio's flexibility has important implications for your work as a copywriter. In the world of classroom assignments, you may have a week or more to turn in a piece of copy. Don't think that this is the pace at which commercial radio operates, especially in local stations. In-class writing assignments due by the end of the class period provide very practical training. Writing under time pressure is typical of work in the real world.

Finally, radio is relatively inexpensive. A sixty-second spot on local radio will sell for considerably less than a thirty-second TV spot in the same market.

The Limitations of Radio

Radio does have limitations. While it can describe a product, radio cannot show the product itself. Radio's lack of ability to show or demonstrate products is its prime limitation. On radio, you can hear the sound of a diet drink being poured from the can into a glass, you can hear the person making sounds of enjoyment as he or she drinks it, but you can see neither the drink nor the person enjoying it.

Motion, too, can only be suggested on radio, not shown. A sound effect can suggest the motion of a sports car, while television gives us the actual picture of the car in motion. Yes, stereo with voice one on one channel and voice two on the other can heighten the suggested effect of motion, but this technique is still only an illusion.

Is the lack of a picture really a limitation? The answer, to a large extent, lies with the product, with the budget available for the production of the commercial, and certainly with the writer. In selling, it is undoubtedly more important to see a bathing suit than it is a tank full of gasoline. But how do we "see"? Remember that radio is a theater of the mind. As we pointed out earlier, when you sell Joe's Steak House on radio, you don't sell the steak, you sell the sizzle.

Another limitation of radio is the inattention of the listener. People often use radio as background music for other tasks. Music plays while we drive, do housework, or study. Most often it doesn't command our full attention, and for this reason the radio copywriter must write well enough to gain and hold attention for the commercial. It's not surprising that sponsors like to run their spots during news and sportscasts—when people are listening rather than just hearing.

Timing Radio Copy

Advertising time on radio, especially local radio, was once sold on a word-count basis. Radio rate cards of the 1940s and 1950s carried prices for ten-, fifty-, and one hundred-word spots. The idea was that it took thirty seconds to read fifty words and one minute to read one hundred words. This practice might have been right in theory, but it did not work in practice. Today, radio (and television) spots are sold by time. Your most frequent assignment in radio will be to write a one-minute spot, not a hundred-word spot.

To illustrate the fallacy that fifty words equals thirty seconds, read the following two spots aloud and time your reading carefully with a stopwatch or a watch with a sweep-second hand. Remember to read the copy using a style of delivery appropriate to the spot.

JOBY'S FURS

ANNOUNCER   Elegance is more than a word at Joby's. Elegance is a Russian sable from Joby's. Even the lining in a Russian sable from Joby's means elegance. These fine furs make Christmas giving an occasion. Joby's showroom is open until 9 each evening. Joby's, Ninth and Congress, where elegance awaits.

WILBUR'S USED CARS

ANNOUNCER   There's nothing more frustrating than a car you can't depend on! That's right, nothing! But you can have a car that will get you there every time. Just visit Wilbur's Used Car lot at Main and Morton. Main and Morton, that's the address for Wilbur's Used Cars. Wilbur has a 1980 Olds Cutlass at a price you'll never believe, and Wilbur has a lot full of good, clean older cars at giveaway prices. It's Wilbur's for dependable used cars at affordable prices. Wilbur's, Main and Morton.

The Joby's spot contains fifty words and can be read comfortably in under thirty seconds using a sincere, dignified delivery. The Wilbur's Used Car spot contains eighty-six words and can be shouted in thirty seconds. Today's radio copywriter must write spots that fit a given time slot. How do you write to time? While experience certainly helps, the only sure way is to read the copy aloud while timing it with a stopwatch.

Ideally, each copywriter should have a soundproof writing area so that he or she can read aloud while writing. The copywriter can then easily time copy and check for combinations of words that are hard to read aloud.

In actual practice, you'll probably work in a congested area with several coworkers. Thus, you'll need to learn to time your copy while reading silently at an out-loud rate.

Again, note the Joby's spot and the Wilbur's Used Cars spot. What type of delivery do you want the announcer to use? Should your copy be read rapidly or slowly? You must learn to time your copy according to the way you want it delivered on the air.

Having emphasized timing copy by the clock, we must admit that some stations still sell and write copy by word count. Some stations even provide copy paper that is ruled for thirty-second and sixty-second spots. As a general rule, seventy-five words can be delivered in thirty seconds and 135 words in sixty seconds. These word counts are not absolutes, however, only a rough guide.

Terminology

The following terms are included because of their relevance to radio writing and production. Other terms are defined in the glossary at the back of the book.

- *Bed*. Music that is played behind a commercial.
- *Board fade*. A decrease or increase in volume made at the audio control board. Could be either *board fade out* or *board fade in*. (See *mike fade*.)
- *Cross fade*. To fade from one sound or music to another. Same as *segue*. This is to *audio* what a *lap dissolve* is to *video*.
- *Echo*. The effect you get when talking in a large, empty room with hard-surfaced walls and ceiling. The effect is best produced by putting a loud speaker at one end of an echo chamber and picking up the sound with a microphone. The amount of echo can be controlled by changing the distance between speaker and microphone.
- *Establish*. To bring sound effects or music to full volume, permitting the listener to hear enough to understand the sound or music.
- *Hold under*. After establishing the sound effect or music, fading it to background and holding it (as in *bed*) behind the spoken message.
- *Mike fade*. Performers move away from mike (*mike fade off*), or move to on-mike position (*mike fade on*), from off-mike position. Mike fade is a decidedly different effect from a *board fade*. In the mike fade, acoustical relationships change because of the performer's movements. In a board fade, only volume changes.
- *Mike filter*. An electronic means for eliminating high and low frequencies. Often used to give the effect of speaking over an unequalized telephone line.
- *Reverb*. Short for *reverberation*. An electronic device sometimes used in lieu of *echo*, but the effects are not the same.
- *Segue*. Same as *cross fade*.
- *SFX*. An abbreviation for *sound effect*.

Radio Copy Formats

The term *format* as used here simply refers to the physical form of your copy on paper. The format governs such points as when to single-, double-, or triple-space, when to type in all caps, and when to use caps and lowercase. Use of a consistent format leads to a uniformity of presentation that all concerned will understand. Unfortunately, no universal format for typing exists for either radio or television spots. Stations tend to evolve their own format peculiarities. Some announcers insist that what they read be typed in all caps, while others prefer the more common practice of using caps and lowercase. The format given here is a common and effective one. You should follow it unless your employer tells you to use a different form.

Here are your two basic rules: Use all caps for directions, instructions, or any other element that is not to be read aloud over the air. Type what is to be read aloud in caps and lowercase and double-space it. Despite its use by Associated Press and United Press International, copy typed in all caps tends to be more difficult to read.

In addition to the basic rules outlined above, format also involves both the number and kinds of voices used, as well as the way sound effects and music entries are typed. These matters are discussed next.

Single-Voice Copy

The basic format for single-voice copy was introduced in Chapter 3, and we'll expand on it here largely as a matter of review. Note the format used in the following copy:

ANCR. URGENTLY	Only 2 days are left to take advantage of the outstanding values at Finger's Department Store. That's right, only 2 days. Everything in the store has been reduced 25 percent at Fingers!

This format tells you that only one voice is required for the spot. The all-caps instructions tell both the producer/director and the announcer what style of delivery to use. The copy itself is typed apart from the production instructions in caps and lowercase.

The practice of using all caps for instructions to the announcer also helps separate what is to be read aloud from instructions that must appear in the body of the copy.

ANNOUNCER	How often do you check the oil in your car? Every fill up? Every six months? Stop and think about it. (SLIGHT PAUSE) Now that we go to self-service stations, we often forget to make that important check on our motor oil.

Within the body of the copy above is the all-caps instruction SLIGHT PAUSE. The writer wants the announcer to pause briefly to let the message sink in. If the entire body of the copy had been written in all caps, this instruction would not stand out to the announcer and his or her delivery might not convey the message fully.

Two-Voice Copy

It's sometimes desirable to have two voices alternate in reading the copy. Two-voice copy (or alternate-voice copy) should be distinguished from dramatic, or dialog copy. In two-voice copy, the two voices merely alternate phrases or statements. The format is as follows:

VOICE ONE	How often do you check the oil in your car?
VOICE TWO	Every fill up? Every 6 months?
VOICE ONE	Stop and think about it. You car's engine can't think about it, but you can.
VOICE TWO	Preston's wants your car to give you the best performance possible, but you've got to help.

In this example, the instructions are again in all caps, indicating the lines for voice one and voice two. The script also introduces a new element: linear spacing. Up to now, you have been instructed to double-space radio copy that is to be read aloud. Triple-space between voice entries. Why? Again, logic dictates the format to use. (Of course, the typeset copy in this book is spaced tighter than your typewritten scripts will be.)

In radio production, the performers do not need to memorize their lines as they do in television. The radio performer—the announcer—stands before the microphone with script in hand, reading from it. He or she reads the script following the format that you have provided and it must immediately make sense. Achieving this immediate communication is the purpose of using a consistent format. Triple spacing between the entries makes it easier for each reader to isolate and identify his or her lines during performance.

Two-Voice Variations

In the preceding two-voice spot, the nature of the content, automotive upkeep, tends to call for two male voices. If the writer wants to indicate the gender of the voices, the format makes it easy to do so.

MAN I	How often do you check the oil in your car?
MAN II	Every fill up? Every six months?
MAN I	Stop and think about it.

It follows that in other commercials, the writer could alternate two female voices, alternate male and female, or even indicate the age of the voices as well, such as ELDERLY MAN or YOUNG CHILD. It also follows that as a writer you may have no control over who is cast to read your copy. These decisions may be left entirely to a production director.

Finally, no rule other than practicality dictates that you are limited to two voices. However, using more than two voices may tend to confuse the listener—and casting more than two good voices may be a problem, especially in smaller stations. Keep these problems in mind when tempted to write a spot with a cast of thousands.

Dialog Copy

A variation on the multivoice spot just illustrated is the dialog spot, which is usually a mini-drama. The format is the same; it is the content that changes. Here is a dialog spot illustrating the consistency in format.

JOHN	What's for dinner tonight, honey?
MARY	Same old question. Same old answer. Leftovers from last night's dinner.
JOHN	I thought that would be the answer.
MARY	So?
JOHN	So I took a tip from the boss.
MARY	The last time you took a tip from him you lost 30 bucks at the track.

JOHN	Yeah, but this is different. Now he's got a working wife like I do who really doesn't have time to slave away in the kitchen.
MARY	You've got that "slave away" part right. Now what's the tip?
JOHN	See this package I picked up at the supermarket on the way home? It's Quick-As-A-Wink chicken and dumplings. Just pour in a pan, add water, heat, and you've got homemade chicken and dumplings.
MARY	Hey, why didn't I think of that? Sue had Quick-As-A-Wink chicken and dumplings when she had me over while you were out of town. Just hand me that saucepan . . . we're gonna have Quick-As-A-Wink chicken and dumplings tonight.
ANNOUNCER	And you can too. Just a quick trip to the supermarket and a quick meal of delicious Quick-As-A-Wink chicken and dumplings.

Again, double spacing is used between the lines spoken by a single performer, and triple spacing is used between the entries. The only really new element in this dialog spot is the use of an announcer at the end.

This approach to radio commercial copy is attractive to write but not always satisfactory when produced. It calls for dramatic talents that the average radio announcer does not necessarily have. Large agencies with comfortable budgets can cast a dramatic dialog spot with little or no trouble, while small-market stations may encounter difficulties. Before you write such a spot, you must know if it can be produced. Is the talent available? If available, how much will it cost? Is the necessary money available? If you can answer yes to these questions, then proceed—with one more caution. Don't become so clever in your writing that the listener remembers the witty dialog but not the product. That has happened with national spots produced by large agencies. Don't let it happen to you. Finally, remember to keep your dialog copy conversational and pattern it after the way people talk.

Sound Effects and Music

Sound effects, or music, or both—when carefully and well integrated into a spot—can do a great deal to make the commercial special and attract listener attention. First, the format. Since sound effects and music are instructions rather than copy to be read aloud, they are typed in all caps and underlined. The underlining is used for clarity; it helps the eye see immediately that here is an element of the production that is different from instructions to the performers. Here is an abbreviated example.

SOUND	FIRE TRUCK WITH SIREN APPROACHING. ESTABLISH AND FADE UNDER FOR:
ANNOUNCER	This can be a terrifying sound, especially when the fire truck stops at your house.

Here are the things to note in this brief example. It took more than two lines to type the complete sound-effect entry and double spacing is used. The entire sound-effect instruction including the word *sound* on the lefthand margins is in all caps and underlined. There are three spaces between the sound effect and the announcer's opening line.

This example illustrates one other important point. Even though a fire engine's siren is a distinctive sound, the announcer identifies it in the first line. The human ear is credulous. It tends to believe what it is told that it hears—but it also likes to be told precisely what it is hearing. Copywriters also commonly write SFX instead of SOUND, so that the previous example might well be written:

SFX	FIRE TRUCK WITH SIREN APPROACHING. ESTABLISH AND FADE UNDER FOR:
ANNOUNCER	This can be a terrifying sound, especially when the fire truck stops at your house.

Music can be most effective in gaining and holding listener attention. Even the smallest radio stations have a music library, and many stations have mood music libraries. The following example uses piano music.

MUSIC	CHROMATIC SCALE PLAYED ON PIANO FROM TREBLE TO BASS ENDING WITH BASS CHORD.
ANCR	Hear that? That's the sound of prices coming down at Al's Furniture Store. Al is cutting prices all week, and . . .

Don't have a piano available at your station? Find one elsewhere and record the music on a portable tape recorder. Or go to the local dime store and buy a trombone whistle. Perhaps the station engineer has an oscillator that will play a descending scale. Or visit the local high school to recruit a clarinet, trumpet, or trombone player.

A word of caution: Your station may have an extensive library of country and western, big band, or classical music, and it may make regular payments to BMI, ASCAP, and SESAC, but you do not necessarily have the legal right to use this music in a radio commercial. Before you make a piece of music part of your commercial, check with The Harry Fox Agency, 110 East 59th Street, New York, N.Y. 10022, for permission. On the other hand, whenever a station purchases a mood music library such as those available from Thomas Valentino, William B. Tanner, CBS EZ-Cue Library, or others, it almost always receives the rights to use this music with its purchase. Also remember that even though a given musical composition is old enough to be in the public domain, the arrangement or performance you want to use may still be under copyright.

Now, back to format. You may wish to use both sound effects and music in the same spot. Again, the basic rule of all caps and underlining pertains. At least two interchangeable terms should be in your writing vocabulary: *cross fade* and *segue*. These terms mean the same thing and they are to audio what *lap dissolve* is to video. As one sound (whether music, voice, or sound effect) fades under, the second fades in over it and comes up to full volume.

MUSIC	CUT 1; SIDE A; MOOD LIBRARY DISC 4652. ESTABLISH FOR 3 SECONDS AND CROSS FADE INTO:
SOUND	RAGING FIRE. FIRE TRUCK SIREN IN BACKGROUND. HOLD UNDER FOR:
ANCR	How up-to-date is the fire insurance on your home? Don't wait for the sound of an approaching fire truck to check your home insurance.

In this example, the writer has selected specific music from the station's mood music library and has given instructions for the location and use of the music. Instructions for the sound effect show that the siren remains in the background, sometimes called the *bed,* while the announcer reads the copy.

It follows that you could write for one piece of music to segue into another or for one sound effect to segue or cross fade into another. The glossary at the end of the book includes production terms often used in writing commercials for radio.

Live Copy

All radio commercials are either read live by a station announcer or are produced on audio-tape (rarely on disc). As a general rule, the smaller the station, the more it uses live copy written by a station employee. The larger the station in size, the more likely it is to use copy prepared by an agency. Each practice has its advantages and disadvantages.

In a radio station in a community of about 15,000, one or perhaps two writers may prepare 80 percent of all copy. Its writer has the advantage of knowing the community and knowing the station announcers who will deliver the copy, including their styles of delivery and their strong and weak points. While writing for the client, the copywriter must also write for them. Another advantage is speed in putting the spot on the air. Small stations avoid the delay involved in producing the spot on tape.

The disadvantages are a tendency for most of the spots to sound alike and a greater possibility of announcer mistakes. Obviously, you can avoid on-the-air mistakes by prerecording a spot.

Some copy does come to stations from agencies in the form of script only, leaving live performance of the commercial to the local announcer. This practice accomplishes two things: It avoids the cost of studio production and it helps make the spot more local, since listeners hear their favorite announcer deliver the message. It is not unusual for the local station writer to prepare a tag for such an agency spot, especially if it is for a national or regional account. Of course, no writer feels he or she is being very creative when writing tags for a commercial such as: "You'll find these fine products at Joe's Drug Store." But it's part of the job.

Donut Copy

A variation on the local tag is *donut copy.* It works like this: The agency produces a sound effect/music open and close for a commercial. The music may be a nationally recognized signature for a product that opens and closes the spot, while the local announcer reads copy prepared by the agency between the opening and closing music/sound. If you are writing for a local station receiving a donut commercial, you may have to prepare a local tag. Timing is critical in this type of spot. Once the tape starts rolling, the announcer has a precise number of seconds in which to read the live message. If the announcer is not finished reading in time, the closing music will quite possibly drown out his or her voice.

Live Ad-Lib Copy

When an announcer has developed a wide listener following and has become a strong air personality, a sponsor may want him or her to ad-lib the sales message. Does this situation require anything of the writer? Often it does. As a writer, you may be asked to prepare a fact sheet for the announcer or dee jay. Such a fact sheet is a list of things the sponsor wants to get across in descending order of importance. These lists are often referred to as *announcer's fact sheets*. The next chapter discusses the topic in more detail.

Production Copy

Any copy that goes through the studio process of being recorded is production copy. Most of these spots come through agencies. Large radio stations offer production services to their sponsors and some serve as production centers for agencies.

Production copy offers the advantages of rehearsing until you get it right, so the result sounds more professional. The chief disadvantage is cost, a factor that may be outweighed by the greater effectiveness of the spot. The disadvantage to small stations is that a spot that reads great on paper may overtax the station's ability to produce it.

Many FM stations follow the practice of prerecording all radio spots, including straight announcements. This practice is due largely to the degree of automation found in quite a few FM operations.

POINTS TO REMEMBER

- Radio is found everywhere you go; it helps us get through drive-time traffic and is a constant companion for many. Still, radio has limitations, chief of which is the lack of a picture. The radio copywriter must therefore make the product or service come alive in the listener's mind by helping create a mental picture.

- The radio commercial comprises three elements: sound effects, music, and voice. You must use these tools to capture the listener's attention and create the desire for your client's product or service.

- Timing radio copy by reading it at the rate at which it will be read on the air is an important part of the copywriter's job, since there is no precise way to time copy by counting the number of words or lines written.

- The term *format* refers to the physical form of your copy on paper. Stations tend to evolve their own formats for writing copy. However, unless your employer directs differently, type instructions in all caps and what is read over the air in caps and lowercase.

- Copywriting for radio involves a variety of formats: single-voice announcements, multiple voice spots, dialog spots, and fact sheets.

This is a drill in writing to time length.

Write a one-minute radio spot for a prestige automobile, stressing its comfort and luxury. First, spend some time researching the product. Indicate in all caps how you want the spot to be read. Have the copy read aloud in class by a classmate, not by you. Time the copy as it is read aloud in class. At the end of the spot, indicate the number of words in the spot.

This is also a drill in writing to time length.

Assume that there is a discount store in your station's market that is overstocked with picnic items: picnic baskets, thermos bottles, paper plates, suntan lotion, and so on. The store wants to move these items immediately and is offering them at a great reduction. Write a one-minute radio spot that will help the discount store dispose of these items. Indicate how you want the spot to be read aloud on the air by using instructions in all caps. Show at the end of your spot the number of words in the commercial. Bring the copy to class to be read by a classmate, not by you. Time the copy as it is read aloud in class.

Convert the following straight announcement into a two-voice, thirty-second radio commercial. Be sure to observe the format recommended in this chapter. Give specific instructions to guide the announcer in reading the spot—for example, URGENTLY or CALMLY.

ANNOUNCER   You are only as comfortable as the shoes you wear. Shoes by Jacobs mean all-day comfort for both men and women. Jacobs shoes for men feature an arch support that lets you stand in comfort, walk with ease. Jacobs shoes for women are both stylish and comfortable. And Jacobs shoes for both men and women are long lasting. Only the finest leather is used in all their styles. You may pay more for Jacobs shoes, but you save in the long run. You save in comfort, you save in the way they wear and never seem to wear out. Jacobs shoes are available at better department stores everywhere.

Convert the following straight announcement into dialog copy. Make the following decisions. For whom is the copy intended? Working wives? Single women? Both husband and wife? What is the best time of day for the spot to be broadcast? How do you identify the performers for the spot? A working woman and her boss? Husband and wife? Two working women? Neighbors? Two working men? To keep the cost of the production within budget, you are limited to two performers plus a closing announcer. The use of the announcer is optional.

ANNOUNCER   Anytime you have company over, you want your house to look its best. With a full-time maid, live-in cook, and yardman, a well-kept house is no problem. What? You don't have a maid? You do your own cooking? Hubby tries to keep the yard in shape? And, oh yes, you work full-time. Howard's Housekeepers has the solution. Howard's offers temporary help for house and yard. One phone call gives you dependable help at reasonable cost. You relax and enjoy your company while Howard's Housekeepers does the work. You can afford help from Howard's. Just call 292-4357. The number is easy to remember: 292-H-E-L-P. Help is what you'll get at a price you can afford. Howard's Housekeepers. 292-H-E-L-P.

You are to write a production spot using both sound effects and music. For this exercise, assume you have clearance to use the music. It is to be a sixty-second commercial. You are limited to one announcer. The client is to be one of the following: a local department store, a hardware store, a prestige automobile, a lawn mower dealer, or a local camera store. Get your information for the spot from a daily newspaper or from brochures.

Student Name _____   Advertiser _____

Date Submitted _____   Commercial Length _____

Student Name _____   Advertiser _____

Date Submitted _____   Commercial Length _____

Student Name _____   Advertiser _____

Date Submitted _____   Commercial Length _____

Student Name _____   Advertiser _____

Date Submitted _____   Commercial Length _____

Student Name _____   Advertiser _____

Date Submitted _____   Commercial Length _____

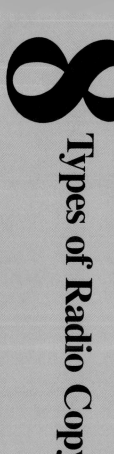

I n the previous chapter, you learned the mechanics for putting a radio commercial on paper. Before that, you considered what motivates people to buy, and you examined the anatomy of a commercial, the A.I.D.A. formula. You also studied the writing style used in broadcast commercials. Now it's time to bring all of these elements together through an examination of the various types of radio commercials. You may wish to think of this as the approach you're going to take for a given radio spot: Will you take a humorous approach, write a hard sell commercial, or use a testimonial or endorsement spot?

The choice may not be entirely yours, of course. The sponsor may dictate the type of commercial desired. In some instances, the nature of the product will help decide. Funeral homes, for example, don't lend themselves to humorous announcements. Used car dealers often prefer hard sell copy, while banks sometimes use institutional spots.

Straight Copy

By far the majority of the spots that you will write for small to medium stations will be *straight copy* commercials. Straight copy (or straight announcement copy) is virtually always written for one-voice delivery, and is perhaps the backbone of local radio advertising. It lacks the urgency of hard sell but doesn't use the understatement of institutional copy. It's written to be delivered in a conversational, informative voice. Straight copy certainly follows as nearly as possible the A.I.D.A. formula. It makes every effort to motivate the listener. There's no definitive definition of straight announcement copy. A U. S. Supreme Court Justice once said, "I may not be able to define pornography, but I know it when I see it." As a copywriter, you'll know this type of radio copy when you encounter it, and you will have to be able to write it. We have selected the following examples to help you know straight copy when you see it.

Writer: Diane	KFOR
Client: DuTeau Chevrolet	1240 AM
	Lincoln, Nebraska

ANNOUNCER	The all-American Cavalier meets the foreign challenge head-on. Drive a Cavalier at DuTeau Chevrolet. Steer it through a curve and understand precision handling. Drive it over a rough road and feel solid construction all around you. Discover the advantages of front-wheel-drive traction in rain, mud, snow, and ice. Cavalier is quality and performance . . . advanced technology and engineering. Cavalier is an exceptional all-American car that meets the foreign challenge head-on. See it today at DuTeau Chevrolet, 18th and "O."

Courtesy KFOR, Lincoln, Nebraska.

Or this example of local copy from a small-market radio station in New Mexico:

Advertiser: Noel's   KWYK

Written by: Dale Felkner   Farmington, New Mexico

ANNOUNCER   Get your lawn mower in tip-top shape for the new season at Noel's, Incorporated. Noel's will sharpen the blade, clean it up, replace filters, change the oil, install a carburetor kit, and replace the spark plug . . . all for just $28.50. Any make or model. Take your lawn mower in now . . . get ready to cut the grass faster and more efficiently . . . $28.50 lawn mower fix-up special at Noel's. They're at 601 Scott Avenue in Farmington.

Courtesy KWYK, Farmington, New Mexico.

Both of these straight announcement radio commercials get the client's message across. Both offer benefits for the product: for the Cavalier, ease of handling in bad weather; for the lawn mower repair shop, ease and efficiency in cutting your grass along with an attractive price. These spots are not screamers, but they do convey information to the listener, and they are persuasive.

It's also possible to classify some station promotion spots as straight announcements. Here's an example from Boston.

BOSTON SYMPHONY BROADCAST

WGBH-FM
Boston, Mass.

ANNOUNCER   Who was Till Eulenspiegel and why were his merry pranks so well-known anyway? "Eulenspiegel" means . . . literally . . . "Owl-glass" and there really was a person by that name who died about 1350 in Germany. He was an itinerant tinker who lived by his wits, and he was an inveterate practical joker. It was Dr. Thomas Murner who wrote about Till and his pranks and it was in this folktale that Richard Strauss found a bit of himself. He once even signed a letter "Richard Eulenspiegel."

You can hear Strauss's musical depiction of Till on our live broadcast from Tanglewood, Saturday at 8:30. Kurt Masur conducts the Boston Symphony Orchestra in a program that also includes the Strauss "Horn Concerto Number 1" with Charles Kavalovski and Beethoven's Symphony Number 2. That's Saturday at 8:30, here on listener-supported WGBH, Boston.

Courtesy WGBH, Boston, Massachusetts.

In this station promo, the writer is appealing to a specific audience, the station's loyal listeners who appreciate inside information about serious music. Note also the point of view in this spot. The announcer is a spokesperson for the station, so a phrase like "our live broadcast" is appropriate.

Hard Sell Copy

Hard sell commercials go by a variety of names: bargain basements, screamers, hard hitters, urgents, quick sale spots. A review of twelve books on broadcast advertising failed to reveal a definition of the hard sell spot, yet nine of them offered examples of this type of commercial. Perhaps the name of this type of spot is itself an adequate definition. The following elements do appear to be present in most hard sell radio copy.

1. *Price reduction.* These examples are typical: "Reduced 30 percent!" "Everything in the store is 30 percent off!" "At Jackson's, we will not be undersold!"

2. *Urgency.* This is communicated by using two techniques—(1) crowding so many words into the commercial that the announcer has to read it at a breakneck pace to finish the spot in the time allowed, and (2) using urgent phrases such as, "This bargain ends tomorrow," "These cars must be sold by midnight," "Madman Mike has done it again," and "You can't beat this!"

3. *Slogans.* Hard sell spots often use the hammering of slogans or the repetition of phrases such as "See it at Goss, the tradin' hoss, located on Ross," "Drive in today and drive out a bargain," or "You always save when you shop at Sampson's."

Hard sell copy lends itself to a variety of formats: one-voice and multiple-voice formats are common. Frequently, the sponsor will elect to deliver his or her own spot. In this latter category, the personal pronoun *I* often predominates: "I want to sell you a car," "I will not be undersold," "I will match any price in town."

There is no consensus on the effectiveness of this type of commercial. In all likelihood, the effectiveness of hard sell spots is related to the educational and economic level of the listener. More research on the value of hard sell commercials is needed. But hard sell commercials certainly exist on both radio and television, especially on small- to medium-market radio and on independent television stations. The following are examples of hard sell radio commercials.

ANNOUNCER   You've just got one day left! That's right . . . just one day remains for Sampson's storewide clearance. Everything in the store . . . sofas, beds, living room suites . . . everything in the store at 30 to 40 percent off. At Sampson's you'll find nationally advertised names like Sealy, Drexel, Grand Rapids, all great names in quality furniture. And at Sampson's, there's no payment for 60 days! And remember, everything in the store has been reduced from 30 to 40 percent! Sampson's, on Highway 80 at Crossline Road where you make no payment for 60 days . . . Sampson's, where everything in the store is reduced 30 to 40 percent. You'd better hurry . . . values like these won't stay in the store for long . . . Sampson's, Highway 80 at Crossline Road!

This Sampson's Furniture spot was written for a thirty-second delivery. Try reading it aloud in just thirty seconds. To get it all in, you'll have to jam the words together. Also note the repetition of the main selling point: price reductions of 30 to 40 percent on every item in the store. Here is another example of the hard sell spot.

Sponsor: Roger Beasley	KASE Radio
Copy by: Carol	Austin, Texas

SOUND	CLOCK TICKING. HOLD BEHIND (USE METRONOME)
ANNOUNCER	Time is running out . . . time is running out! Roger Beasley Mazda's offer of a great little truck for only 5,590 will soon be over! Supplies are running out, and Roger Beasley soon won't have any left to offer! Imagine, the greatest little truck in Austin with steel-belted radials, five-speed transmission, fully carpeted, with tinted glass, and many more features. Hurry while supplies and color selection are good.
SOUND	TICKING SOUND UP AND UNDER
ANNOUNCER	Time is running out! Time is running out! Roger Beasley Mazda, 1918 Burnet Road.

Courtesy KASE, Austin, Texas.

Again, this thirty-second radio spot features urgency and repetition coupled with a sound effect suggesting time running out. The hard sell example below uses two announcers.

CLIENT: BUDGET USED CARS

VOICE ONE	Budget has done it again!
VOICE TWO	Yes, Budget Used Cars has done it again!
VOICE ONE	And here's what they've done . . . Budget Used Cars has reduced every car on the lot by 20 percent!
VOICE TWO	Fords, Chevys, Dodge! Even imports!
VOICE ONE	Trucks, vans, family cars . . . they've all been reduced 20 percent at Budget Used Cars!
VOICE TWO	Budget Used Cars has done it again . . . But . . . and get this . . . for 3 days only!
VOICE ONE	That's right . . . for 3 days only starting tomorrow.
VOICE TWO	When Budget does it, they do it right . . . but these prices won't last.

VOICE ONE	Twenty percent off every used car on the lot!
VOICE TWO	Budget Used Cars . . . Fourth and Jackson . . . remember the address . . . Fourth and Jackson.
VOICE ONE	Budget Used Cars has done it again!

Institutional Copy

The *institutional* spot has as its chief aim keeping the client's good name before the public. Some products and services are closely tied to the image of the producer. As a result, what is advertised is the institution, not the product or service. Power companies, for instance, have no competition. They want their customers to use electricity and thereby increase the company's profit; but since power companies are regulated by state or local agencies, they are more concerned that they project a favorable image to both the public and the regulators. Institutional, rather than product, advertising can be used to maintain that image. Banks use institutional ads to project an image of strength and stability, while petroleum companies use them to tell the public of innovations that promote better living, quite apart from the selling of gas and oil.

Institutional copy may even be thought of as soft sell advertising. Yes, there is a sales message in an institutional spot—it just doesn't hit listeners over the head. Consider the following commercial, which is one of a series of spots for Franklin Savings featuring Mack and Karen.

NEAL SPELCE COMMUNICATIONS

Client: Franklin Savings

Copy: :30 radio "Gas Station"

MUSIC	UP BRIEFLY AND BED
MACK	I remember Grandma's big old Packard . . . driving to the service station . . . wishing I were big enough to run and pump gas . . . polish the windshield . . . know all the customers by name. It's sure different now . . . attendants in glass boxes . . . mechanical voices . . . computer pumps. I just can't imagine my Grandma pumping her own gas!
MUSIC	UP SLIGHTLY
MACK	I guess that's why I bank at Franklin Savings . . . They always have time for a smile and a cup of coffee . . . Franklin knows me. They want my business and they show it with every banking service I need . . . plus good, old-fashioned friendship and concern.
KAREN	At Franklin Savings . . . you come first. Ten locations and extended business hours make it easy for you . . . for all the service you deserve . . . with a smile.

MUSIC	UP AND OUT
MACK	Franklin Savings. Your Austin savings and loan.

Courtesy Neal Spelce Communications, Austin, Texas.

This Franklin Savings commercial offers several examples in one piece of copy. First, it uses a low-key institutional approach. We can also examine the spot for its ability to position the client, as discussed in Chapter 4. It's a spokesperson spot. It uses two voices and music. And note the use of nostalgia—the reference to the "good old days"—to create listener interest.

Institutional copy is still common today, and its most frequent appearance on the station's log comes during the Christmas–New Year's season. Here's an example.

ANNOUNCER	Williams Furs wants to take this opportunity to thank all of you for your patronage during this past year. As we all enjoy the Christmas season, Williams Furs wishes all of you a joyous holiday season and a happy New Year. Williams Furs will be closed from December 23 through January 5 so that our staff can be with their loved ones. The entire staff of Williams Furs joins in extending holiday greetings.

Many radio stations' traffic logs are filled with similar messages during the Christmas season. Often these soft sell, institutional spots are followed after the first of the new year by white sale, inventory clearance, or other sales promotion that is either hard sell or close to it.

Spokesperson Copy

In its simplest definition, the *spokesperson spot* features someone speaking in the first person for the client, its product, or its service. It may be the sponsor, it may be a celebrity, someone portraying a man in the street, or a member of the station's announcing staff who receives a talent fee to speak for the client.

The Sponsor Speaks

Sometimes called the *ego trip commercial,* this type of spot often takes a hard sell approach, especially in small to medium markets. The owner of Joe's Used Cars comes on mike or on camera to tell the audience, "I want to sell you a car. I will not be undersold." On a national scale, it might be the president of an automotive company telling about the values of his automobiles or the owner of an electric razor company offering to give you his company if his product does not shave as close as a blade.

In either instance, local or national, someone has to write the words the client reads in presenting his or her message. That someone might well be you, especially on the local level.

In writing a client-as-spokesperson spot you want to observe the standards of good commercial copy, you want to gain attention, hold interest, and sell the product or service—but you also need to write a spot that fits the client's delivery. If at all possible, visit the client and listen to how he or she talks. Does the sponsor have favorite phrases? Does the person use short, choppy sentences? Is his or her normal delivery slow and deliberate, or fast and rapid-fire? As far as possible, you should strive to make the sponsor sound normal. And don't be surprised if the client rewrites your copy.

Endorsements

A fine line separates *endorsements* from testimonial commercials. Endorsement copy features a well-known personality, while testimonials come from the man in the street. Sometimes both are found in one commercial. An example of this approach is a Roger Staubach commercial for Rolaids. Staubach, a celebrity, asks unidentified people how they spell relief, and they answer R-O-L-A-I-D-S.

The motivational aspect of celebrity endorsement was discussed in Chapter 5. Today, by far the majority of endorsement commercials appear on television. The effect of seeing John Madden, Bob Lilly, Billy Martin, and the rest of the Lite Beer gang adds an impact that radio can hardly equal.

On the local level, endorsement radio copy tends to flourish during political campaigns. The local banker may endorse a candidate for sheriff, or someone else who is well-known in the community may go before the local microphone to endorse a candidate for county judge. In many instances, the person making the endorsement may write the copy together with the candidate. As a copywriter, you will rarely receive assignments to write political commercials for your station. These spots usually come from an agency or from the candidate's campaign staff.

Local endorsement copy often uses a popular station personality. A local disc jockey may appear in first-person commercials that constitute an endorsement of the client's product or services. Whether or not the disc jockey is paid a talent fee for these spots depends largely on station policy. If the disc jockey receives a talent fee, the station usually passes the cost on to the sponsor.

In many instances, the air personality ad-libs the spot from a fact sheet prepared by the copywriter. Below is a fact sheet prepared by a station writer at KNDN, Farmington, New Mexico.

UTE MOUNTAIN RODEO

JUNE 21, 1984

* 3rd ANNUAL UTE MOUNTAIN TRIBAL RODEO!
* TOWAOC, COLORADO—JUNE 23 & 24, SATURDAY AND SUNDAY AT 1:00 P.M.
* ALL INDIAN AIRCA—NNRCA APPROVED
  * SADDLE BRONC
  * BAREBACK
  * BULL RIDING
  * CALF ROPING
  * STEER WRESTLING
  * TEAM ROPING

* BARRELL RACING

* JUNIOR BARREL RACING

* GREASED PIG

* CALL INS—JUNE 18 & 19—5:00 P.M. to 8:00 P.M.

* UTE MOUNTAIN RODEO!

Courtesy KNDN, Farmington, New Mexico.

Talk radio often abounds in endorsement commercials. This approach to radio programming may feature regular programs built around a handyman, a horticulturist, or a sports specialist. They take calls from listeners and give helpful advice on home repairs or backyard gardens, or answer questions about sports. Here's an example from a local handyman talk program.

> We'll be back to the phone in just a minute, but for right now, I'd like to tell you about the friendly folks at Huggens Hardware. They aren't just another hardware store, and they hire only employees who know hardware. When Huggens Hardware signed up as one of our sponsors, I thought I'd better check them out, and I did. I went in the store, didn't tell anyone who I was, and looked for the youngest helper on the floor. He looked like a kid just out of high school . . . but you know what? He explained to me the difference between a Jordan anchor and a molly bolt . . . told me when to use which for what. He knew his business. And that's the way it is with all the helpful people at Huggens Hardware. Huggens is easy to get to on Highway 377 just past Riggins Road. That's where I go for my hardware needs and you should too. Huggens Hardware . . . they're not just friendly, they know what they're doing.

Who writes this copy? Station practices vary. In the example for Huggens Hardware, the handyman wrote his own. But you as the station's copywriter might be assigned to prepare a fact sheet or to write the full copy. In the latter case, your copy must fit the delivery, style, and personality of the person making the endorsement.

Testimonials

Testimonial copy is rarely found on the local radio, largely because of cost. It would be possible to prepare a local spot in which noncelebrities testified in favor of a product or service, but note what such a project would involve. First, you would need to locate a number of townspeople who would be willing to go on mike and state that they had used and liked the product or service. A recording crew would have to visit them or they would need to come to the station to record their testimonials. Either approach involves considerable time and money. A straight copy spot that could be written and on the air in thirty minutes has now become a project for several days—and few local sponsors would be willing to spend the extra money required.

Humorous Copy

Humorous copy should be treated with care and respect. It's serious business. This type of radio copy can be very effective, but it can also backfire. Some sponsors seem to have little or no sense of humor, especially concerning their product or service. You should never put humorous copy on the air without first checking with the sponsor. Keep in mind also that humorous copy is difficult to write. You may indeed be the life of the party, but putting your wit on paper in a manner that will effectively sell a product is another thing. Or you may have a gift for writing good, humorous radio copy, but do you have local talent available to execute what you've written? Humorous copy is pointless if it just stays there on your copy paper. And it's even worse if it falls flat because of inept delivery.

If you must write humorous radio copy, consider this checklist:

1. Can the listener identify with the humor? Or is the humor so far outside your audience's experience that no one can relate to it?
2. Does it sell? Or does the listener remember the comedy and not the product? Does your wit hide the sales message?
3. Will it stand up under repeated airing? Listeners tire quickly of the same joke told over and over.

The following spots use humor to reach their audience.

ANNOUNCER	We don't. But then again, we do. The Greensheet delivers interested buyers and sellers right to your doorstep, even though we don't deliver the paper there.
	Finally . . . and this really gets me . . . people think the Greensheet is run by elves.
ELF 1	I'll buy that.
ELF 2	You can't, it's free.
ELF 3	Which is why it's read.
ELF 2	But it's still green.
ELF 1	You got a point there.
ANNOUNCER	Find out for yourself how every week the Greensheet delivers classified ads that are read.
ELF 2	And green.
ANNOUNCER	All over.
MUSIC	UP AND OUT

Courtesy Fogarty and Klein, Inc. Houston, Texas.

NEAL SPELCE COMMUNICATIONS

Client: TPEA

COPY: :60 radio "Dental Plan"

Characters: Patient: Neophyte, a real "Golly-gee'er"
                Doctor: Scatterbrain, a W. C. Fields type
                Nurse: Sarcastic, Mae West delivery
                Anncr: Warm, believable

MUSIC	ESTABLISH MUZAK TYPE, DENTIST OFFICE SETTING
PATIENT	Gee, my first dental checkup in 26 years.
NURSE	Really? Whew! Mind turning your head, hon?
PATIENT	I almost forgot what a dentist office is like.
NURSE	Honey, you don't need a dentist, you need an exterminator.
PATIENT	Ya see, the Texas Public Employees Association has this great dental plan . . .
NURSE	Yeah, but did they plan on getting you?
PATIENT	. . . any state employee can join!
SFX	DOOR OPENS. ENTER DR. ROUTER. DENTAL DRILL
DOCTOR	All right, where's the action, er, patient?
PATIENT	(SHEEPISHLY) Uh, right here.
DOCTOR	Ahem . . . Okay, we're going in. Open wide!
PATIENT	AaaaaaHhhhhhh!!!
DOCTOR	Mother of Pearl! Bring me my five-iron.
SFX	DENTAL DRILL
PATIENT	(MAKES GURGLING SOUND)
DOCTOR	What did he say?
NURSE	He's bringin' the kids in for braces.
DOCTOR	Holy molars!
SFX	DENTAL DRILL UP
PATIENT	(MAKES MUMBLING, GURGLING, CHOKING NOISES)
ANNCR	Join the Texas Public Employees Association and get a dental plan your whole family can sink its teeth into. Plus other great benefits like personal loans, legal service, and auto and home insurance . . . at a price that won't take a bite out of your wallet.
SFX	DENTAL DRILL UP BRIEFLY AND UNDER PATIENT STILL MUMBLING
NURSE	We'll never get this finished.
DOCTOR	Patience, my dear. It's cuspid's last stand.
SFX	DRILL UP BRIEFLY AND OUT
ANNCR	Join TPEA today. Write TPEA, Austin, Texas, 78711.

Courtesy Neal Spelce Communications, Austin, Texas.

Both of these humorous commercials were effective on the air. Why? First, they're well written, but more than that, they featured professional actors and were produced under good radio studio conditions. Both spots contain plays on words . . . "read" for "red" in the Greensheet copy and "It's cuspid's last stand" in the dental plan copy. This approach to humor can work well on radio. Both spots straightforwardly present a selling message. Neither has a hint of derision about the product or service. Note that in neither of the examples does the humor interfere with the sales message. On the contrary, the humor serves its purpose of holding listener attention while the sales message is delivered.

POINTS TO REMEMBER

- For the copywriter, style can best be defined as the approach being used to sell the client's product or service. You must remember that, regardless of the approach you use, it should fit the product or service.

- The straight announcement—a commercial, station promo, or PSA—is the most commonly used type of radio commercial. It requires only one announcer and presents no production difficulties. When written well and delivered on the air in an effective manner, it can be an effective sales message. Hard sell radio commercials are also fairly common, especially in smaller markets.

- Institutional copy takes the dignified approach of soft sell, keeping the sponsor's good name before the audience.

- Humorous copy can be very effective, but has to be treated with care. Writing humorous copy is serious business. You should not write this type of copy without first having the client's approval—and also be sure that your station's announcers can handle the humorous approach in delivery. Agency writers are probably on safer ground with this type of copy than are station writers because an agency is more likely to be able to cast the right voices for the spot.

- All four approaches to radio spots may be written for a single voice. It's possible, however, to write for multiple voice delivery. Hard sell copy is frequently written for two alternating voices. Humorous copy often lends itself to dialog delivery.

Write a straight announcement, sixty-second radio spot for Budget Used Cars, using the following copy information.

Ninety-day warranty on all used cars. Fords, Chevys, Dodge, imports. Many late models. Open until 10 P.M. every Thursday. Budget Used Cars is located on Airport Blvd. at Beltline. This is the only car dealer in town with lady salespersons to talk to lady buyers. It only takes a small down payment at Budget Used Cars and you don't make your first payment for sixty days. If you buy your used car from Budget before the end of the month, you will get a certificate good for 50 gallons of gasoline.

Remember, this is a straight announcement, not hard sell.

Rewrite the Budget Used Cars commercial for the owner, Jake Benson, to read himself. Make it a hard sell spot. Jake likes to use the expression "Other dealers jack up the price—at Budget, we jack up the quality!" He also likes the expression "We stand behind our name . . . Budget Used Cars . . . quality cars to fit your budget."

Convert the Budget Used Cars copy into a two-voice hard sell spot using two of your station's staff announcers.

If your college or university operates a radio station, write a thirty-second promo for some aspect of the station's programming. You may wish to hold a class competition to determine which of the spots go on the air.

Willard's Department Store will close for one month for extensive remodeling, but the firm wants to keep its name before the public while it is closed. The remodeled store will include a larger parking lot, a comfortable coffee shop, and a new computer center. Write a thirty-second institutional spot for Willard's. It is located in the Richland Shopping Center.

Pick a national celebrity to endorse one of the following products: Leica R-4 camera, Lawn-boy lawn mower, Sears radial arm saw, Norelco electric shaver for men, or Amway products for women. (Your instructor may wish to choose other products or services.) Research the products using brochures or talk to a dealer. Write a sixty-second celebrity endorsement spot for radio.

Analyze the following humorous radio commercial. Answer these questions: Does the copy satirize all travel agencies, including the client? How is the client's service positioned? Does the humor detract from the sales message? (Be specific in your answer to this important question.) Then try producing the spot yourself. Yes, this is a book on writing, but writers can benefit from production experience. If possible, tape-record your production efforts and let your classmates judge your efforts.

DEEP SEA DISCOUNTS

By ___Neal Spelce Communications___

Client ___American International___

	(ESTABLISH PIRATE MUSIC, BOAT SFX, ETC.)
PIRATE	Ahoy, mateys. Welcome aboard "Deep Sea on a Discount" Cruise Lines . . . har, har, har.
ARNOLD	This isn't like their brochure.
WIFE	This is the luxury cruise you promised me?
PIRATE	Why sure it be a luxury cruise. Here's yer "welcome cocktail," madam. (CORK POPPING OUT OF JUG SFX) Jest wipe off the neck when yer through . . . har, har.
WIFE	Oh, really . . .

ARNOLD	May I see your brochure?
PIRATE	Not now, trim the mainsail. Then I'd like to trim yer mainsail, lady . . . har, har.
WIFE	Oh, I can't believe it. (FADE UNDER ANNCR)
ANNCR	If you travel through American International Traveler, you'd always have smooth sailing. With nothing but firsthand fact from our large, experienced staff. Whatever the budget, destination, or time of year, we've been there. We know. So don't get lost in a sea of blind offers. Call A-I-T at 459-5401.
WIFE	When is dinner served?
PIRATE	Oh, whenever ya catches it . . . har, har, har.
WIFE	Ohhhhh.
HUBBY	Oh fishy, here fishy, here fishy.
JINGLE	The choice is so rational, American International. The most priceless free service in town.

Courtesy Neal Spelce Communications, Austin, Texas.

Student Name _____   Advertiser _____

Date Submitted _____   Commercial Length _____

Student Name _____   Advertiser _____

Date Submitted _____   Commercial Length _____

Student Name _____   Advertiser _____

Date Submitted _____   Commercial Length _____

Student Name _____   Advertiser _____

Date Submitted _____   Commercial Length _____

Student Name _____   Advertiser _____

Date Submitted _____   Commercial Length _____

Student Name _____   Advertiser _____

Date Submitted _____   Commercial Length _____

9 The Television Commercial: The Mechanics

I t's no secret that Americans love TV. People spend many hours a day watching TV, and special network programs regularly set viewing records. But television is not the personal and portable companion that radio is. A few people have small, portable TV sets that they can take to a sporting event or on a picnic. More often, the television set is the chief element in the living room decor, a large immovable piece of furniture. Still, whether a family has one TV set or several, its members usually watch a lot, often over six hours a day. This makes television an attractive vehicle for advertisers.

While radio relies on sound to reach its audience, television adds sight, movement, and usually color. When you write a commercial for TV, you therefore have the opportunity to approximate face-to-face communication more directly than you have in any other means of communication. In fact, local advertisers often want to appear in their own commercials to speak directly to customers.

Television Today

While radio programming is highly specialized, just the opposite is true of TV. Television is a mass medium, and generally each network affiliate offers something for everyone—sports for men, soap operas for housewives, and cartoons for children. In fact, the typical program cycle of a TV station's broadcast day corresponds to the audience available at a particular time: news and information for adults in the morning; variety shows, movies, and soaps for housewives at midday; reruns of comedy series after school; news and information for adults in early evening; and the most popular current series during evening prime-time hours when the entire family is available to watch. This pattern creates an attractive structure for advertisers, who can buy time to reach the specific viewers likely to buy a product.

Network Affiliates

The programming pattern described above is largely the product of network scheduling. While networks are not influential in radio programming, they control much of the programming on TV. Many local stations affiliate with a national network (ABC, CBS, or NBC), which supplies the bulk of the station's programming. Network affiliation results in relatively little local programming, but it does give local advertisers the opportunity to advertise adjacent to highly rated network programs. In addition, the high ratings of the network can pull in viewers to watch the local affiliate and often its own programming as well.

Independent Stations

Independent stations (those not affiliated with networks) follow a program cycle that is somewhat similar to that of network affiliates. Independent stations, however, rely heavily on syndicated reruns, movies, and sports programming. Since the station does not rely on a network to supply programming and advertising, there is much more opportunity for local advertisers to buy time. Often, the number of people viewing an independent station will be smaller than the audience of the lowest rated local network affiliate. Still, independent stations are often popular and successful.

Even though much TV programming comes from a network or is syndicated, local spot announcements are still important. Individual commercial messages are purchased separately from programs. The local advertiser buys this commercial time to promote its business. In some cases, you, the station copywriter, will write these commercials. Others, however, will be written and produced by local advertising agencies.

Cable Television

Cable television operates quite differently from broadcast TV. A cable system must fill a number of channels—anywhere from twenty to one hundred—while a broadcast station has only a single channel. Cablecasters fill their channels with satellite networks, retransmissions of local and distant TV stations, and local programming. Although cablecasters rely on fees from subscribers for their revenue, advertising support is becoming increasingly important.

A number of the cable networks such as ESPN, USA, and MTV provide availabilities in which local cablecasters can sell advertising. These networks target a highly specific audience, such as the young adult (eighteen- to thirty-four-year-olds) audience sought by MTV. As a part of this narrowcasting, the cable networks design programming specifically for that audience.

In addition, many cablecasters place advertising on a local channel. Cable systems can sell advertising time for much less than broadcast stations, enabling small businesses and special interest groups to buy time. Cablecasters may present electronic classified ads using alphanumeric information (words and numbers) to present a *screen,* a single visual frame of information. These classified ads may be scheduled jointly with newspapers to offer the client both print and cable television exposure. The copy is prepared and presented much like a classified newspaper ad.

Cable systems might use a local channel to present commercials prepared by the cablecaster's production department. Such spots may be as professional as the local spots seen on television stations, or they may be rather simple ad-lib spots shot on location. The client, for instance, may be shown standing in front of his or her place of business. These spots may be unsophisticated, but they appeal to small business operators because they are inexpensive and give the advertiser a chance to appear on TV.

Some cable systems place advertising by establishing an interconnection among cable systems via satellite and microwave to create a cable network. A group of cable companies can then carry the same programming and receive income from the advertisers whose messages will be shown throughout the network.

Advertisers can also lease time on a cable channel to present magazine programs that develop a theme built around the advertiser's message. This is a form of program-length advertising, since the entire program advertises the investment, medical, real estate, or other services of the advertiser. Such programs are often called *infommercials,* since they provide a low-profile way for the advertiser to blend a message into the program. A food manufacturer, for example, might sponsor a cooking show. The dishes prepared on the show could use ingredients manufactured by the sponsor. Traditional commercials for the sponsor might also be shown during the program.

The Advantages of Television

Television is a flexible advertising vehicle. A national advertiser can purchase network advertising and reach the entire country seven days a week and most hours of the day. In like manner, a local advertiser can cover an entire individual market with spot announcements. Since almost all Americans watch TV, it is possible to reach almost all of them.

The primary advantage of television as an advertising vehicle is that television can use sight, sound, and movement. This allows you to show a product and to demonstrate it in action. You can also show people enjoying the benefits of a client's product. Radio has to rely on sound to stimulate the listener's imagination. You don't. You can show the stripes in the toothpaste, the tread of a new tire design, or the roominess of a new automobile. You can show people using the toothpaste and commenting on its great taste. Not only can you show the tread design of a new tire, but you can show a car equipped with the tire as it safely maneuvers through corners on a rain-slick highway. You can also show a family of five riding comfortably in their new car.

Television is a visual means of communication. Certainly, the audio should not be ignored, but the video is crucial. People don't like static scenes on television. Consider your own reaction when a television station experiences technical difficulties and is forced to put an identification slide on the screen while its technicians solve the problem. How long does it take before you become impatient with the interruption and lack of movement? Ten seconds? twenty seconds? We each have our levels of tolerance, and the significance of the program will make a difference. Still, just as we don't like static interruptions in programs, most of us also have a low tolerance for a television spot that requires scene changes but doesn't have them. A balance of sight, sound, and movement is required in every spot if it is to be effective.

The Limitations of Television

Even though people watch television many hours a day, they are not glued to the set. Viewers often leave the room at breaks in the program—precisely when your best effort comes on the air. Viewers may also mentally tune out commercials even while sitting in front of the set. Thus, your greatest challenge is to present a sales message that people will want to watch. To produce such a spot, you will undoubtedly need money for commercial talent and production. TV spots can be much more expensive to produce than radio spots, and the budget for a spot determines what type of production you can do. Slick nationally produced TV spots often have a budget of $20,000 to $150,000. The budget for a locally produced spot is often small, sometimes as little as several hundred dollars.

A television commercial is much more difficult to produce than a radio commercial. It's possible for one person to write and record a radio spot. Producing the very simplest television commercial requires a writer, an announcer, an artist, and a technical crew. Television is simply more complex than radio. Not only does producing a TV spot require more people, but the advertiser can't expect to make quick changes in most television commercials. Once the television commercial is produced, it's costly and time consuming to change it. Some local spots using very modest production techniques can be altered quickly, but they're the exception, not the rule.

Don't be misled into thinking that you'll have unlimited time to write a television commercial. As in radio, you'll have deadlines. You must get one spot written and ready for production while knowing that you have other copy orders waiting to be written. Writers at advertising agencies are likely to have more time to prepare a spot, but they must meet deadlines, too.

Timing Copy

Like a radio spot, a TV spot must be timed carefully. The advertiser is paying for twenty, thirty, or sixty seconds and should get the exact amount, no more, no less. But timing a TV spot is not easy—especially when you're timing the draft of a spot at your typewriter.

The best practice is to do the same thing you would do with a radio spot—read it aloud as it will be presented on the air. This means that you will have to act out portions of dialog or business that require more visual time than audio presentation. If you don't allow sufficient time for the visual portions, the spot almost certainly will run too long when it's produced.

Some television writers count words to time a spot. A word count can be a rough guide if the spot does not have scenes that last longer than the audio copy. The general rule is that a ten-second TV spot may have about 25 words. A twenty-second spot may have 45–50 words, a thirty-second spot about 65–75 words, and a sixty-second spot 125–145 words. The pace and the visual nature of a TV spot will alter the word count. For example, a spot with a number of sound effects or musical insets would use fewer words. As a result, we recommend that if you use a word count, use it only as a guide for your initial draft of the spot. It's much better to time the spot as you want it presented.

Television Commercial Production Styles

Television commercials are usually classified according to their means of production. Although production styles are not mutually exclusive, here are the major styles you might write in a small- to medium-market station (not necessarily in this order).

1. *Studio production.* A variety of commercials, often low budget, are produced in the studio using the station's cameras, control room equipment, and talent. Some spots may involve live talent who perform a scripted on-camera presentation. The talent often consists of nonprofessionals such as owners and managers of auto dealerships, furniture stores, and certain services who believe in publicly representing their business. The script is usually presented on a teleprompter or on cue cards. Live talent spots are often supplemented with studio technique. Camera movement such as pans, tilts, or zooms may be used to create visual movement. Special effects such as dissolves or wipes may also be added to achieve visual variety. Often the live talent will not appear on the screen for the entire duration of the spot but will be interspersed with still photographs or slide pictures. This mixing of production techniques can help achieve visual variety on a low budget.

2. *Voice-over.* Voice-overs involve both talent and studio production. In a voice-over, the talent (often a staff announcer) is heard but not seen. The entire visual portion of the spot may consist of slides or videotape.

    Slides are inexpensive and easy to produce. Further, they can be done in color. This type of spot is common in local production, since it does not require use of the studio or studio cameras. Only the control room, slide projector(s), and announce booth are required.

A similar approach is to use a voice-over videotape. This involves shooting and editing silent videotape. The announcer's voice is then inserted over the tape. Again, the studio and studio cameras are not needed. While film was once used in such commercials, it has been almost totally replaced with videotape, which is inexpensive and easy to use. Unlike slides, videotapes have the advantage of showing products in motion.

3. *Electronic field production.* An electronic field production (EFP) spot is similar to a taped voice-over spot except that all voice and video can be done on location. Small portable cameras (minicams) and portable video-tape recorders are used to record the commercial on location and in color. The tape can be replayed immediately to judge the quality of the production. If it is not satisfactory, the spot can be retaped because videotape is reusable. If the EFP videotape recorder is equipped with editing capability, it is possible to edit on location—for example, when a car dealership shows its service department, sales staff, and inventory of automobiles.

As a further variation, electronic field production spots can be enhanced with postproduction special effects in the TV studio. Wipes or dissolves can be added, and items such as phone numbers, prices, or addresses can be inserted over the tape produced in the field. This approach produces a more sophisticated commercial, but one that is more complicated and costly than the other techniques discussed.

Television Commercial Formats

A television commercial can be presented as a script, a storyboard, or a photoboard. One or more may be prepared for a given spot. If the spot is to be fairly routine, production will probably require only a script. If the spot is more complex, or if the advertiser needs or wants to visualize the spot, a storyboard or photoboard may be prepared.

The TV Script

There is a major difference between a TV script and a radio script: The TV script is divided into two columns. The left column is for visual instructions, and the right is for audio (including spoken copy, music, and sound effects). The columns have no prescribed size. In some cases, a standard-sized sheet of paper will be divided half for video, half for audio. In other cases, one-third of the page will be for video and two-thirds for audio.

It is best to capitalize all video instructions. Video instructions tell the director what you want the visual scenes to look like. Assume that you won't be present when the commercial is produced (often you won't). Give the director sufficient instructions so that each change in video or audio can be understood. Abbreviations are used liberally in instructions to conserve space. Figure 9.1 illustrates a completed script on standard two-column paper.

The audio portion of the script should be written as a radio script would be. Type in lowercase everything to be spoken. Capitalize, label, and underline sound effects, music, and special instructions. Example: SFX: THUNDER. You will find exceptions to these suggestions. Some stations capitalize both audio and video portions of the script; some put both in lowercase.

TELEVISION CONTINUITY ⓐⓑⓒWFTV9

CLIENT:		TIME:	COPY CODE:	START DATE:	END DATE:
WINTER PARK MALL		30	WPM-8	11/26/84	12/20/84

SPECIAL INSTRUCTIONS:			VIDEO		AUDIO	
			VTR ☐		VTR ☐	
			F ☐		SOF ☐	
			SLI/C ☐		AT ☐	
			SLI/BW ☐		B ☐	

VIDEO	TIME	AUDIO
SLO MO VIDEO OF SANTA PUTTING ON HAT	:00-05	CHRISTMAS DONUT OPEN: GET READY FOR THE HOLIDAYS AT THE WINTER PARK MALL.
EXTERIOR WIDE SHOT OF STORE	:06-:15	INSERT: GREAT GIFT IDEAS ARE YOURS AT THINGS REMEMBERED
CU OF CROSS PENS WITH PRICE SUPER: $11. and up		WHERE CROSS PENS ARE FEATURED AT $11. AND UP WITH FREE ENGRAVING TIL CHRISTMAS. ENGRAVED GIFTS ARE... THINGS REMEMBERED.
WIDE SHOT OF EXTERIOR WITH PUSH TO INSIDE DISSOLVE TO MED. SHOT OF PICK-UP COUNTER	:16-:25	SPICE UP YOUR SHOPPING WITH A BREAK AT TACO VIVA. GET VARIETY IN QUALITY MEXICAN FOOD AT REASONABLE PRICES AND YOUR
EDIT TO SLIDE SHOWING CU OF FOOD WITH TACO VIVA LOGO SUPERED IN UPPER HALF OF SCREEN		CHOICE OF 6 SAVORY SAUCES! WHEN YOU SAY TACO...SAY VIVA!
	:26-:30	CLOSE: A JOYOUS SEASON TO ALL FROM THE WINTER PARK MALL, YOUR FAVORITE PLACE TO SHOP.

RP-105

FIGURE 9-1   Typical script for a TV commercial. *(Courtesy SFN Communications of Florida, Inc.)*

The TV Storyboard

Since television is visual, it is often desirable for the producer or the client to see a graphic depiction of what each scene (called a *frame* in TV jargon) in a script will look like. This is accomplished in a *storyboard,* which shows section by section what the creator of the commercial had in mind, using a series of panels much like a cartoon strip. Storyboards for high-budget agency presentations are often elaborately produced with photography or artwork.

They may be prepared by an individual, but more typically they're prepared by a creative team, often a writer and an artist. A carefully produced storyboard can help a producer or client decide on the suitability of an idea for a commercial. A storyboard is well worth the cost and effort when an advertiser is planning to spend thousands of dollars on a commercial. Figure 9.2 illustrates a professional storyboard. Note that the script is typed below the frame. By contrast, the storyboard in Figure 9.3 illustrates the visual portion of a spot that will accompany a musical jingle.

Small-market stations usually do not prepare a storyboard for a commercial. However, they may do so if the client wishes to see what the commercial will look like, either to clinch a difficult sale or satisfy a demanding customer. It probably won't be as elaborate as one done for a national agency. It may even be sketched. Still, the goal is the same: to help the writer and others visualize the commercial message in a step-by-step fashion, allowing them to judge its structure, cohesiveness, and flow. Figure 9.4 shows the storyboard form used by a television station for generating quick, stick-figure storyboards.

In this class, you'll function as both writer and artist. It's not necessary that you be a skilled artist. Stick figures and rough drawings of settings and special effects will be adequate. Simply place video and audio instructions under each frame. The drawing in Figure 9.5 is an example.

How many frames should you use in a commercial? A beginning copywriter should plan on using one frame for each four or five seconds of commercial time. Thus, a ten-second spot would have two video changes, a thirty-second spot six to eight scene changes, and a sixty-second spot would involve twelve to fifteen scene changes. Of course, the actual number of scene changes depends on the pace of the spot. Avoid long, static scenes. Exposure to one scene for more than ten seconds will cause the viewer's attention to wander. Yet too many

LISTEN!

THE FIRST (HOME LOANS)
TV :30
CONCEPT (SPOKESMAN).
VIDEO: EXECUTIVE CHARGING
DOWN CORRIDOR
OTHER EXEC'S AROUND HIM.

SHOPPING FOR A HOME LOAN TODAY CAN BE CONFUSING.

ECU  MCU

MANY PLACES TRY TO LURE YOU IN WITH LOW FIRST-YEAR MORTGAGE RATES.

 ECU

BUT WHO KNOWS HOW MUCH THE LOAN WILL COST AFTER THAT?

THAT'S WHY MORE AND MORE PEOPLE COME TO THE FIRST, FIRST, THE ONE YOU CAN BANK ON.

HOLD UP LOGO 'FOLDER' GOING INTO OFFICE.

WE DON'T PLAY GAMES, WE DELIVER WHAT WE PROMISE. HOME LOANS AS COMFORTABLE AS YOUR HOME INSELF.

 IN OFFICE

IF YOUR IN THE MARKET FOR A HOME LOAN.

 MCU

COME TO THE FIRST, FIRST.

 FOLDERS

THE ONE YOU CAN BANK ON.

 FOP ON
THE ONE YOU CAN BANK ON

FIGURE 9·2   Typical storyboard. *(Courtesy Fry-Hammond-Barr, Inc.)*

FIGURE 9·3   Storyboard keyed to a musical jingle. *(Courtesy Frailey & Wilson, Inc.)*

scene changes can confuse the viewer. Act out your first draft aloud. If it's too fast or has too many changes it may leave viewers behind.

Building a Storyboard

Which part of a storyboard comes first, the words or the pictures? There is no definitive answer, and you should experiment with both ways to find the best pattern for you. Still, it is always important to think visually in planning a spot. The storyboard focuses more directly on the visual element of the spot and can be planned more efficiently if you follow these steps:

1. Identify the distinctive feature you want to get across in the spot. This feature must stand out clearly, so it's important that you identify it at the out-

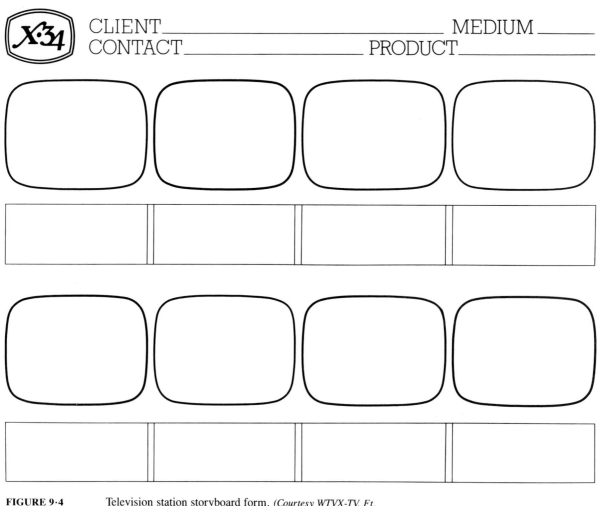

FIGURE 9·4   Television station storyboard form. *(Courtesy WTVX-TV, Ft. Pierce/West Palm Beach, Florida)*

set. Look closely at the spot for the U.S. Navy in Figure 9.6. The distinctive feature is spelled out in the logo "Navy. It's not just a job, it's an adventure." This idea must be presented visually, and not just in the logo, but in the rest of the spot as well.

2. Determine what benefit stems from the distinctive feature. In the Navy spot the benefit is twofold: the adventure and glamour of a job on the high seas.

3. Decide what setting will help convey the distinctive feature and its benefit(s). You must visualize a setting that will be appropriate to carry the spot. The Navy spot could do that best by showing activity on an aircraft carrier steaming in Hawaiian waters. Both the glamour and excitement are communicated with this setting.

4. Build on the setting to convey the message. A logical, reasonable progression of visual scenes is necessary. Remember: If the visual could carry the spot alone, you've done a good job. The Navy spot does that. It sets a general scene, follows with a number of shots of specific jobs on the carrier, and concludes with a launch of aircraft. The spot then turns to the distinctive feature at the conclusion. The progression of scenes is logical and easy to follow.

VIDEO: MS OF BOY WITH BASEBALL GLOVE

Audio: Playing baseball is hot work.

FIGURE 9·5   Example of a student storyboard frame.

These four steps can help you prepare a TV spot that accomplishes the job visually and establishes the framework for your script. Use them each time you prepare a storyboard, and you'll be more likely to prepare spots that sell.

The Photoboard

It is fairly common practice for national and regional advertising agencies to go one step beyond the storyboard and the actual production of the spot. This step is to prepare a *photoboard*. It usually consists of photocopies taken from the actual tape or film and mounted on heavy paper. The audio track is indicated under each frame. A photoboard of this type is really the reverse of the storyboard. Since still pictures are lifted from the tape or film, the photoboard provides the client and advertising representatives with a static picture of the completed commercial. Figure 9.7 illustrates a photoboard prepared from a nationally produced public-service announcement.

Photoboards do not always come from a completed commercial. In some instances, the creative team may want to evaluate certain concepts or visual effects before final production. In this case, still photographs are shot and included in the storyboard.

TV stations and advertising agencies rarely prepare photoboards from a completed commercial for local advertising accounts. The cost is prohibitive, and arrangements can more easily be made for the client to see the complete commercial on tape.

Producing TV Commercials

As in the case of radio, it's essential that you know the jargon of the television industry so your words and sketches can be translated into the desired movement on the screen. In some cases, you'll need to know the specific terminology for desired effects or camera movement.

U.S. Navy Public Service TV

"FLIGHT OPERATIONS": 30 Seconds (also available in :20 and :10 versions) QUAQ 0837

ANNCR: Flight Operations - Hawaiian Islands

155 is the

go bird. 10° right rudder.

Bring up 155 on No. 2 elevator.

Cloud tops at 28,000 feet. Alpha Hotel your wind is down the deck

at 28 knots.

Launch aircraft.

Stand clear. Stand clear. Most jobs promise you the world.

The Navy delivers. See your recruiter.

Navy. It's not just a job, it's an adventure.

NAVY. IT'S NOT JUST A JOB, IT'S AN ADVENTURE.

FIGURE 9·6   A logo can help identify a spot's distinctive feature.
(Courtesy U.S. Navy)

We support the National
Citizens' Crime Prevention Campaign.

TAKE A BITE OUT OF
CRIME™

"JENNY"

Public Service Announcements
Available in :60, :30, :10 Versions
60 SECONDS
Please use until Sept. 15, 1984.

MC GRUFF: Ahh -- that's
Jenny.

But that's not Jenny's dad.

If she gets into that car --
you may be lookin' at Jenny
for the last time.

I'm McGruff, the crime dog.

Let me show you something --

See that playground? Lots-a
kids there. Every day in this
country sixty kids --

disappear.

Some run away, but a lot are
kidnapped by strangers or
even by people they know.

Almost 20,000 kids a year.
20,000 kids: one kid at a
time.

Maybe your kid. On your
street.

Just like Jenny.

You know, your kids can
learn to protect themselves
against crime -- at home, at
school, on the street.

Very nice going, Jenny.

She's gonna tell her folks
about this.

And you can write to
McGruff. Learn how to keep
your family and your
community safe.

And help take a bite out of
crime.
(RUFF)

FIGURE 9·7   Photoboard of a public-service announcement. *(Courtesy
The Advertising Council)*

In other cases, you'll use a form of shorthand, especially in designating a desired camera shot. For example, *MS* is the abbreviation for *medium shot*. This is the jargon by which you, the copywriter, communicate visual instructions to the artists and producers. Your instructions should be specific and sufficiently detailed so that the producer can understand exactly what you intend. If the instructions do not include enough detail, the producer will have to guess at what you want. You may be present at the production session, and you may have the opportunity to offer advice and clarification. But the director usually has the final say about what's done once the copy is written.

Television audio terminology is basically the same as that used for radio, so it will not be covered here. To help you understand the major terms you need to know, we'll cover four categories of video terminology with which you should be familiar. These include (1) shot composition, (2) physical camera movement, (3) technical descriptions, and (4) special effects.

Shot Composition

To write a shot-by-shot description of a TV commercial, it is necessary to use composition terminology to describe how much of the scene the viewer will see. The actual composition of the shot will be achieved by moving the camera or manipulating lens components (subjects we will discuss later).

- *Long shot (LS) or wide shot (WS).* This shot provides a full view of a set or background, usually including a full-length view of the actor or actors. Since this shot provides a distant perspective it should be used sparingly. However, this type of picture has one advantage. Since it can show the total visual setting, it can be used at the beginning of a commercial as a cover or establishing shot that will introduce the entire scene.

- *Medium shot (MS).* This shot is the approximate mid-point between a close-up (CU) and a long shot. Medium shots show talent from approximately the waist up. They show more detail of the setting than a long shot because they are not as wide. A medium shot can thus be an effective establishing shot, since it will have fewer distracting elements.

- *Close-up (CU).* The close-up is a narrow-angle picture that will present a full-screen image of an object or the talent's face. This shot is also used to focus on individual elements such as the talent's mouth or eyes. It can be used to show an entire object or parts of it. By focusing attention, the close-up gives added emphasis to key elements of the sales message.

There are also variations of the shots just described. A long shot may be varied to become a medium–long shot (MLS), a medium shot may become a medium–close-up (MCU), and a close-up may become an extreme- or tight-close-up (ECU or TCU).

Finally, more specific shot composition may be called for in some instances. Anatomical and grouping designations offer more precise shot specifications. Terms such as *one-shot, two-shot,* and *three-shot* refer to a scene with one performer, a scene with two performers, and a scene with three performers. Terms such as *bust shot* and *waist shot* have obvious meanings. An *over-the-shoulder shot* uses the camera to look over a person's shoulder at another person.

Physical Camera Movement

A number of terms refer to instructions that call for movement of the entire camera and its base or movement of the camera alone while the camera base remains stationary.

- *Pan (left or right).* To pan is to move the camera either left or right without moving the camera base. A pan might be used to follow a moving object or person. It might also be used to move the camera's focus from one stationary object to another.

- *Tilt (up or down).* To move the camera either up or down without moving the camera base.

- *Truck (right or left).* This term refers to movement of the camera base parallel to the scene being shot. This is a difficult move that requires a skilled camera operator.

- *Dolly (in or out).* To dolly is to move the entire camera base either toward or away from the subject. When a dolly is called for, the subject usually remains stationary. A dolly is best avoided, since it is difficult to achieve a smooth shot while pushing or pulling the entire camera. You can achieve a similar effect with better results by using a zoom lens. Most stations have a zoomar lens available.

- *Zoom.* Movement of a camera lever that adjusts the focal length of a zoomar lens to move either toward or away from an object. The effect is similar to that achieved by dollying in or out, but the result is perfectly smooth. A zoom can be used to create all shots, from a long shot to a close-up, without moving the camera.

- *Arc (right or left).* Movement of the camera and base semicircular to the scene being shot. This is a difficult move and not often used.

- *Boom or pedestal (up or down).* To move the camera up and down using the studio boom or pedestal. This movement can be used to create dramatic perspectives—for example, to move the camera up to look down on a subject.

Transitions

To arrange an orderly change of scenes, you should provide for transitions from one scene to the next. As a copywriter, you'll use transition terms to tell the director whether you want a rapid scene change, a slow scene change, or certain special effects.

- *Dissolve (DS or DISS).* This term refers to the overlapping fade-out of one picture and the fade-in of another. Dissolves are used for slow scene changes, although the speed of the dissolve can be controlled to fit a particular mood. Dissolves may also be used to indicate a change in time or to move from one place to another.

- *Cut or take.* This technique is the most simple transition from one TV commercial scene to another. The final frame of one scene changes instantaneously to that of another.

- *Fade (in or out).* To fade in is to gradually increase the intensity of a video picture from total black to full strength. A fade out decreases the full brightness of a picture until the screen is dark. Fades can be used to achieve such effects as passage of time. In commercials, fades are used to fade in the opening and fade out the closing.

Special Effects

A number of terms used in television refer to electronic effects produced by the control room switcher. Most special effects are either a combination of images or a manipulation of them. Since such effects are indeed special, they should be used only as needed in order to preserve their effectiveness.

- *Wipe.* A wipe is an optical effect in which a line or object appears to move across the screen revealing a new picture. A wipe may stop midway and become a split-screen. Wipes may be horizontal, vertical, diagonal; they may come from either side (closing doors) or sweep around like the hands of a clock (iris or circular).

- *Super.* This effect (short for superimpose) is a very useful sales tool for showing one object over another picture.

- *Split screen.* In this special effect, two or more scenes are visible simultaneously on separate parts of the screen—for example, the screen is split to show two families independently reacting to a given problem.

- *Freeze frame.* A technique for holding a particular scene on the screen for a desired length. It is often used at the close of a commercial to highlight the advertiser's name or slogan.

- *Character generator (CG).* An electronic device using a typewriterlike keyboard to produce printed words optically.

- *Key.* An electronic effect that permits an image (usually lettering) to be cut into a background image. Phone numbers, addresses, and so forth are best produced by keying in the additional material.

- *Matte.* An electronic process similar to keying. Often the terms *matting* and *keying* are used interchangeably. In commercial production, matting often refers to the electronic laying in of a background scene, such as a client's showroom or storefront, behind a foreground image such as an announcer.

- *Chromakey.* An electronic device that allows a given color to be removed from an original scene; the color is replaced by a visual element from another source. For example, the color blue may be removed from an in-studio scene and a shot of the product put in its place.

- *Digital video effects (DVE) unit.* A device that permits manipulation of the image by expanding or compressing it, thus modifying its size, shape, and position in a variety of ways. The DVE enables the director to apply a variety of visual effects, such as image rotation, bouncing, or splitting the video, to achieve a special effect in a spot.

Additional Terminology

Television commercial production has so much specialized jargon that much of it is difficult to categorize. The following terms are included to provide a fuller understanding of the language of TV commercial production.

- *Aspect ratio*. The standard dimensions of the television screen—three units high by four units wide.

- *Crawl*. A technique that places printed words (credits, short public-service announcements, or news items) on the screen in a gradual horizontal or vertical movement.

- *Depth of field*. The distance within which a subject can move toward or away from a stationary camera without going out of focus.

- *Film chain*. Slide and film projectors linked together to permit the showing of 35-mm slides and motion picture film on television.

- *Frame*. The field of view in any particular shot.

- *A-B rolling*. Switching between two or more videotape machines to prepare a composite tape.

- *Montage*. A sequence of short scenes, usually cuts or wipes, that together convey an idea more effectively than could any one of them.

- *Postproduction*. Any production work that occurs after filming. In making TV commercials, postproduction activity is usually either editing videotape or adding special effects to tape already shot.

- *Slide*. A title or picture on a single frame of 35-mm film mounted in a suitable frame for projection into the camera of the film chain.

- *Still-frame-storage unit*. A digital device used to store individual frames, any of which can be electronically recalled instantly. It is often used in place of slides or camera cards.

- *Studio card/camera card*. A posterboard of any size that can be shot by a live studio camera. It must conform to the three-by-four aspect ratio, and may be a pasteup picture, a printed message, or a combination of picture and message. Studio cards provide an inexpensive way to televise artwork.

- *Titles*. Letters or other printed material appearing on the screen such as a telephone number, store name, or address.

- *Voice-over (VO)*. A narrator who is not seen.

- *VTR*. Abbreviation for videotape recorder.

Film versus Tape

Local television stations seldom shoot their commercials on film, but film is often used by advertising agencies to produce commercials for national and regional distribution. Such commercials are usually shot on 16-mm or 35-mm film when a larger budget is available for commercials with wider distribution.

Film has several advantages over videotape. It tends to give products, actors, and settings a softer, more cinematic image than videotape. Film editing can also be more precise than videotape editing, and film is preferred if certain optical effects are desired.

Despite these advantages, videotape is the choice of local TV stations. The primary reason is speed. Tape requires no processing, so it produces an immediate product that directors and advertisers can examine. If retakes are necessary, they can be done immediately—no need to wait until the tape is developed, printed, and copied. Further, videotape produces a sharp, realistic, but sometimes stark picture that few can distinguish from film.

Animation

In animation, movement is created by drawing a number of still pictures and exposing them one frame at a time on film or videotape. Animation is costly because it requires considerable artwork and production effort. Still, it can be useful if live action cannot produce the intended message. For example, cartoon characters such as Tony the Tiger and Smokey the Bear have been used successfully. The same effect could hardly be achieved by having an actor dress in costume and appear in a live commercial. Animated characters can be used to produce a unique approach, either by appearing alone or in combination with actors. Either approach requires a substantial budget that most local accounts won't be able to afford. The spot in Figure 9.8 illustrates the use of animation.

Keeping the Spot Producible

The technical sophistication of your station or cable system will determine the nature of the effects you can use. Get to know the directors and learn what is possible at the station for which you work. You may not have to do production as a writer, but you're expected to write a spot that can reasonably be produced. Budget, studio time, and the type of special effects the station can accomplish will determine what you can do. However, even on a low budget, you can create considerable action by moving the camera. You can have the camera pan or tilt, zoom in or out. Virtually any TV station should be able to accomplish such movement. Many stations, however, won't have all the specialized production equipment you might want to use.

A warning: Keep the production simple and to the point. Don't assume a tricky effect will sell the product. Demonstrate the benefits of the product or business and don't let production techniques get in the way.

If the client wants to appear in a commercial with his or her family, be very cautious. People off the street are obviously not professional actors. In this case, ask the family to say and do very little. Show them, but don't give them speaking lines unless you're sure they can handle them. If you really want to show a typical family on a shopping spree, you'll need a budget to hire professional actors.

Remember also that the spots you write will appear adjacent to higher budget national or regional spots. Your local, low-budget commercial must look and sound sufficiently professional if your viewers are to pay attention.

In many cases, television scripts are prepared with a minimum of video instruction. In these commercials, the director either has considerable latitude in producing an acceptable spot, or the copywriter is present during production and gives verbal instructions. While this happens in the real world of television, it is not a wise practice for the student of copywriting. Make it a point to include detailed visual instructions. That way a director can interpret what you want if you're not at the production session, and you save time for your primary task—writing copy.

The Production Budget

Another factor that determines whether your spot can actually be produced is the amount of money the advertiser is willing to spend for production (beyond the station's charge for time). Advertisers want their spots to look professional and to sell the product. But they also want

GENERAL 🄖🄔 ELECTRIC

GE WX ELITE PLUS HEAT PUMP

TV Spot for Local Dealer use
:25 with :05 open tag
Produced for Trane CAC, Inc., by Caraway Kemp Communications, Jacksonville, Florida

Hot weather . . .

and rising utility bills are on their way again!

But now you can help beat 'em both with a new,

GE super efficient Elite Plus heat pump system. It cools in summer . . . heats in winter and can save on energy costs all year long.

The GE Elite Plus . . . our most efficient heat pump line . . . and it's a Weathertron® !

Beat the heat this summer . . .

and help save on energy costs all year.

(Dealer name, address & phone)

FIGURE 9·8   Animation in a TV spot. *(Courtesy Caraway Kemp Communications, Inc.)*

their advertising dollar to buy them the maximum number of appearances on the air. For example, the advertiser that spends $5,000 on your station probably won't want to spend $1,000 of that amount to pay for producing the spot. That wouldn't be cost-effective unless the advertiser planned to use the commercial for a long time, or planned to use the spot on a number of stations simultaneously. Even then, production costs would be kept to a minimum.

The account executive will often determine the amount of money the client is willing to spend for producing the spot before a contract is signed. If the account executive is knowledgeable about production, the contract may specify the method—studio production, field production, or other means. In other instances, the account executive may consult with the copywriter before signing the contract to determine what method of production can be used for a given amount of money. In yet other cases, you may be given the production budget with the responsibility of selecting the best method of spending it.

While it is difficult to generalize, the following methods, in descending order, represent the least costly approaches to spot production:

1. *Slides with announcer voice-over.* Slides are inexpensive to prepare and use of the studio is not necessary for production. A staff announcer can deliver the audio portion of the script.

2. *Studio production.* This method requires use of the studio and its cameras and might include slides or other graphic aids. The complexity of the production and the talent involved—staff announcer or outside talent—will affect the cost of studio production.

3. *Electronic field production.* The cost of EFP production is high because the portable videotape equipment must be transported to location. Costs will be even higher if special effects are added from the studio switcher during postproduction.

Production costs vary widely according to the size of the market, production methods used, talent involved, and special editing effects added during postproduction.

Advertising agencies also handle production for their clients, but the majority of agencies do not have their own studios and production crews. Depending on market size, agencies negotiate the cost of production with specialized production firms or with local television stations. Representatives of the agency then attend the production session as supervisors.

Guidelines for Writing Television Spots

Most of the rules for writing radio commercials also apply to television audio, but the emphasis on video requires elaboration. The following sections provide guidelines for writing television content.

Gain Attention

Gaining attention early in a television spot is just as important as it is in a radio commercial. The opening seconds either gain viewer attention or lose it. Since television is primarily a visual medium, let's begin with the opening shot of a TV spot. One school of thought maintains that the opening shot should be a long, establishing shot that sets the scene for the viewer. In other words, the video sets the scene, and the audio introduces the sales pitch.

Suppose that you're asked to sell the large selection of used cars at Honest John's Emporium. An establishing shot with John standing in front of a row of cars may be the best way to orient viewers.

A second approach is to use a close-up shot in the opening—a shot that will focus on a specific person or item. In this approach, the location may not be important, or you may wish to hide it until later in the commercial. If your goal, for instance, is to convince the viewers of Honest John's integrity, it may be preferable to begin the commercial with a close-up shot of John dressed in a business suit. The car lot can be shown later or not shown at all.

Study this spot for *TV Weekly*. Close-up shots are used until the final scene. The goal of this spot is to focus attention on the magazine, so close-up shots are appropriate. The Jack Rabbit commercial begins with a close-up for another reason. It begins with a video of fingers walking into the picture that can only be accomplished with a close-up.

VIDEO	AUDIO
TABLETOP IN LIVING ROOM SETTING . . . HAND PLACES OLD VERSION OF TV WEEKLY ON TABLE. HANDS COME FROM THE SIDE AND SQUEEZE THE MAGAZINE VERTICALLY . . . HANDS COME IN FROM TOP AND BOTTOM AND SQUEEZE THE MAGAZINE HORIZONTALLY . . . MAGAZINE DISSOLVES FROM OLD SQUEEZED VERSION TO PRESENT ONE.	(ANNCR:) The State and Columbia Record's popular television guide, TV Weekly, has been transformed into a thicker, new compact size that you can keep at your fingertips all week long.
CUT TO CLOSEUP OF TITLE AND ZOOM OUT TO SHOW HAND OPENING COVER, TURNING PAGES . . . DAILY PROGRAM LISTING PAGE SQUEEZES OUT FROM TURNING PAGES ON CURVED TRAJECTORY. PICTORIAL EXAMPLE OF FEATURE . . . EDITORIAL HEADLINE . . . LOGOS FROM HBO, CINEMAX, THE MOVIE CHANNEL, USA NET, CNN, AND ESPN SLIDE ACROSS THE SCREEN FROM RIGHT TO LEFT IN RAPID SUCCESSION.	This 56-page magazine contains weekly listings for 18 channels on programming from 7:00 A.M. to 2:00 A.M. daily. TV Weekly offers feature articles, editorial reviews, plus extensive movie and sports information. It's the only television guide you'll need.
SQUEEZE SPLIT REVEALS SATURDAY RECORD AND SUNDAY'S STATE . . . HAND DROPS TV WEEKLY ON TOP OF DISPLAY.	Look for it Saturdays in the Columbia Record, and Sundays in the State.
CUT TO SHOT OF PAPERBOY RIDING BICYCLE WHO THROWS NEWSPAPER AT CAMERA LENS . . . SCENE FREEZES, AND TV WEEKLY LOGO WITH SUPER: SUBSCRIBE TODAY 771-8380 SQUEEZES FROM NEWSBOY'S HAND TO 80% FULL FRAME, LEAVING FREEZE SHOT AROUND EDGE.	Call today and have it delivered to your doorstep.

Courtesy WIS-TV, Columbia, South Carolina.

VIDEO	AUDIO
SHOT OF CAMERA AND FILM WITH FINGERS WALKING BY AND PICKING UP THE FILM.	So you've taken some pictures and now you have to have them developed.
SUPER DISCOUNT AND DRUG STORE. EXTERIOR SHOT OF JACK RABBIT.	You could take them to a discount store or drug store, wait a few days, and hope for the best. Or you could take them to Jack Rabbit one-hour photo lab.
VARIOUS SHOTS OF FILM GOING THRU LAB.	Imagine, film developed while you watch, with no extra charge!
PRINTS COMING OFF ROLLER.	At Jack Rabbit, you get high quality prints on Kodak paper in just one hour!
PAN OF PILE OF FILM.	And for a limited time when you have film developed, we give you a fresh role of Jack Rabbit film Free!
LOGO AND LOCATIONS.	Jack Rabbit, where good things develop fast!

Courtesy WSPA-TV, Spartanburg, South Carolina.

Of course, there is no single "correct" shot that will gain attention in a television commercial. Careful analysis of the client and its sales goals will help you determine whether a wide shot or a close-up is most appropriate in a given spot.

Don't forget the Attention-Interest-Desire-Action formula we discussed in Chapter 6. It applies as much to television as to radio.

Identify the Client or Product Name

Just as you must interest people in watching the commercial, you must also make certain that you identify the name of the client, product, or service clearly. The message will be ineffective if people can recall some of the action, and perhaps even the general product category, but not the name of the advertiser.

Implant the advertiser's name early and repeat it as often as you can without making the commercial dull. Since the product or client name can be presented by both audio and video, you'll have sufficient opportunity to include it. It's also wise to include the name of the client or product in a slogan used in a commercial. For example, the slogan "There's more for your life at Sears" is short, catchy, easy to repeat, and includes the client's name. Above all, don't expect the viewer to remember the client or product name if it's presented only once. Include it as often as you reasonably can and conclude the spot with the client or product name. The conclusion is the part of the spot that viewers are most likely to remember, so it's essential that you conclude with strong sponsor identification.

Examine the photoboard for the Car Vac commercial in Figure 9.9. Notice that close-up shots of the Car Vac are used to show both the product and the product name. The product name is established early in the commercial, and the spot concludes with both the product name and the advertiser's sales theme.

BBDO
Batten, Barton, Durstine & Osborn, Inc.

Client: **BLACK & DECKER**

Product: **CAR VAC**

Title: **"GREAT PICK-UP"**

Time: **30 SECONDS**

Comml. No. **BKPT 4013**

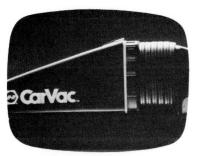

This is Car Vac. . .
from Black & Decker's Car Care Series.

Plug it in,

rev it up,

feel its power. Black & Decker's Car
Vac starts fast,

It's great on the curves,

great on the straightaways.

Its 16 foot cord really goes the distance.

Watch it corner,

maneuver through tight spots.

Car Vac handles like a dream and even
stops on a dime.

Car Vac. It's got great pick-up

because it's the only car vacuum that's
built like a Black & Decker.

FIGURE 9·9   Photoboard with strong product identification. *(Courtesy
Michael L. Ianzito/Batten, Barton, Durstine & Osborn, Inc.)*

Balance Audio and Video

The two vehicles of television communication—audio and video—must relate to one another if a commercial is to be cohesive. Nothing is more distracting than to have what is shown conflict with what is said. For example, if the audio for a restaurant spot says, "Choose from the selection of terribly tempting desserts," the video should not show people entering the restaurant, a family eating dinner, or a smiling waitress. Showing the items as they're described lets the viewer comprehend them.

A balanced audio and video presentation can also be used to establish the client's or product's name. When you first mention the name, you should show it.

For example:

VIDEO	AUDIO
OPEN ON WS OF COUPLE STUDYING MENU IN RESTAURANT WINDOW. SLOW ZOOM IN AS THEY TURN TO CAMERA AND SHAKE HEADS "NO."	ANNCR (VO): You don't have to be wealthy to dine out.
CUT TO FESTIVAL HOUSE LOGO	At Festival House you can get delicious home-cooked meals at affordable prices . . .

With this approach, you show the client's name as it's said. You've also introduced the client's name early. As a result, you have a good start in presenting a message that will sell.

You should also balance the audio and video in the closing shot. Either present the client's logo as the final shot and reinforce it with audio, or accompany the final shot with a superimposed title that repeats the audio script word-for-word. If the announcer's final line is "Festival House . . . fine food at affordable prices," show that wording on the screen either by itself or supered over a visual. This balances the audio and video and reinforces the sales key that you hope to leave in the mind of the viewer.

Examine the script for this commercial for Charles Towne Landing. The spot is built around a slogan, "Families doing things together," which is presented both aurally and visually at the close of the commercial. Notice how each line of audio is balanced by a compatible visual scene.

VIDEO	AUDIO
A-&-B-ROLLS FOR DISSOLVES BETWEEN SHOTS AS NOTED:	(Music under . . . #105 "Feelin' Free". . .)
FAMILY WALKS UP TO PAVILION; START SHOT BETWEEN LITTLE BOY'S LEGS & FATHER'S DAD AT GRILL W/HOT DOG TO BOY; PULLOUT TO MOM & KIDS.	At Charles Towne Landing, families do things together! They picnic—Dad can grill hot dogs or hamburgers. . . .
FAMILY BIKES PAST LAGOON.	Or bicycle the many trails as a family. (Music up for split second . . .)
CLOSE-UP MAST OF ADVENTURE SHIP & PULLOUT TO FAMILY COMING TO IT.	Imagine ghosts of sailors past on board the Adventure . . .
FAMILY WALKS ACROSS BRIDGE IN GARDENS; USE TODDLER HELD UP.	Reflect on the beauty of the English Park gardens . . .

PUMA CAT & PULLOUT TO FAMILY.	Discover native animals in Charleston's only zoo . . .
FAMILY LEANS OUT FROM LOG FORTRESS.	Roam the 1670 fortifications . . .
FAMILY WATCHING SETTLERS' ACTIVITIES.	Visit dwellings like those of the first settlers!

FAMILY W/FEET IN FOUNTAIN. SCRIPT SUPER:
    CHARLES
    TOWNE
    LANDING . . . FAMILIES DOING
      THINGS TOGETHER
	Charles Towne Landing is . . .
	
	FAMILIES DOING THINGS TOGETHER!

Courtesy WCIV-TV, Charleston, South Carolina.

Emphasize One Main Idea

As with a radio spot, you should limit a television spot to one main idea. Analyze the information and break it into major and minor selling points. Once you have done this, identify the single strongest sales key and emphasize it in your spot. Don't try to include a number of selling points. Even if you can logically include a number of ideas in the spot, viewers probably won't remember them.

A commercial for a restaurant illustrates what should not be done. The commercial begins by describing the food and service at the restaurant. Midway through the spot a second idea is introduced. The words "Use our executive limousine service" are supered over shots of the food available at the restaurant. It's a second idea, one that has no clear relationship to the first, and one that would better be presented in a separate spot. It draws attention away from the main idea and weakens the sales message.

Don't Overwrite

Since television is a visual medium, you should use the video to present more than half the message. The old cliché says that pictures are worth a thousand words, and it remains true of television commercials.

Of course, you'll want audio copy, but don't use more words than you have to. Circumstances will vary: In some spots you'll have to rely heavily on audio. This may be true when you have a lot of complicated material to present and will also be true when you want a version of the TV spot to be used on radio. Then the audio must stand alone, reinforced only by exposures to the spot on television, where both audio and video present the message. In other situations, you'll want the video to be the primary message, supplemented only with a minimal amount of audio.

Also keep in mind that television spots as a rule are shorter than radio spots, making it all the more important that you make each word and scene count. While sixty-second spots are common in radio, thirty seconds is the most common length on television. Television occasionally uses one-minute spots, but many agencies and advertisers believe that shorter spots are more appropriate in terms of cost and viewer attention. Ten-second spots are often used when the message is uncomplicated, and fifteen-second spots, usually run back-to-back as split thirties, are gaining popularity with advertisers.

Not only are television spots shorter than those on radio, but they're almost always presented in a cluster with at least two other spots. As a result, you must be certain that your spot is clear and easy to grasp. If it isn't, viewers probably won't get the message.

POINTS TO REMEMBER

- The primary advantage of television as an advertising vehicle is that it can use sight, sound, and motion.

- Television scripts are best timed by reading or acting them aloud.

- The major styles of television production are (1) studio production, (2) voice-over, and (3) electronic field production.

- The television script is divided into two columns. The left column is for visual instructions, and the right is for audio.

- A television storyboard shows what the creator of a spot had in mind frame by frame.

- TV spot production should be kept simple. Trick effects may not make for good selling.

- The least costly approaches to TV spot production are (1) slides with voice-over, (2) studio production, and (3) electronic field production.

- The opening seconds of a TV spot are crucial since they either gain viewer attention or lose it.

- The name of the advertiser or product should be presented early in a spot and repeated as often as possible without boring the audience.

- Audio and video must relate to one another in a television spot.

- A television spot should be limited to one main idea. Secondary ideas should be used only if they have a clear relationship to the main idea.

This is an exercise in visual planning. On the form provided at the end of this exercise section, prepare the video portion of a thirty-second television commercial for Yourtown Lawn and Garden Shop. Your task is to produce a visual sales message. *Do not* use audio! Be certain that the client's name and the sales theme are clear.

Copy Information

Advertiser: Yourtown Lawn and Garden Shop; three locations in Yourtown. Ask the audience to see Yellow Pages in phone book for locations.

Product: Store wants homeowners to see the Majik Mower by Lawncleaner. Dealer will demonstrate the mower.

Features: Variable height settings, self-propelled. Its 4.5-hp engine can cut all types of grass, wet or dry. Majik Mower is a rear bag model (the bag that picks up clippings is in rear of mower, not on its side). This feature allows for closer mowing near bushes, fences, and buildings.

Special safety feature: The easy-starting engine automatically shuts off if pickup bag is dislodged while engine is operating.

Write a thirty-second television spot for Yourtown Lawn and Garden Shop. Be sure the spot includes movement and demonstrates product or advertiser benefits.

Copy Information

Advertiser: Hometown Spas and Fitness Center, with four locations in greater Hometown.

Facilities: swimming pools, steam rooms, hot mineral whirlpools, sun rooms, and inhalation rooms.

Features: This weekend, a special offer for women only—a figure-proportioning special. Twelve visits for $5.00. The twelve visits must be at the same spa and must be used over the next two weeks. See the Yellow Pages for locations.

On the form provided, prepare a complete storyboard (including both audio and video) for Hometown Spas and Fitness Center. The commercial should be thirty seconds long. Develop a sales key that stresses figure proportioning. Assume you have a modest budget but strive to include as much movement in the spot as possible.

On the form provided, prepare a complete storyboard (including both audio and video) for Hometown Spas and Fitness Center. This commercial should be sixty seconds long. Develop a sales key that stresses the special offer. Assume you have a modest budget. Keep the spot producible.

Write a thirty-second television spot for Lodgepole Park. At this park visitors can see replicas of Old West buildings while enjoying the out-of-doors. The park consists of twenty-five acres of grasslands with several streams and plenty of trees. Two restored buildings are open to the public (one includes historical data on the area, the other depicts a typical house in the 1850s). The old bridge on Walnut Creek, which wagon trains once crossed heading West, has also been restored. The park has plenty of picnic areas, plus trails for hiking, and camp-grounds are available (by request only). Lodgepole Park charges no admission fee and is located five miles east and two miles south of Yourtown. Signs point the way.

Develop a slogan for use in your spot. Be certain that the slogan and the client's name appear early. Reinforce the audio with video and vice versa.

Prepare fifteen-second spots for Lodgepole Park and Yourtown Lawn and Garden Center. Remember that you can't use much information, so be certain that you identify the client's name and/or product clearly.

Develop ten-second TV spots for Yourtown Lawn and Garden Center and Hometown Spas and Fitness Center. Be certain that you identify the client's name and/or product. Don't cram the spot with information. A ten-second spot tells little more than who and what.

STORYBOARD
FOR: _____   _____   _____

Class Name   Project or Assignment   Page

BY: _____   _____   _____

Student Name   Class Number   Date

EXERCISE 2

Student Name _____   Advertiser _____

Date Submitted _____   Commercial Length _____

VIDEO   **AUDIO**

STORYBOARD

FOR: _____   _____   _____

Class Name   Project or Assignment   Page

BY: _____   _____   _____

Student Name   Class Number   Date

AUDIO: AUDIO: AUDIO:

VIDEO: VIDEO: VIDEO:

AUDIO: AUDIO: AUDIO:

VIDEO: VIDEO: VIDEO:

STORYBOARD
FOR: _____   _____   _____
                Class Name   Project or Assignment   Page

BY: _____   _____   _____
              Student Name   Class Number   Date

AUDIO:

VIDEO:

AUDIO:

VIDEO:

AUDIO:

VIDEO:

AUDIO:

VIDEO:

AUDIO:

VIDEO:

AUDIO:

VIDEO:

Student Name _____   Advertiser _____

Date Submitted _____   Commercial Length _____

VIDEO   **AUDIO**

LODGEPOLE PARK

VIDEO   **AUDIO**

YOURTOWN LAWN AND GARDEN CENTER

VIDEO   **AUDIO**

YOURTOWN LAWN AND GARDEN CENTER

VIDEO   **AUDIO**

HOMETOWN SPAS AND FITNESS CENTER

VIDEO   **AUDIO**

10 Types of Television Commercials

To the typical television viewer, commercials may seem easy to prepare. That's almost never the case, however. A television commercial whose message grabs the viewer's attention and is remembered requires careful planning, writing, and production. Gimmicks alone won't sell. The mind best remembers a cohesive idea that is presented in an interesting and relevant manner. That's where careful preparation comes into play.

Your primary task as a television copywriter is to interest the viewer in each spot you write. Your task is somewhat easier than that of the radio copywriter because you can use both sight and sound. But simply pointing a television camera at a person or object usually doesn't produce an effective sales pitch. You must structure the video and audio so that the message involves the viewer and sells the product or service.

If the commercial you've written is weak—if it's uninteresting, confusing, or poorly defined—you'll have lost your sales opportunity. But viewers don't have to leave the room to miss a commercial message. They can simply pay limited attention to a spot that doesn't involve them. You must strive for viewer involvement with each spot you write. In this chapter we'll examine what you must do to organize and structure a television commercial that will interest and involve the viewer.

The Copy Platform

To write a cohesive television spot, you need to know as much as possible about the client or service. Who does the firm wish to reach? What geographic area does it wish to cover? What are the product's main selling points? Who are the principal competitors, and what approaches do they use? Gather as much information as you can. To avoid being overwhelmed by it, develop a copy platform that helps you identify the most important items in developing your sales theme.

As you'll recall from our discussion in Chapter 4, the sales theme is the key to a persuasive message. It can be especially effective if it is developed as a sales slogan, a memorable idea presented in an original phrase. A sales slogan helps viewers recall the advertiser or product name and its selling features. Television can present the sales slogan aurally, visually, or both. A carefully developed sales slogan can be your best aid for recall.

The spot for Luvs Diapers in Figure 10.1 illustrates the effective use of a sales slogan that is presented both aurally and visually. The slogan, "New Luvs," is presented in a song. The music accompanies visual presentation of the slogan in four different frames of the commercial. Audio reinforces the video for a simple but easily remembered sales slogan.

Choosing the Approach

After you've analyzed your material and planned your sales theme, you're ready to choose an approach to deliver the information. The approach is the blueprint, the pattern you follow in presenting your sales message. This is the last phase of your planning, and it requires care because using the proper style is a key part of creating an effective commercial.

Television spots, like radio spots, may be either hard sell or soft sell. Hard sell, you'll recall, refers to direct selling of the client's product or service, while soft sell spots use an understated, suggestive approach to create a positive image of the client or its products. Only

Client: PROCTER & GAMBLE CO.   Title: "TOUGH CHRISSY"
Product: LUVS   Commercial No.: PGLU 2656
As Filmed/Recorded: COLOR   Date: 5/4/84   Length: 60 SECONDS

1. (MUSIC UNDER)

2. ANNCR: (VO) Luvs proudly announces America's first diaper

3. with double gathers

4. for your baby's comfort.

5. SONG: New Luvs.

6. DAD: Who ever thought they could improve Luvs?

7. MOM: But they sure did...

8. up till now diapers had only one row of elastic...

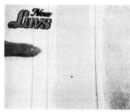

9. but New Luvs has two rows of gentle, flexible gathers.

10. SONG: New Luvs.

11. ANNCR: (VO) Besides, other diapers can sag and gap.

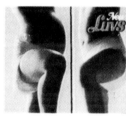

12. But New Luvs fits without sags or gaps.

13. New Luvs helps stop leaking better than those wider bargain brands.

14. 'Cause you can't be comfortable if you're soggy.

15. SONG: New Luvs.

16. DAD: And they snuggle gently and more comfortably than ever around Chrissy's legs.

17. MOM: Luvs double gathers are great!

18. 'Cause when it comes to keeping Chrissy dry and comfortable...
DAD: It's double or nothing!

19. (SFX: BABY)

20. SONG: New Luvs.

FIGURE 10·1   Merging audio and video. (*Courtesy The Procter & Gamble Company*)

a few basic styles or approaches are used in television commercials, though there are many variations. We'll stick to six of the most common styles used to present television spots. They work equally well for local or national copywriters.

Note that the approaches overlap. Almost all spots, for example, include a problem, solution, and result. Still, use one style as your primary method of presentation. You'll find that choosing an approach will direct your thinking and help you to write a spot that will be noticed. Note also that while we use the terms *style* and *approach,* other professionals use such terms as *technique, format,* or *structure.* The words *style* and *approach* seem most helpful to us in describing ways of organizing commercial data.

The Problem-Solution Approach

One of the commonest types of TV commercial is the problem-solution spot. It has been used successfully for a variety of products. It works best when the qualities of the product can be demonstrated. A situation might be part of the spot, but it should be subordinate to the problem-solution approach.

Here are some characteristics of an effective problem-solution commercial.

> ▪ The problem identified in the spot must be believable. Whether it is bad breath or water spots on fine crystal, it must be a problem the target audience can relate to. If the problem isn't one the viewer has experienced, heard about, or wants to avoid, the commercial could be offensive.
>
> ▪ The product must be introduced as a natural, realistic solution to the problem. Too many gimmicks or incredible solutions do little for the credibility of the product. The product's ability to solve the problem and the manner of presentation must seem reasonable to the viewer.
>
> ▪ Not only should the product be introduced as a solution to the problem, but the solution should show the user experiencing benefits or achieving satisfaction after using the product. That is the high point of this type of commercial. The user may feel better because he or she has solved an annoying problem, saved money, or increased his or her status. Just as the problem must be believable, the demonstration of benefits must also relate to something familiar to the viewer.
>
> ▪ The name of the product or service must be identified clearly, and it must be associated with the problem the product claims to solve.

The Rid-A-Bug commercial in Figure 10.2 illustrates a problem familiar to homeowners. Not only is the problem evident, but the spot dramatizes the feelings associated with it. The product is quickly and easily identified as the solution to the problem. The family in the commercial is shown deciding to use the product, and in an "after" decision scene, we see a happy, confident homemaker in a bug-free kitchen.

The Demonstration Approach

The demonstration spot is one of the mainstays of television because it uses TV's greatest strength—its ability to show the product being used. It is easiest to demonstrate functioning products like a lawnmower or a reclining rocker. But products whose operation is not observable, like a flashlight battery or an animal flea collar, can also be demonstrated, although it

Rid·a·Bug®
HOME INSECT KILLER
30 Second TV Commercial
"Embarrassed Home Owner"

WOMAN: Sure...we've got plenty of sugar...

ANNCR (V.O.): Rid·a·Bug doesn't want you to be embarassed by dirty, nasty bugs...

SFX: Slam of cabinet.

We're out!

MAN: The bathroom's right here.

ANNCR (V.O.): Rid·a·Bug doesn't want you to have bugs at ALL.

Uh...It's out of order!

ANNCR (V.O.): That's why Rid·a·Bug Home Insect Killer is the strongest, longest-lasting spray you can buy...at any price!

MAN: Hmmm...Rid·a·Bug...

WOMAN: To get RID of bugs!

ANNCR (V.O.): Now get 23% more Rid·a·Bug at no extra cost!

WOMAN: Of COURSE we have sugar!

(Alternate tag)
ANNCR (V.O.): Now from Rid·a·Bug...Flea and Roach Fogger and Quick Kill Aerosol.

The Rid·a·Bug Company
P.O. Box 6246, Jacksonville, FL 32236   ©1984

FIGURE 10·2   Problem-solution commercial. *(Courtesy Caraway Kemp Communications, Inc.)*

takes more imagination. If a demonstration is properly executed, it can involve the viewer in the commercial message and provide convincing reasons to buy the product.

A word of warning: Televised demonstrations must be true and authentic. As we'll discuss further in Chapter 12, false and misleading demonstrations are illegal.

Follow these rules in using a demonstration in a commercial:

- Be certain the significance of the demonstration is clear to the viewer. If you think viewers might not understand, tell them what you plan to do before you do it.

- Write more video into a demonstration spot than audio. The video portion of your spot must be strong because it carries the demonstration. Check your final draft. If the point of the demonstration isn't clear from the video portion alone, rework the spot.

- Use close-up and extreme close-up shots to enhance the demonstration. Let the viewer see the product as he or she would see it in person. Don't show parts of the product that are too small for the camera to show clearly.

- Don't use a lot of technical jargon in the audio portion of the script. Show the viewer how the product works.

- If possible, show the demonstration from beginning to end. Don't cutaway unless necessary. Cuts may create doubts in the viewer's mind and draw attention from the sales message. If you must cutaway—for example, to allow for passage of time, tell the viewer what you're doing. Don't make the viewer guess about your use of the cutaway.

- Keep your message simple and direct. A complicated message and a complicated demonstration won't be remembered.

- Be certain the product name is displayed prominently. Use the demonstration to show the benefits the viewer might realize from using the product.

- Prove that the claims for the product are true. Use the demonstration to show the product doing what you've promised.

The Heat 'N Strip spot in Figure 10.3 both shows and tells the audience what the demonstration will do. The spot has a strong visual sell that could carry the spot by itself. Extreme close-up shots are used to show the product at work. A concluding shot offers proof that the product works by showing a beautifully restored mantle. The product name is clearly established at the beginning and end of the spot.

The Situation Approach

The situation commercial tells a story that establishes a reason for the presence of the product. The story must have a simple plot that can be easily understood—for example: Boy meets girl in laundry room. They share a washer and use her detergent because his leaves ring-around-the-collar. The detergent solves that problem. Boy asks girl for date. She declines.

A carefully developed story can gain attention and involve the viewer in the situation. If viewers find the story believable, they will probably feel the product will work as well for them as it did for the characters in the story. Here are some guidelines for writing situation commercials:

BBDO
Batten, Barton, Durstine & Osborn, Inc.

Client: **BLACK & DECKER**   Time: **30 SECONDS**

Product: **HEAT 'N STRIP**   Title: **"MANTLE"**   Comml. No.: **BKPT 4023**

Somewhere in this room is a beautiful antique,

hidden under layer upon layer of paint.

Now Black & Decker will find it with Heat 'n Strip

the remarkable paint stripper that works with hot air, not caustic chemicals.

Heat 'n Strip bubbles away years of paint

with less work

and a lot less mess.

It makes all other ways of stripping paint antique.

Heat 'n Strip. . .
It's built like a Black & Decker.

FIGURE 10·3   Product demonstration. *(Courtesy Michael L. Ianzito / Batten, Barton, Durstine & Osborn, Inc.)*

■ Develop a situation that is logical, believable, and easy to follow. Zany, unrealistic situations aren't appropriate. Even though most anything goes on TV, the situation must be plausible. Since you'll have less than a minute to develop the situation, you must keep it simple. The situation is the key to the spot. Present the product subtly.

- The opening of your story must attract attention and involve viewers. The opening sets the stage for the rest of the spot, often by introducing a problem.

- The middle of your story should elaborate on the situation, usually by introducing the product as a solution to the problem.

- In the final stage, the product solves the problem. The situation concludes with the characters displaying the satisfaction they've achieved from use of the product.

- A logical development of the situation is essential. Each step must relate to the one that precedes it and the one that follows it.

- The story should present the product in a way that it promises a beneficial result—the viewer will be healthier, more secure, more confident, and so forth.

- Identify the product name clearly.

The Ætna commercial in Figure 10.4 uses a believable setting. The client's name is introduced early and logically. The situation is developed to show a happy event—the wedding—with the father of the bride displaying satisfaction because he's used Ætna's services.

The Spokesperson Approach

In a spokesperson commercial, an individual delivers the sales message on camera. It's a common approach both nationally and locally (where automotive dealers seem to love it). Advertisers often use the spokesperson approach because they feel that consumers will respond to a commercial if they identify with the personality or admire the person delivering the message.

As we noted in Chapter 8, a spokesperson may be a well-known person who endorses the product or service, or a person who claims to have used the product and cites personal experience in the form of a testimonial. Most of the factors in choosing a spokesperson are the same in television as they are in radio. However, there is one difference. The television spokesperson is seen and not just heard. This factor adds a visual concern that can bear on the credibility of the spokesperson.

It is important that the spokesperson be appropriate to the product or service and look and sound sincere. A beautiful actress may be a suitable spokesperson for a line of cosmetics, but the same person might be inappropriate in a spot for vacuum cleaners. You must decide what kind of person is appropriate for the product you're selling, whether it is someone characterized by warmth, humor, glamour, or authority. Here are some guidelines:

- Describe the person before you write the commercial. What do you want the person to look and sound like?

- Prepare the copy with your spokesperson in mind. Write for his or her style of delivery. Write copy that seems extemporaneous and can be delivered conversationally.

- Show and mention the advertiser's name or product throughout the spot. If the name isn't mentioned prominently, the spokesperson may upstage the product.

- Keep the spot straightforward. Movement and shot changes should be minimal. Focus on the person and his or her presentation of the sales message.

30-Second Television Commercial Titled: "THE WEDDING"

FATHER OF THE BRIDE
He's not the father of the bride. I am.

He's my Ætna Agent. I met him when my Susie

was her size. And my business wasn't much bigger.

From day one, he's worried as much about my business as I have.

Do I have enough insurance? Or too much insurance? Do I have the right insurance?

Thanks to him, I'm free to worry about other things.

Like how I'm gonna pay for all this.

AVO: Call your Ætna Agent.

FATHER: Ætna, I'm glad I met ya!

FIGURE 10·4 Situation commercial. *(Courtesy Ætna Life and Casualty)*

The spokesperson commercial in Figure 10.5 is a buyer's guide that gives consumer information. The presentation uses an anonymous actor who appears knowledgeable and serious. The spot presents information that consumers may not know. The advertiser's name is presented prominently in both the audio and video portions of the commercial.

The Product-as-Star Approach

In this format, the product is the star of the commercial. It is displayed prominently, naturally, and made to appear irresistible.

This approach works well for any product or group of products you wish to put on display. It's a favorite for dairy products, other food items, and soft drinks. If the budget permits, the audio portion will often be a musical background. The commercial may include live action shots of people enjoying the product. Here's how to make the product the star:

- Present the sales message with restraint. Hard sell terms such as *hurry* or *buy now,* are best avoided. Use the suggestive approach and build the spot around the sales theme.

- Use realistic settings and a simple, straightforward message. The advertiser wants the product to be remembered, so the setting should not upstage it. The audio portion shouldn't be complex either, and it should reinforce the video.

- Use close-up and extreme close-up shots of the product to make the video strong. They give the viewer the best view of the product and enhance its appearance.

- Show happy, satisfied people enjoying themselves as they use the product. Make the results of using the product rewarding.

- Explain the characteristics of the product: Communicate its taste, feel, appearance, or other feature. Show these characteristics when they appear in the audio.

- Emphasize the name of the product.

The Red Lobster commercial in Figure 10.6 features shrimp, showing them up close and in color. A musical jingle reinforces the attention drawn to the product. Lighting, setting, and the choice of music and announcer are all important in making shrimp the star of the spot.

The Direct Response Spot

A direct response spot tries to persuade the viewer to order a product directly from the advertiser, either by mailing in a coupon or calling a telephone number. Direct response spots are very popular on both television and cable, with the telephone response (usually featuring an advertiser's toll-free number) being the most common.

Direct response spots are often per-inquiry advertisements. That means the station or cablecaster is paid for each response. These spots hit hard and use every possible inducement to get the viewer to respond. They may advertise an unbelievable kitchen tool, an album of songs by a favorite singer, magazine subscriptions, or jewelry. Direct response spots are often as long as two minutes in length. Here are some guidelines for writing a direct response spot:

- Remember that the video is key. You must show the product at its best. If you're selling records, the artist should be shown and heard. Show household

AMERICA'S FAMILY DRUG STORE

"PRIVATE LABEL GUARANTEE" TV:30

MAC OC: Store brands. There are hundreds of them. And they're not all the same.

In fact there's one that's tested to such high quality national brand standards . . . it comes with a guarantee.

Eckerd Brand. If you're ever dissatisfied with any Eckerd Brand product . . .

we'll replace it with the comparable national brand free.

With a guarantee that strong, we have to make sure Eckerd Brand is as good as you can buy. Period.

If your store brand isn't guaranteed . . . ask yourself . . . why? Eckerd Brand products. You're going to like them. We guarantee it.

W. B. Doner and Company Advertising

FIGURE 10·5 Spokesperson commercial. *(Courtesy The Eckerd Drug Company)*

FIGURE 10·6   Product as star! *(Courtesy Red Lobster Inns of America)*

or shop tools doing as many jobs as you can put into the spot. Jewelry should be made to look attractive and durable. Show the product in as many appealing settings as possible. Make the offer appear desirable.

▪ Don't ridicule the product. As a writer you should be aware of the product's limitations: Are some of the record cuts made from worn masters? Will the tool work only for one adept at woodwork? If you've accepted the job of writing such spots, you have an ethical responsibility to write a positive message for the client even if you know the shortcomings of the product. Direct response writing is not for the squeamish or the beginner. Some direct marketing companies sell products of questionable value. Others sell quality items at real savings. A few direct marketing companies are careless about quality and provide little customer assistance. Others are ethical and make every effort to resolve problems. Writing spots for an unscrupulous direct marketing firm is a tough test of your integrity.

▪ Reach for the impulse buyer. Direct response spots seek the person who buys on impulse. It's your job to make such a person grab the phone. Stress that this is a limited offer, that credit cards are welcome, that the item can't be found in stores. Repeat the phone number at least three times. Stress that operators are waiting. Make the offer appear so good that viewers won't want to pass it up.

The photoboard in Figure 10.7 illustrates a direct response spot. It presents a product that can be effectively advertised on TV.

A variation of direct response advertising now exists on the videotext systems in use in some cities. These systems provide a complete shopping and bank-at-home service by allowing the viewer to choose items from those presented on the television screen. The viewer enters the required code on a personal computer terminal to order an item and can charge the purchase to his or her bank account. Some videotext systems are available at extra cost as an additional service to cable TV subscribers.

Variations on Six Themes

As we noted earlier, you can devise other approaches or use variations of the six we've covered here. For example, humor can be injected into many approaches, such as a situation approach, a problem-solution approach, and possibly a spokesperson approach. Animation could be considered a separate approach, but it can be adapted to any of the styles we've discussed. (Tony the Tiger, for instance, is a spokesperson for a product.)

You might also use an institutional approach. An institutional commercial is designed to enhance the image of the company and to build goodwill toward it. This form of advertising, which is related to the public-service announcement, does not promote specific products or urge the viewer to go to a store or dealer. Instead, it informs viewers about the company's achievements, standards, and activities. Institutional commercials are a favorite of the major oil companies.

The spot in Figure 10.8 is an institutional commercial used by Martin Marietta, an aerospace company. The commercial does not sell a specific product, but generates goodwill for the company by illustrating a service that the company provides.

A final reminder. Before you begin writing a television spot, visualize what it will look like. This point cannot be stressed enough. It's your responsibility as a copywriter to visualize

TIMES MIRROR MAGAZINES
OUTDOOR LIFE

TITLE: "MOST DANGEROUS GAME"   COMM'L. NO.: XXGR 0222 (:120)

(MUSIC UNDER)
MAN: You can see it in their eyes. They are some of the most dangerous animals in the world.

The lion -- if it's hungry, it will eat you.

The leopard -- it's a deadly killer because it's small and almost totally silent.

The grizzly -- it stands nine feet tall. Now you can come face to face with them in this special gift from Outdoor Life.

Incredible stories on the animals that strike the deepest terror in man.

It's the Most Dangerous Game -- from the editors of Outdoor Life --

a special free gift for you with a low cost introductory subscription. A full year of Outdoor Life for only $6.97.

Call this number, 1-800-228-2080 and bring home the great outdoors. The action. The information. The pride...

Outdoor Life. I'm talking about hunting and fishing the way you like it --

pages of tips and tactics you can use to enjoy the outdoors even more. Articles on fish and game in your neck of the woods...

on the big ones that didn't get away and the little secrets that make it happen.

Outdoor Life. It's all you need to know -- from what's new in hunting equipment to where the bass are hitting big.

Lures. Boots. Boats. Fathers and sons. Adventure. Close calls and long shots.

That's the Outdoor Life for you. Equipment. Camping. Hunting. Field guides and updates and special reports on everything

from trout to turkey to white tails to mallards.

It's the tradition of caring for the wilderness, of making it on your own, through strength and smarts.

Outdoor Life. It's the man's magazine you can depend on -- every month, every issue. Come with us today and get Outdoor Life's Most Dangerous Game -- free with your paid subscription.

Call now. 1-800-228-2080 and save 53% off the $15.00 cover price. That's 40% off the regular subscription rate of $11.94.

So you get 12 great issues -- for just $6.97.

1-800-228-2080. For the Most Dangerous Game. For the great outdoors. For Outdoor Life. (MUSIC OUT)

FIGURE 10·7   Direct response commercial. *(Courtesy Times Mirror Magazines)*

what the spot will look like when it's on tape or on the air. If you need help, use a storyboard sketch, or have a colleague critique your first draft. Either way, be certain the visual elements of your spot will be appealing to the viewer. Television is a visual medium, and if the video portion of your commercial is weak, the entire spot is likely to be ineffective.

One way to give a spot visual strength is to write the visual portion before you write the audio portion. If the video portion will carry the message by itself, you'll know that you have a good television spot. Audio can be added as needed.

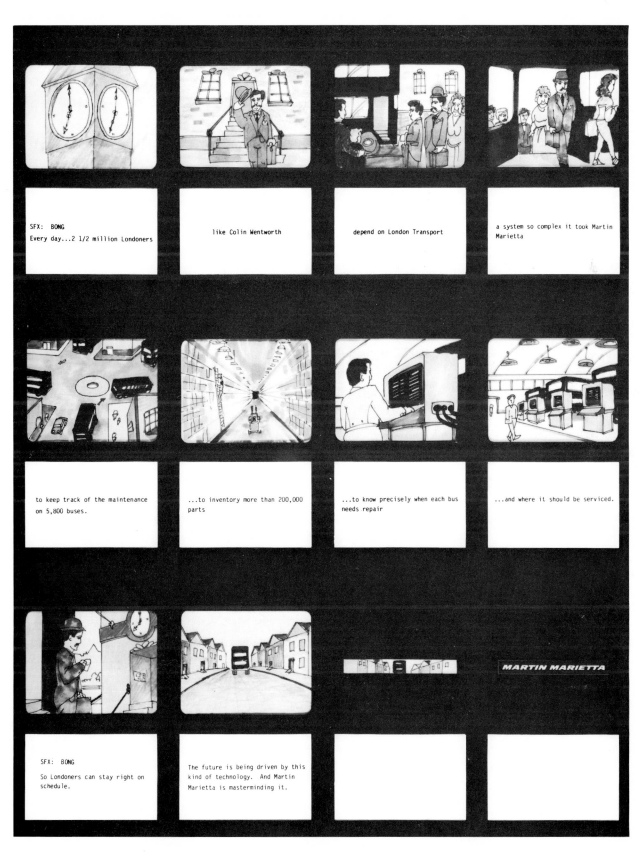

FIGURE 10·8   Institutional commercial. *(Courtesy John H. Boyd, Jr., Martin Marietta Aerospace)*

POINTS TO REMEMBER

- A spot must have a structure that involves the viewer and sells the product or service.

- The problem-solution approach lets you depict a realistic problem and show someone solving it with the product.

- The demonstration approach lets you show the benefits of the product in action.

- A situation commercial tells a story that establishes a reason for the presence of the product.

- The spokesperson approach uses either a well-known person to endorse a product or an unknown person who claims to have used the product and delivers a testimonial for it.

- The product-as-star approach seeks to display the product prominently and make it appear irresistible.

- A direct response spot persuades the viewer to order something directly from the advertiser.

- The visual must be very strong in a direct response spot.

- An institutional approach is designed to enhance the client's image and build goodwill.

Write a thirty-second problem-solution television spot using the following facts:

The Dynamic Corporation is offering a new type of light bulb. This three-way bulb, dim-medium-bright, deals with the problem of having one element burn out. If one element of this bulb lights, all three work. The bulb is guaranteed to work for 1,500 hours.

Write a thirty-second problem-solution spot. Show the problem and introduce the product as a solution. Be certain to show people enjoying the benefits of using the product and establish the product name clearly.

Accompany your script with a storyboard that illustrates the spot.

Grandma's Home-Style Ice Cream has a new flavor, Butter Up. This new flavor combines butterscotch and walnut. Stress that Grandma's ice cream is made with real cream and does not contain artificial ingredients. Grandma's picture is on the label.

Write a thirty-second product-as-star television spot for Grandma's Butter Up Ice Cream. The product should be the star of this commercial. Follow the rules in the chapter. Devise a slogan for use in the spot.

Accompany your script with a storyboard that illustrates your spot.

Waterworld, a recreation complex in Yourtown, wants to advertise on your television station. Stress that Waterworld has something for all members of the family. It has real waves in a gigantic pool, several kinds of water slides, special attractions for toddlers, and paddleboats on the Waterworld lake. One slide, called "The Zoomer," is almost four stories high. Waterworld is open from 10:00 A.M. to 9:00 P.M. through Labor Day.

Write two thirty-second spokesperson television spots for Waterworld.

1. One spot should be a testimonial by one or more Waterworld visitors. Assume that you have videotaped comments by people leaving Waterworld. You also have videotaped scenes of Waterworld. Use a voice-over announcer for any segments of the spot not using actual visitors.

2. The second spot should use a celebrity as spokesperson. Choose the type of person you feel would be appropriate to endorse this client. This spokesperson should lend his or her credibility to the message but not be an actual visitor. Assume that you have videotaped scenes of Waterworld.

Accompany each script with a storyboard.

Prepare a thirty-second situational television spot for the Rapid Fire Microwave Oven. Be certain the spot tells a story with a definite plot. Don't dwell on details. Instead, use the story to introduce the microwave oven in a believable setting. You may wish to base your situation on some of the following features of microwave ovens: They are good for preparing light meals (a portion of lasagna) or quick snacks (a hot dog), or for heating leftovers. They're also good for defrosting frozen foods. Microwaves don't heat up the kitchen and usually cook foods faster than a conventional range can. Your goal is to create a situation in which the Rapid Fire Microwave Oven is used for one or more of these reasons.

   Prepare a storyboard to accompany your script.

The Dynamic Corporation has produced a new battery-operated shoe shiner called the Eze-shine. It's about the size of a hair dryer and comes with brushes of different textures. Because of its size and portability, it can be used anywhere. It operates on four "D" size batteries.

   Write a thirty-second television commercial that demonstrates the shoe shiner in action. Your goal is to show what the product can do, so don't spend time developing a situation.

   Prepare a storyboard to accompany the script.

Write another thirty-second television spot for the Rapid Fire Microwave Oven. Choose an appropriate spokesperson to demonstrate the features of the oven. Develop a sales theme that includes the product name. Use the sales theme prominently in the spot. Use a balance of audio and video to present the sales theme.

   Prepare a storyboard to accompany your script.

Write a ninety-second direct response spot to sell these two products. Prepare a storyboard to accompany the script.

   Product one is a shoe insert called Kushonfoot. It is available in all sizes for both men and women, and slips easily into shoes. It is designed to keep feet dry and warm in the worst weather. The revolutionary design features an insert with millions of tiny air pockets that let your feet breathe naturally. The insert holds warm air in and keeps cold air out. Kushonfoot is treated with new ingredient Chapahol, which repels moisture by working in combination with air pockets. Natural body heat pushes cold and dampness out but keeps heat in. Price: $4.95 a pair. Kushonfoot is suitable for construction workers, police officers, joggers, or anyone else who must be on their feet in cold, wet weather.

Product two is Wondersock, a lightweight, cool stocking. It is suitable for jogging, hiking, yardwork, and so on. It is so lightweight it will feel like you're not wearing a stocking. Wondersock stays cools and dry no matter what the activity. The stocking will not stretch and lose shape, and is made of a combination of wool, linen, and cotton. Wondersock is available in men's and women's sizes. Color: white. Price: $6.95 a pair.

Order both for just $8.95. Call toll-free (800) 123-1234. All credit cards accepted. No postage and handling costs on phone orders. Customers can send $8.95 to Kushonfoot, Box 001, Downtown, New York 10001.

Student Name _____   Advertiser _____

Date Submitted _____   Commercial Length _____

VIDEO   **AUDIO**

EXERCISE 1 *(continued)*

STORYBOARD
FOR: _____   _____   _____
              Class Name   Project or Assignment   Page

BY: _____   _____   _____
              Student Name   Class Number   Date

AUDIO:

VIDEO:

AUDIO:

VIDEO:

AUDIO:

VIDEO:

AUDIO:

VIDEO:

AUDIO:

VIDEO:

AUDIO:

VIDEO:

Student Name _____   Advertiser _____

Date Submitted _____   Commercial Length _____

VIDEO   **AUDIO**

EXERCISE 2 (continued)

STORYBOARD
FOR: _____   _____   _____

Class Name   Project or Assignment   Page

BY: _____   _____   _____

Student Name   Class Number   Date

AUDIO: AUDIO: AUDIO:

VIDEO: VIDEO: VIDEO:

AUDIO: AUDIO: AUDIO:

VIDEO: VIDEO: VIDEO:

Student Name _____   Advertiser _____

Date Submitted _____   Commercial Length _____

VIDEO   **AUDIO**

STORYBOARD
FOR: _____　_____　_____
　　　　　　Class Name　　　　Project or Assignment　　　　　Page

BY: _____　_____　_____
　　　　Student Name　　　　　Class Number　　　　　　　Date

AUDIO:　　　　　　　　　AUDIO:　　　　　　　　　AUDIO:

VIDEO:　　　　　　　　　VIDEO:　　　　　　　　　VIDEO:

AUDIO:　　　　　　　　　AUDIO:　　　　　　　　　AUDIO:

VIDEO:　　　　　　　　　VIDEO:　　　　　　　　　VIDEO:

Student Name _____   Advertiser _____

Date Submitted _____   Commercial Length _____

VIDEO   **AUDIO**

EXERCISE 3 *(continued)*

STORYBOARD
FOR: _____   _____   _____
              Class Name   Project or Assignment   Page

BY: _____   _____   _____
              Student Name   Class Number   Date

AUDIO:

VIDEO:

AUDIO:

VIDEO:

AUDIO:

VIDEO:

AUDIO:

VIDEO:

AUDIO:

VIDEO:

AUDIO:

VIDEO:

Student Name _____   Advertiser _____

Date Submitted _____   Commercial Length _____

VIDEO   **AUDIO**

EXERCISE 4 *(continued)*

STORYBOARD
FOR: _____   _____   _____
               Class Name   Project or Assignment   Page

BY: _____   _____   _____
            Student Name   Class Number   Date

AUDIO: AUDIO: AUDIO:

VIDEO: VIDEO: VIDEO:

AUDIO: AUDIO: AUDIO:

VIDEO: VIDEO: VIDEO:

Student Name _____   Advertiser _____

Date Submitted _____   Commercial Length _____

VIDEO   **AUDIO**

EXERCISE 5 *(continued)*

STORYBOARD
FOR: _____   _____   _____

　　　　　　　Class Name　　　　　　Project or Assignment　　　　　　　Page

BY: _____   _____   _____

　　　　　　Student Name　　　　　　　Class Number　　　　　　　　Date

AUDIO:　　　　　　　　　AUDIO:　　　　　　　　　AUDIO:

VIDEO:　　　　　　　　　VIDEO:　　　　　　　　　VIDEO:

AUDIO:　　　　　　　　　AUDIO:　　　　　　　　　AUDIO:

VIDEO:　　　　　　　　　VIDEO:　　　　　　　　　VIDEO:

Student Name _____   Advertiser _____

Date Submitted _____   Commercial Length _____

VIDEO   **AUDIO**

STORYBOARD
FOR: _____   _____   _____
           Class Name   Project or Assignment   Page

BY: _____   _____   _____
         Student Name   Class Number   Date

AUDIO: AUDIO: AUDIO:

VIDEO: VIDEO: VIDEO:

AUDIO: AUDIO: AUDIO:

VIDEO: VIDEO: VIDEO:

Student Name _____   Advertiser _____

Date Submitted _____   Commercial Length _____

VIDEO   **AUDIO**

EXERCISE 7 (continued)

STORYBOARD
FOR: _____   _____   _____
       Class Name   Project or Assignment   Page

BY: _____   _____   _____
       Student Name   Class Number   Date

AUDIO: AUDIO: AUDIO:

VIDEO: VIDEO: VIDEO:

AUDIO: AUDIO: AUDIO:

VIDEO: VIDEO: VIDEO:

11 The Copywriter as Image Maker

If a broadcast station is to be successful, it must develop a favorable image in the community it serves. This image may be created by broadcasting public-service messages of interest to the community and by using promotion and publicity to let the public know about the station's programming.

You may be asked to help the station develop the image it seeks, either by taking a position as a PSA or promotion writer, or by handling these duties in addition to your regular responsibilities as a commercial copywriter.

Writing public-service or promotional copy presents a special problem. If you're selling a product in a commercial, some of your audience will probably need the product or could benefit from using it. But people don't really *need* to give time or money to a nonprofit organization, nor do they *need* to watch or listen to your station. There are probably other stations they could choose. You hope that people will respond to a charitable organization or a broadcast station because of the concrete services it provides, but often it's the image that must be sold to the public. This chapter sets forth guidelines that will enable you to write promotional and public-service announcements that will sell both service and image.

Promotion

Like any other business, a radio or television station must promote its product. For a broadcaster, the product is programming. Promotion seeks to gain a larger audience. Successful promotion of the station's programming is important to its advertisers, because a client's message may not be seen or heard unless the station has an established audience.

Promotion has two interrelated goals. One is to tell the audience about upcoming programs, and the other is to keep it interested in regularly scheduled programs.

Program originators usually supply stations with promotional information. The major television networks—NBC, CBS, and ABC—prepare promotional packets for every show on their schedules. These packets are sent to the local affiliates before the programs are shown. One major mailing occurs before the fall season, and updates and additions follow as needed. The packet includes publicity releases, star biographies, photos, fact sheets, suggested on-the-air announcements, and prepared print ads.

The networks also supply the stations with timely news and promotional information—for example, adjustments of the evening schedule due to a presidential news conference or material for special programs. Such information is commonly sent to the local affiliate by closed-circuit two-way teletype between the local station and the networks.

The networks also send their affiliates prepared on-the-air promotional announcements for both radio and TV. Scripts may be mailed to the station, sent by teletype, or sent as produced promos in a closed circuit feed from the network to the local station. Networks may also provide their affiliates with the opportunity to interview a celebrity from a network program. The interview is conducted in the station's studio with a local announcer, who talks to the celebrity by satellite. Since the celebrity will usually do a number of interviews in one sitting, the local station will generally tape the interview. Arrangements are made by mail or teletype.

Syndicated program producers also send promotional packets to local stations, but they're usually not as extensive as those supplied by the networks. They typically include slides, a synopsis of each episode, photos, and prepared print advertisements. Syndicated film companies supply television stations with even less information, usually a synopsis of each movie and photos. Syndicators of special programs—talk shows and news features—supply local stations with on-air promotional material, often fed to the station by satellite along with the programs. Promotion packets are usually also sent to local stations.

The promotional department of a syndicated film or program company often supplies recommended copy for stations to use. Syndicators do this to insure a consistent level of promotion quality in all markets carrying the program. All that needs to be done is to fill in the blanks with your station's call letters and the time of the program. Similarly, program excerpts are sometimes supplied either by satellite feed or as a part of the promotional packet. If prepared material is not supplied, the promotion writer must write the copy and screen episodes of the program for suitable excerpt material. Screening film or tape is a time-consuming process that the station may choose not to pursue.

Radio stations rely on the networks for a much smaller percentage of their programming than television stations. Many radio stations aren't affiliated with a network, and many that are receive only news from it. Others receive network news and/or talk shows. Stations with a network affiliation generally receive a daily closed-circuit audio feed consisting of scheduling information, and, where appropriate, promotion and publicity material.

Some radio stations carry syndicated programs in which well-known disc jockeys present the week's top records. The station usually receives a promo in which the show's host urges people to listen to the program on the local station.

When the goal is to promote a locally originated program or a programming format, you, as copywriter, will work from firsthand knowledge. In this case, you cannot rely on material prepared by network professionals. Instead, you must use your own insight and creativity. There are a number of ways in which a full-time promotion manager or a copywriter handling promotion and publicity can reach the public.

Promos

The *on-the-air promotional announcement (promo)* is one of the primary methods of reaching the public. The promo reaches the station's established audience, the people most interested in your message. As with the other types of copy covered in this chapter, you have a different product but the same goal as a radio or TV commercial writer.

There are two types of promos—specific and generic. The specific approach aims at the audience's decisions; it asks viewers or listeners to make up their minds, to do something—for example: "Watch Channel Five News tonight at six!" A specific promo may ask viewers to watch a given episode of a program, to watch a special program, or to watch the station's evening program lineup. A specific promo might also ask viewers to watch a given individual such as the weatherperson or, in the case of radio, to listen to the morning wakeup announcer.

A generic promo might be used to create an image of competence for a television station's news team or an image of reliability for the weatherperson. In the case of radio, a generic promo could help communicate the feeling of relaxation created by the songs played on the station.

On-the-air promos may be any length—as short as three-second logos or as long as one-minute promos. The commercial load and programming philosophy of the station's management will determine the length. Unsold commercial slots (called availabilities) are often filled with promos.

Writing Specific Promos   The following promo illustrates the specific approach. It's a direct appeal for viewers to watch a program. It includes the name of the program, the day and time it runs, the station on which it appears, and a direct request for viewers to tune in.

VIDEO	AUDIO
CG: CARNIVAL BOAT STARRING GINGER ROGERS AND WILLIAM BOYD	WFTV presents this week's chapter of the FRED ASTAIRE–GINGER ROGERS FILMOGRAPHY. In the first film of our double feature, the rugged men of the turbulent North struggle to survive in CARNIVAL BOAT, starring Ginger Rogers and William Boyd. Then, in their first film together, Astaire and Rogers dance "The Carioca" in the musical comedy, FLYING DOWN TO RIO. Join host Walter Windsor for the FRED ASTAIRE–GINGER ROGERS FILMOGRAPHY, Sunday afternoon at 2:30 on WFTV, Channel 9.
CG: FLYING DOWN TO RIO STARRING FRED ASTAIRE AND GINGER ROGERS.	

Courtesy SFN Communications of Florida, Inc.

The news promo that follows also uses the specific approach. Notice how the spot sells the advantages of listening to this weather forecaster and urges viewers to tune in.

VIDEO	AUDIO
BOYLAN DELIVERS CONCEPT SCRIPT BOYLAN ANIMATION	When you need the most accurate weather forecast in town, Ray Boylan delivers! He's the only weatherman in town with Skytrack color weather radar! He tells you what's best to do, come rain or shine. Twenty-five years of weather forecasting experience, working for you on TV-12 Action News. See for yourself, weeknights, at 6 and 11!
SKYTRACK C.K. SKYTRACK CONSOLE/EXTERIOR	
WEATHER MAP IN OFFICE WEATHER MAP C.K. BOYLAN ANIMATION	

Courtesy WTLV, Jacksonville, Florida.

The specific approach can also make strong use of the balance of audio and video, as illustrated in the promo in Figure 11.1.

Writing Generic Promos   The generic approach is not as direct as the specific approach. Since it is designed to promote images, a generic promo need not present so much specific information about the day and time of a program. Instead, its goal is to develop an overall feeling about the station or its program content. That's what this news promo does: It communicates the dedication and commitment of a television news department.

VIDEO	AUDIO
00 MS SLIGHTLY HIGH ANGLE BOB OPSAHL AT SWITCHER TURNS TO CAMERA	At Channel 9, there's a spirit, a commitment that makes us Central Florida's leading news station.

WTSP TV

PROMOTIONAL COPY

GOOD THROUGH :_____

LENGTH :_____

TITLE :_____   ACTION NEWS AT NOON   :30 _____

AUDIO CART   :_____

VIDEO	AUDIO

IN

OVER-STUFFED SANDWICH
EDIT TO SAME SANDWICH
LESS MEAT . . .
EDIT TO SAME SANDWICH
EVEN LESS MEAT
EDIT TO SANDWICH, BREAD
ONLY.

QUANTEL OUT FROM
SANDWICH NEWS VIDEO
DENNIS REPORTING . . .

WEATHER SHOT WITH MENARD

SCHWARTZ ON LOCATION AT
BUCS PRACTICE

LEACH W/CONSUMER REPORT
DEESON W/ACTION LINE

FONDA INTERVIEW

ANTIQUES DETECTIVE/
DR. ____ HEALTH REPORT

OVER STUFFED SANDWICH
EDIT TO SAME SANDWICH
WITH BITE TAKEN OUT . . .

LOGO AND C.G. INFO.

OUT

ANNCR: A mid-day newscast should be piled-high

with all the news you need. But some

stations only offer news by-products, and

don't get to the meat of the issues . . .

(Pause)

At Channel 10's Action News At Noon, we

serve you a hearty helping of the most

current news . . . up to the minute weather

forecasts . . . and a taste of sports you

won't get anywhere else . . . and, news for

the consumer, problem solving with Action

Line, personality interviews, and helpful

hints to fill you day.

Action News At Noon. We make all the

news, easy to swallow. Weekdays on

Channel 10.

FIGURE 11·1   A specific promo. *(Courtesy Cyndie Reynolds, WTSP-TV, St. Petersburg, Florida)*

06 MS EYE LEVEL, ALYCE AT PAY PHONE.
   MAN WITH CAMERA ON SHOULDER
   WALKS BETWEEN HER AND CAMERA.
   SHE HANGS UP, MOVES FORWARD A
   STEP. MOVES OUT OF FRAME AT END.

It starts with reporters who know their
subjects . . . who dig deeper to develop
stories you won't see anywhere else.

10 MLS, DANNY ON WEATHER SET WITH
   ACCU-WEATHER GRAPHICS TERMINAL.

and that commitment shows, in the way we
cover the news . . . from Accu-Weather . . .

12 MS, MARSHA AIRBORN IN SKYWITNESS
   OVER EPCOT.

. . . to Skywitness

13 MLS, STEVE TRIGGS IN FRONT OF INSTANT EYE AT CAPE. MAN WITH CAMERA SET UP. TRIGGS TURNS AS THOUGH TO DO LIVE REPORT.	to live satellite and instant eye reports.
16 MLS BOB JORDAN IN COURTROOM. BENCH BG.	Central Florida's largest television news team covers the important stories.
18 MS MIKE STORMS DRIVING RACE CAR PAST DAYTONA SIGN AT SPEEDWAY. SHOT FROM OUTSIDE DRIVER'S WINDOW.	And the interesting ones.
22 TRUCKING SHOT, MLS GEORGE RYAN, CAMERAMAN BG MOVING DOWN BEACH	Wherever the news happens.
26 CU BOB OPSAHL, INSTANT EYE	We work hard to bring you Central Florida's best newscast.
WS, BOB OPSAHL, SKYWITNESS, 2 INSTANT EYES, SATELLITE DISH, AND MEMBERS OF TEAM BG. MUSIC FULL. SUPER	And that's the Eyewitness advantage.

Courtesy SFN Communications of Florida, Inc.

Radio stations can also use the generic approach to create a feeling or image, as the following promo does in promoting WGBH's Summer Radio Festival.

NEW ENGLAND SUMMER RADIO FESTIVAL/generic spot

SFX: SOUND OF CRICKETS IN BACKGROUND, NOT CLOSE UP. AUDIBLE THROUGHOUT; UP FULL BEFORE TAG, OUT UNDER
Sorry about the crickets. After all, they are the longest-running musical tradition of the New England summer. And here we come, right into the heart of cricket country, with our mikes and mobile studios and nervous producers, intent on capturing summer music of another sort. The NEW ENGLAND SUMMER RADIO FESTIVAL series with host Phyllis Curtin, takes you to the most popular regional music festivals in the Northeast—from the seaside: Newport's Music Festival; inland: to the Connecticut Early Music Festival; then north to Vermont's Mozart Festival . . . and that's just a taste. Because summer in New England is an endless celebration of music . . . and if you sort of "squint" your ears, you'll hear the faint, unmistakable music of crickets.
The NEW ENGLAND SUMMER RADIO FESTIVAL . . . Sunday at 6 . . . here on listener-supported WGBH Boston.

Courtesy WGBH, Boston, Massachusetts.

A feeling or image can also be created with a touch of humor. The following promo promotes a TV station's movies on radio.

ANNCR   You want free movies? Okay, let's talk free movies on WMOD
                         TV-43. WMOD's got midday movies, 8 P.M. movies, Saturday
                         movies, Sunday movies, late movies, all-night movies. TV-43

gets you in free to the movies you want to see! We fill your TV with comedy, drama, romance and passion, fast-moving adventure with plenty of action, and musicals too. We've got war movies, spy movies, and the best of the westerns with good guys in white who win all the fights! We've got movies with monsters who crawl in the window and scare off your pants. So don't take a chance and miss the movie you want to see in full living color—TV-43! What else? We've got the greatest in classics, the box office winners with your favorite stars. Sit back and relax with all the free movies on WMOD, TV-43. M-O-D brings M-O-V-I-E-S into your living room, den or (gasp) bedroom, free! You'll see what you've been missing when WMOD TV-43 brings Hollywood home to you, don't you see? That's WMOD, TV-43 . . . B-Y-O-P, Bring your own popcorn!

Courtesy Chapman and Castello Advertising, Inc.

Instead of promoting a specific program or a category of programming, some promos may be used to promote a station's special programming, as this generic promo does.

(SFX: JINGLE, CUT #9) Take Me Out to the Ballgame
One of America's favorite pastimes developed from the game of cricket and an old English sport called rounders. In 1839, Abner Doubleday laid out a diamond-shaped field with four bases and named the game baseball. Six years later Alexander Cartwright established standard rules and designed the game almost exactly as it is played today . . . and for over one hundred years Americans have enjoyed the excitement and thrills of major league baseball! Join the fun yourself this season with us, as KFOR brings you Kansas City Royals baseball!
VOCAL CLOSE

Courtesy KFOR Radio, Lincoln, Nebraska.

More Promo Basics   In a promo, the sponsor is the station, and the station should be clearly identified. Television stations find that viewers identify them most readily by channel number. As a result, you can usually omit the station's call letters.

Radio stations may or may not seek identification by their call letters. Many music stations prefer a verbal logo using a letter from their call letters, or a word in combination with their location on the dial. For example, station WHLY might become Y106, or a station may call itself Hits 106. These are promotional logos and should be used in promotional copy. They will also be used on the air by the disc jockey. They cannot be used as the station's legal ID (identification), which by law must include the station's call letters and city of license.

A promotional announcement publicizing a specific program, event, or the evening's program schedule should include the name of the station, the title of the program(s) or event, and the day and time of the broadcast. The following spot is typical of promos used by television stations to promote an evening's program lineup.

VIDEO		AUDIO
T.J. HOOKER	8	ABC and Channel 9 present Saturday prime-
LOVE BOAT	9	time entertainment. At 8, on "T.J. Hooker,"

| FANTASY ISLAND | 10 |
| EYEWITNESS NEWS UPDATE | 11 |

Vince goes undercover as a male stripper to get evidence on a drug dealer. Then, at 9, Celeste Holm plays a widow who turns the Love Boat into a gambling cruise for charity. JoAnn Pflug costars. Next, on "Fantasy Island," Mickey Gilley is a country star who gets the cold shoulder at his own family reunion. The Eyewitness News update follows at 11. For the tops in prime time, it's ABC and Channel 9.

Courtesy SFN Communications of Florida, Inc.

IDs

The shortest form of on-air promos are IDs. Identifications are short, usually no more than three to five seconds long. The most obvious form of the ID is its use to give the station's legal identification announcement, as required by the U.S. Federal Communications Commission (FCC). This announcement must be given once each hour, close to the top of the hour. It must include the station's call letters and place of signal origination (city or area of dominant influence). Stations often use the legal ID spot to include brief program promotions as well. Radio stations include their frequency, while television stations include their channel number. A promotional theme may also be included. A music/information AM station in Orlando, Florida, uses this legal ID: "This is WDBO, Newsradio 58, Orlando. Count on us for news every hour, on the hour."

Television stations can use audio, video, or both to present their legal ID. A TV station can thus super its legal ID over program content, insert an audio recording at the proper spot, or broadcast a complete ID with sight and sound. In the latter case, TV stations often use a shared ID to share the legal information with a promotional announcement. This can be done by combining a slide with prerecorded audio on cartridge. Another way is to combine a short excerpt from a syndicated program with a topical audio announcement. The legal portion of the ID can be supered under a station logo. For example:

> Audio: Next on the MERV GRIFFIN SHOW.
>
> Video: Excerpt from MERV GRIFFIN SHOW.
>
> Audio: Watch the MERV GRIFFIN SHOW tomorrow at 4.
> Video: Station call letters, name of city, and location.

IDs that are not necessary for legal identification also appear throughout a station's schedule. Radio stations have their DJ's mention short generic IDs to promote the station's format. Television stations may insert IDs in commercial availabilities. They may be the same IDs used for legal identification or modified versions that do not include the legal information (call letters and city).

An ID may also be shared with the network. Networks supply their affiliates with topical ID material. A local voice announcement and a visual logo are all that must be added to complete the ID.

Teasers and Bumpers

Another type of television promotional announcement is the teaser or bumper. These are brief visual announcements, sometimes as short as two seconds, designed to stimulate interest in an upcoming program or event. Bumpers are used in network or syndicated programs at the beginning and end of a series of commercials. For example, in the syndicated showing of "Fantasy Island," a station precedes and follows each commercial cluster with a slide showing the house on "Fantasy Island," the name "Fantasy Island" imposed across the top of the screen, and the call letters and location imposed across the bottom.

Teasers are used at the end of a program or a program segment to promote interest in an upcoming program, such as the local newscast. The written copy for a teaser might be very brief, but the wording is crucial. Your task is to write interesting copy that will gain attention without giving away the outcome of the show or news item. For example, a teaser for the late evening sportscast should not say, "The Jackrabbits win by one in overtime. Details at 10." With that wording the suspense is gone, so there's no reason for the audience to stay tuned. A better teaser would say, "The Jackrabbits had a fight on their hands tonight. Details at 10." This teaser doesn't provide the outcome and thus maintains suspense. Teasers for syndicated shows or movies call for the same rigorous writing: Tease the viewer with the story line but don't give it away.

Logos

A logo is a brief, identifiable signature representing a station, network, or program syndicator. Visuals are commonly used on television to create effective associations with promotional themes developed by the station. Figures 11.2 and 11.3 show typical station and network logos. Radio stations may also use brief verbal logos to establish their identity, especially when similar formats exist, or to gain listener identification through repetition. One album-oriented rock station may refer to itself as the "real rocker," while another in the same market calls itself the "hot rocker."

FIGURE 11·2   A station logo. *(Courtesy Cyndie Reynolds, WTSP-TV, St. Petersburg, Florida)*

FIGURE 11·3   A network logo. *(Courtesy American Broadcasting Companies, Inc.)*

Use of a station's logo in its promos is another example of positioning. Just as advertisers seek to position their products in relation to those of their competitors, broadcasters seek to establish a stance for their station in the market. Positioning a station's sound or appearance is especially useful when the market has several stations with similar programming. As a promotions writer you may be asked to create ID campaigns with logos that will help position your station. In this assignment, you'll have to evaluate your station and its primary competitors to find a characteristic that can differentiate your station in the mind of the listener.

Tie-in packages are available to network-affiliated TV stations. Tie-in packages involve custom animation and music packages developed by the network and made available to its affiliate stations at modest prices. These materials allow the affiliates to include their own call letters, channel number, and local or syndicated program promotions in on-air promotional packages developed around network themes (Figure 11.4 shows a typical example). Tie-in packages can be used to increase the potential of a promotion budget.

Jingle and Image Packages

Both radio and television stations purchase ID/station image packages from various production companies. Stations use the packages with their own programming and in external advertising.

Radio stations use television rather than print as their primary advertising medium. Radio stations want to promote their format and sound, and television is thought to be a primary source of potential radio listeners.

Conversely, television stations advertise on radio stations. For the TV station, this may consist of co-op advertising, which splits the cost between the station and the network. Since TV stations often advertise a schedule of evening programming, as in the evening line-up promo on pages 261–262, the network is willing to share the cost of promoting its programs. As a copywriter, you will need to write the copy to fill in a donut—a recorded musical bed with the local station designation sung at the beginning and end. Your staff announcer can usually record the entire spot. Television stations also advertise their evening newscasts on radio, often having one of their news anchors record a summation of the stories to be covered that evening.

Some radio stations produce their own image spots, while others turn to ad agencies. Often these spots are not of satisfactory quality or are very costly. Preparing an effective

"WE'RE WITH YOU" CUSTOM MUSIC

For the fourth consecutive year, Frank Gari Productions has produced the promotional campaign music for the ABC-TV Network and its affiliates.

Frank Gari Productions has an impressive track record. "Now Is the Time, ABC Is the Place" won a Clio Award in its music category in 1982. "Come On Along With ABC" and "That Special Feeling on ABC" were Clio finalists in the 1983 and 1984 awards competition. Additionally, Frank Gari Productions produces all music for ABC-TV's "Good Morning America," as well as themes for "PM/Evening Magazine," Lifetime Cable Network, Eyewitness News, and 150 local television and radio station campaigns, including the popular "Hello" promotion.

Frank Gari brought together a wealth of talent to provide music for the new ABC-TV campaign, "We're With You." Co-writer Barbara Morr is represented on national commercials and some of the top 40 hits recorded by "The Manhattans." Co-lyricist Marty Winston won a Clio, with Frank Gari, for his contributions on "Come On Along With ABC." His lyrics are also represented nationally on over 70 television station campaigns. Lead vocalist Florence Warner may be recognized from her many national commercial songs (American Airlines, Hellman's, etc.) as well as her close work with television station campaigns across the U.S. and Canada. Fifty-two musicians, production, and engineering talent were utilized to produce the "We're With You" campaign.

Frank Gari, Bruce Breslau and the rest of the staff at Frank Gari Productions are available for consultation with promotion managers/creative service directors to help them customize lyrics to the new ABC campaign, or to help fine-tune the network campaign to local station campaigns.

Examples of basic music customization, and full music customization will follow to show you how the "We're With You" campaign can apply to news, programming, public service, sports, and community involvement aspects of your station.

The following are materials participating affiliates will receive with basic or full customization orders. Please remember that the original network version musicians and singers are utilized on affiliate custom tracks.

:60 FULL VOCAL
:60 DONUT
:60 INSTRUMENTAL
:30 FULL VOCAL
:30 DONUT
:30 INSTRUMENTAL
:10 VOCAL
:10 INSTRUMENTAL
:05 OR :03 VOCAL
:05 OR :03 INSTRUMENTAL

Some of the people behind the music:
Frank Gari (center) of Frank Gari Productions, Lead Singer Marty Nelson, Arranger/Singer Danny Baker, Singers Peter Thom, Valerie Wilson, Kathy Ingraham, and Lead Vocalist Florence Warner (left to right) in a recent recording session for the 1984-85 ABC-TV Network campaign "We're With You." Frank Gari Productions, Inc. has been the exclusive music producer for ABC for the past four years.

FIGURE 11·4   A network promotional package. *(Courtesy American Broadcasting Companies, Inc.)*

image spot to run on television is not easy. The following list identifies some of the pitfalls to avoid in developing a TV campaign for a radio station.[1]

---

1. "How to Afford an Effective TV Campaign," *Radio Only* 2 (November 1983): 33.

Stations ordering a *basic music customization* will receive the following lyric. Lines in Italic represent those which can be altered to reflect your channel number/call letters. Please note that this year you receive customization in several sections.

We're with you
On Channel 2 with you (we're with you)
We're with you on Channel 2
Come on America
Let's get together
'Cause when we're with you
There's nothing better
We're with you
On Channel 2 with you (we're with you)
We're with you on Channel 2
Feel the spirit young and old
We're going for the gold
We'll give you all we've got
This year we're red hot
There's magic day and night
With every star in sight
With you for fantasy, with you for laughter
With you to share your dreams and all that you're after
We're with you
On Channel 2 with you (we're with you)
We're with you on Channel 2
We're with you on Channel 2

Stations that have been using their own local campaign may want to incorporate their slogan into the new network theme. This can be easily accomplished by further customization.

For example:
Stations utilizing a "Here's to the Team" concept may alter lines to sing *"We're with you, part of the team with you."*

"Hello" promotion stations could say, *"We're with you, we say "Hello" to you."*

Stations could also incorporate city location, personality or other programming information. There are additional charges for further customization.

This year, Frank Gari Productions post-scored many of the spots for the "We're With You" campaign with a variety of :30 instrumental pieces that contain :05 "We're With You" vocal tags. These promos are available for local customization at an additional cost.

1. Don't overproduce the spot with exotic effects and a dazzling cast. People may remember the spot but not your station.

2. Don't include too many points about the station's format. Stick to one sales point.

3. Don't use a lengthy lead-in that wastes the opening of the spot.

"WE'RE WITH YOU" CUSTOM ANIMATION

The following elements will be offered as part of ABC's affiliate custom animated graphics package:

The Custom ID — An animated version of your station logo in the style and length of the network master logo.

The Donut — 30 second donut opens with network opening graphic slogan and closes with your custom logo.

The Title Package — 29 animated titles in the style of this year's animation. This package includes DAYS OF THE WEEK, TONIGHT, TOMORROW, NEXT, WEEKDAYS, WEEKNIGHTS, TODAY, SPECIAL, SPECIALS, SPORTS, NEW SHOW, EDITORIAL, MOVIE, COMEDY, NEWS, DRAMA, NEW, PREMIERE, RETURNING SHOW, CHILDREN'S MORNING & DAYTIME, ONE WEEK FROM TONIGHT, TWO WEEKS FROM TONIGHT.

Custom ID Center — Custom logo center frame on black background for 5 seconds.

Custom ID Lower Right — Custom logo lower right on black background for 5 seconds.

Custom ID Lower Left — Custom logo lower left on black background for 5 seconds.

Slides — 4 slides of your station's logo on black background.

Novocom Inc. will be producing the customized graphics package for affiliates.

Novocom is a Los Angeles based firm specializing in state of the art graphics and film effects for television, commercials and motion pictures.

Unlike many design studios, Novocom offers a complete design and production service. Our motion-controlled graphics camera allows us to shoot anything from a simple logo treatment to complicated model set ups. Our exclusive relationship with Joblove-Kay (formerly the computer animation arm of Marks & Marks) enables us to produce 3-dimensional computer-generated images directly onto film.

Combining the talents of a creative and production staff with extensive experience in television graphics, cosmmercial production and feature film effects with the latest in commercial animation technology, Novocom has produced work for ABC, Fiat Oil (Italy), Pennzoil (Eisaman, Johns, & Law/Houston), Olivetti (GSD&M/Dallas), Twilight Zone The Movie (Warner Bros.), Paramount, Walt Disney Productions, Activision (J. Walter Thompson), Pacific Bell (Foote, Cone & Belding/ Honig), Ford Mexico (J. Walter Thompson/Mexico) and many others.

All questions regarding the customized graphic elements and price quotes should be directed to:

Mark Trugman,
Vice President/Executive Producer,
Novocom Inc.,
1545 N. Wilcox Ave., Suite 201,
Los Angeles, CA 90028,
(213) 461-3688.

4. Use radio personalities in TV spots with care. They may not transfer well to TV.

5. Keep the call letters prominent. They should be on the screen for most if not all of the spot.

6. Avoid inside information about the station that may not be meaningful to the TV audience.

Rather than risk producing a costly and ineffective TV spot, many radio stations use syndicated packages instead. They are cost-effective because the quality of the spots is usually high and stations using the package in other markets in effect share the cost. Figures 11.5 and 11.6 illustrate the kinds of image packages available to radio stations. Preproduced image packages are also available for TV stations.

Cable Promotion

Promotional efforts for cable systems do not differ greatly from those of television broadcasters. Promotion attracts new subscribers, communicates positive images to current and potential subscribers, governmental officials, and local advertisers, and reduces disconnects. Cable systems can use on-air promotion, as well as paid promotion and publicity. Together these efforts (1) inform viewers about the full array of channels available, (2) convince the public that this complement of channels is the best available, thus reducing disconnects, and (3) creates an image of the cable service as the source of desired products—such as MTV.

Cable networks provide local systems with a wide range of consumer marketing and sales materials to aid low-budget local promotions. These materials include on-air spots and IDs, direct mailers, program guides, subscriber information kits, and bill stuffers.

Many national cable networks pay cablecasters for local joint promotion of the system and network. Payment may be made at sign-up time or on an annual basis. Both pay and basic networks use cooperative advertising in which the network and the local system split the cost of radio and print promotion. The major pay cable networks, such as HBO, also supply local systems with camera-ready materials for use in local print promotion. This service is a great cost saver because many local systems do not have art departments and must hire outside advertising or art firms to prepare print advertising.

Cable systems also want to get maximum use of availabilities in pay cable networks. Cablecasters will usually use any commercial time that has not been sold for self-promotion. These spots may promote some of the system's pay services or some of the system's customer services.

Cable systems can also devote a channel to program listings, public-service announcements, and information about services offered by the system. Program promos will focus on locally produced cable programming, and may promote offerings on other channels of the system. The information is usually presented by on-air print crawls created by a video character generator. A musical background usually accompanies the visual material, often the signal of a radio station.

Cable systems have unique problems that affect their promotional efforts. The script that follows is part of a paid promotion for an "amnesty period," during which a cable system sought to convince people who were receiving cable service illegally to call the cable system and subscribe. Read the script closely to examine the appeal that successfully dealt with the problem of cable signal theft.

VIDEO	**AUDIO**
MOVING DAY, BOXES, WRAPPING PAPER IN EVIDENCE. OPEN WITH TS OF DAD WITH CABLE IN HAND. SLOW ZOOM OUT AS HE STARTS TO HOOK CABLE CONNECTION TO TELEVISION. SUPER ON AND OFF: © 1985 AMERICAN TV & COMM., CORP.	DAD: Honey, look at this! I wonder if the cable is still connected!

(continued on page 271)

FIGURE 11·5   An image package for country music stations. *(Courtesy Buddy Scott, TM Productions)*

HOT LIPS

You should hear how she talks about you...

The kiss my lover brings, she brings to me...

Yes, you're once, twice, three times a lady...

Do you really want to hurt me...

Just once can we figure out what we keep doing wrong...

I've been waiting for a girl like you...

Private eyes are watching you...

It's a little bit funny, this feeling inside...

Doo wop, diddy wop, diddy wop doo...

TM Productions

You should hear what HOT LIPS from TM has to say about your station.
Better yet, you should see how HOT LIPS presents the music you play
to promote your station on TV. And you can, right now.
Call TM collect at 214-634-8511, and order your HOT LIPS demo today!
HOT LIPS. Get it to do all the talking for your station.

1349 Regal Row   Dallas, Texas 75247   214-634-8511

FIGURE 11·6   An image package using excerpts from records. *(Courtesy Buddy Scott, TM Productions)*

MOM WALKS OVER TO CONFER WITH DAD.	MOM: Does it work? DAD: Yeah, we can get cable and HBO without paying!
DAUGHTER WALKS INTO SCENE. (SCREEN SHOWS HBO LOGO MOVING ON SCREEN.)	DAUGHTER: But Daddy, isn't that like stealing?
MOM AND DAD LOOK AT EACH OTHER AND REACT.	SILENCE.
DAD LOOKS AT DAUGHTER AND AGREES TO CALL FOR CABLE SERVICES. <u>SUPER: CALL NOW! OFFER ENDS MAY 15.</u>	ANNCR. V.O. (PAUL HAYES): Using cable services without paying for . . .
ACTION SHOWS DAD AND GIRL LOOKING THROUGH PHONE DIRECTORY, MAKING CALL.	. . . them is a crime. Cablevision of Central Florida urges you to . . .
CU OF DAD ON TELEPHONE. SQUEEZE FRAME TO UPPER 1/3 EFFECTS WINDOW AND SUPER BELOW:	. . . call us—and get connected legally.
(CABLEVISION LOGO) ORLANDO: 291-2500 S. SEMINOLE: 834-4031 SANFORD: 322-8512 ORMOND BEACH: 677-1232 KISSIMMEE: 847-8001 MELBOURNE/COCOA: 254-3300	ANNCR. V.O.: Call us, before May 15th, and we'll sign you up with no questions asked.
FADE TO BLACK. SUPER ON: STEALING CABLE IS A CRIME. <u>SUPER: CALL NOW! OFFER ENDS MAY 15.</u>	After that, we'll take action.

Courtesy Cablevision of Central Florida.

Public-Service Announcements

Public-service announcements are messages broadcast free of cost for nonprofit organizations. Broadcast stations air PSAs to respond to community needs and to build their own prestige in their community.

Since stations carry PSAs without charge, they have discretion in the number and nature of the PSAs they broadcast. Stations generally won't devote a lot of costly production for PSAs, and they usually won't schedule many PSAs in prime time. As a general rule, the easier the PSA is for the station to use, the more likely it will be broadcast.

Broadcast stations are flooded with requests for public-service air time. The requests, including some PSA announcements themselves, come from several sources. Large charities like the Red Cross and the Cancer Society have their own staffs to prepare PSAs, or they may hire an advertising agency to write them. Many other requests come from local charities, religious, educational, and civic organizations. In addition, advertising agencies or individuals in the advertising business donate their time to prepare PSAs. Finally, a national public-service organization, the Advertising Council of America, produces public-service messages for worthy organizations. PSAs prepared by such professionals are sent to the station ready for broadcast or requiring only a tag to identify the local chapter or affiliate of the organization.

The Public-Service Message

A PSA is really not different from a commercial. You're still delivering a sales message but not for a product. For example, instead of selling a car you may be selling people on the idea of using their seat belts.

When writing a PSA, you go through all the steps you would in preparing a commercial. Once again, the copy platform can be an effective guide. Here is a summation of the points discussed in Chapter 4.

1. What objective does this client want to achieve? Is it to raise money, seek volunteers, or create a favorable image?

2. What is the target audience for this message? Men, women, families, teenagers?

3. What sales theme can be developed to promote this client? What selling point can be developed and tied to a strong consumer benefit? Is a slogan appropriate?

4. What bonus items, if any, can be introduced?

5. How can you position this public-service client to establish a separate identity among competing nonprofit groups?

6. What approach (tone, mood, or style) will match this client's message?

Writing a PSA may be more difficult than writing a commercial because you're not selling a product people need or want. A PSA generally tries to sell an idea that people agree with in theory. But it may be an idea they have trouble putting into practice or one to which they won't give time or money.

Types of Public-Service Announcements

There are two types of public-service announcements: the informational announcement that tells the audience who, what, when, and where; and the announcement that advocates an idea or goal. Local organizations tend to disseminate more informational PSAs, while national organizations more commonly seek to sell ideas to the public.

The PSA that follows is an example of an informational announcement. While the spot establishes a framework to gain the attention of the audience, its primary goal is to convey information about an event of interest. This spot used the wife of Florida's governor as the spokesperson.

VIDEO	AUDIO
MRS. GRAHAM HOLDING BOUQUET OF YELLOW ROSES	Recently, there was a very popular movie about a lovable creature from outer space who could bring dying flowers back to life.

SUPER: MRS. ROBERT GRAHAM

CLOSE-UP: OF ROSES

CUT TO MRS. GRAHAM

Now, I'd like to tell you how these flowers can help you give the gift of life to children who are dying of cystic fibrosis.

The Florida Federation of Women's Clubs is selling yellow roses like these to raise money that will help give more years of life to children with cystic fibrosis. Please buy all that you can. If your children were dying, what wouldn't you give to give them life?

SUPER: CYSTIC FIBROSIS LOGO

Courtesy Cystic Fibrosis Foundation, Florida Chapter.

The two announcements in Figure 11.7 illustrate the selling of an idea. The idea—that drug abuse can be prevented—is approached in two different ways. The "Teddy Bear" spot presents a set of concerned parents preparing for a tough task—talking to their child about drug use. The "Davey" spot is quite different. It shows a teenager confronting the pressure of peers who want him to use drugs. These spots do not present their main idea—that parents can help their children avoid drug use by discussing the problem with them—in a straight sell. Instead, miniature dramas are used to illustrate the idea. Obviously, these spots were prepared with a substantial budget. As a result, they exhibit the characteristics of a good television message: a strong balance between audio and video, an appropriate number of scenes, and a forceful sales message presented both aurally and visually.

Researching the Organization

When you write a public-service announcement, you need answers to the same questions the major charities ask. However, you won't have their budget. You'll have to do your own checking and planning to determine the objectives of the organization.

Your first goal is to determine what the organization hopes to accomplish in its messages. Does it want to inform the audience about an upcoming event or a new service? Does it want to recruit volunteers? Does it want donations? Does it want people to change their behavior? Like a commercial, a PSA should present only one main idea.

Once you determine the goals of the organization, you must consider the public's image of the charity. The image may not always be favorable. People have reasons for disliking charitable organizations, just as they dislike certain businesses. The distrust may be greater when people are being asked to give money or change their behavior out of altruism.

Negative images may stem from a number of factors. People may dislike an organization because its work runs counter to their own beliefs. For example, people are not likely to be favorable to a group that advocates birth control when they oppose it. People may also believe that the money given to a charity goes to administration rather than the work of the charity. And people may distrust a charity that they feel didn't deliver: "I've always given, but where were they after the flood?"

You probably can't change a strong negative image, but you must be aware of it. Your public-service announcements must present a positive approach and should counter negative images as much as possible.

DRUG ABUSE PREVENTION CAMPAIGN

Sponsor: National Institute of Drug Abuse, U.S. Department of Health and Human Services.

Please do not run after March 31, 1985

| "TEDDY BEAR" | (CNDA-3130) | 30 SECONDS | |

DAD: Look, you're 12 years old now -- Sooner or later, you're going to run into a situation --

MOM: Someone's going to offer you drugs.

DAD: Ask you to smoke a joint with them.

MOM: So, we just want to say that -- we care about you and your health.

DAD: We love ya. What-a-ya think?

MOM: Pretty good. We'll try it for real with Kevin tomorrow.

ANNCR. (VO): Talking to your kids about drugs isn't easy. You might even want to try it first with a friend. But you can do it.

Get involved with drugs before your children do. For free information write: Get involved, P.O. Box 1706, Rockville, MD. 20850

Get involved with drugs before your children do.

| "DAVEY" | (CNDA-3330) | 30 SECONDS | |

BOY 1: Hey, Davey, get lost, will ya?

BOY 2: Hey, hey, let the kid in. (I know.) Hey, Davey, want to try something?

BOY 3: Come on, man, let him alone.

BOY 2: Come on. Try it, Davey. (I don't like this guy.) Come on, take it.

DAVEY: No thanks.

BOY 3: Kid's gonna be all right.

ANNCR. (VO): If someone offers you drugs --
BOY 2: What is it with you guys?

Just say no. For free information write: Say no to drugs, P.O. Box 1635, Rockville, MD. 20850

ANNCR. (VO): just say no.

Volunteer Coordinator: Nathan Kelne, Vice President-Public Relations, New York Life Insurance Company.
Volunteer Advertising Agency: Needham, Harper & Steers, Inc.

A Public Service of
This Station &
The Advertising Council

FIGURE 11-7   Two public-service announcements. *(Courtesy The Advertising Council)*

Audience Sensitivities

Some public-service announcements will touch the fears and dislikes of the audience. If those feelings are touched too deeply, people may be turned off by the message. For example, some charities ask for money to fight diseases that can leave people crippled or dead. Most of us don't like to think about death, and we don't like to think of the possibility of being crippled. To talk vividly of death or show crippled people may make a point that many don't want to see. The same problem may occur when a spot shows people getting shots or giving blood. The cause may be worthy, but many people are afraid of needles.

A PSA designed to draw attention to animal cruelty used a startling message. The message focused on the hazards of leaving pets in closed autos during summer days. The car's surface, according to the PSA, becomes hot enough to fry an egg. The heat inside the car could quickly "fry the brains" of a dog. The spot got attention.

You must understand the fears and discomforts of your audience. Don't play on their fears or leave them with a feeling of despair. Impart a feeling of hope no matter how unpleasant the topic maybe. But themes that gain attention by startling or disturbing viewers can work—if they're prepared with care. Careful writing and selection of visual material for TV is important if you are to get your message across without frightening your audience away. The problem-solution approach to spot development discussed in Chapter 10 is appropriate for such a PSA. Notice how the spot in Figure 11.8 introduces a problem and provides a solution.

Appeals

A public-service announcement, like a commercial, must appeal to a human need. In fact, the appeal may have to be stronger in a PSA because you'll often be asking people to give for the good of others, not to buy something for themselves.

The human need to which you appeal will relate to the goal of the organization—raising money, recruiting volunteers, disseminating information, and so forth. Supplying information to the public will be the easiest task. Asking people to give time or money will be harder. Asking people to change their behavior—for example, to actually use their automobile seat belts—will be difficult, if not impossible.

The human needs you appeal to will be the same ones discussed in Chapter 5. Some human needs to which you might appeal include needs to give and receive love and to feel self-esteem.

Love and family appeals touch emotions to which we all respond. PSAs have focused on the need to protect infants riding in a car by using a safety seat. Parental love for a child is a strong appeal. Other campaigns urge individuals to use a sensible diet to avoid high blood pressure or to be aware of the early signs of cancer. These campaigns appeal not only to our instinct for self-preservation but also to the love of family members for one another.

PSAs often appeal to our sense of self-esteem, since people like to feel they're willing to give to others. You can do this by reminding people that supporting a worthy cause increases their value in the eyes of others. You can provide such recognition by using the announcement to publicize badges, ribbons, or other symbols that people can wear to show they support a given cause.

A message can also challenge viewers' self-esteem. The Red Cross did this with the slogan "We'll help! Will you?" Examine this spot in Figure 11.9.

Finally, a PSA can appeal to self-preservation. The slogan "The life you save may be your own" does that. So does the PSA for the Drunk Driving Campaign illustrated in Figure 11.10.

A PUBLIC SERVICE MESSAGE — THE EPISCOPAL CHURCH

<u>For Information:</u> Armstrong Information Services, Inc., 141 East 44th St., New York, N.Y. 10017 (212) 986-0910

<u>SILENT NIGHT</u> -- :30 PSA -- #84-152

(SFX) VOICE OVER: Silence...
doesn't stop teenage suicide.

Families that <u>deal</u> with the
problem succeed in reducing
the incidence of suicide.

So, look for the warning
signs. Ask the probing questions.

Don't be afraid. You can't
give them ideas they haven't
already thought of.

You can give them the
attention and help

that might save their life.

FIGURE 11·8   Problem-solution PSA. *(Courtesy Armstrong Information*
Services, Inc.)

American Red Cross

Public Service Announcements
Available in :60, :30, :10 Versions
60 SECONDS

"HEALTH UMBRELLA"

Please discontinue use: JULY 27, 1984

SINGER: (VO) WHEN
YOU'RE WEARY,

FEELING SMALL --

WHEN TEARS ARE IN
YOUR EYES,

I WILL DRY THEM ALL:

I'M ON YOUR SIDE.

WHEN TIMES GET
ROUGH --

ANNCR: (VO) When you
need a helping hand,
Red Cross is there.

If you're old, we'll show
you how to feel young
again.

If you're young, we'll
teach you how to stay
that way.

And if you're working
hard, Red Cross can
keep the job from getting
the best of you.

We'll help you make it
on your own.

SINGER: (VO) LIKE A
BRIDGE OVER
TROUBLED WATER,

I WILL EASE YOUR
MIND.

LIKE A BRIDGE

OVER TROUBLED
WATER,

I WILL EASE YOUR
MIND.

Conducted by THE ADVERTISING COUNCIL
for the American Red Cross

FIGURE 11·9   PSA based on an appeal to self-esteem. *(Courtesy The Advertising Council)*

DRUNK DRIVING CAMPAIGN

Public Service Announcements
Available in :30 & :10 Versions

for National Highway Traffic Safety Administration

"Skeleton"   Use expires Dec. 12, 1985.

30 SECONDS

SONG: "Beat It."
FRONT SEAT GIRL:
C'mon John!

BACK SEAT GUY: Just get
in...we'll talk about it.
BACK SEAT GIRL: I've got
to go home.

FRONT SEAT GIRL: Oh,
c'mon Carey, we're goin'
to a new place.

DRIVER: I bet she wants
to go home, right?
BACK SEAT GUY: Shh...
let's go.

DRIVER: Here, hold this.

BACK SEAT GUY: Hey,
you okay to drive?
DRIVER: I'm fine.
BACK SEAT GUY: Are
you sure?

DRIVER: What's a few
beers?

ANNCR: (VO) If you
don't stop your friend from
drinking and driving,
(key turns)

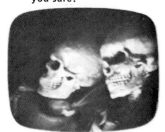

you're as good

as dead.

Drinking and driving

can kill a friendship.

A Public Service Campaign of the Advertising Council

VOLUNTEER ADVERTISING AGENCY:
Leber Katz Partners

VOLUNTEER COORDINATOR:
Michael Fink, Block Drug, Inc.

FIGURE 11·10   PSA based on an appeal to self-preservation. *(Courtesy The
Advertising Council)*

Remember also that the station is *giving* time for public-service announcements. As a result, the station can't be expected to supply much money for writing and production. The local charity organization will probably have a limited budget as well. Keep PSA scripts simple and easy to produce. Do, of course, make them interesting. They must gain viewer attention as much as any commercial spot. Don't let a limited budget be an excuse for an uninteresting production.

Radio PSAs

Since radio stations seek specialized audiences, not every station will be appropriate for every cause. Radio stations usually analyze the PSAs they receive and air only those they feel are appropriate for their listeners. For example, a station with adult listeners may not be eager to promote a program to teach toddlers to swim if most of its listeners no longer have children at home. If you're writing PSAs it's best to send stations topics and versions that they're most likely to run. Otherwise you may waste a good deal of time. If you work for a radio station, be aware of its target audience. If you're asked to analyze the PSAs sent to your station, choose those most suited to the station's listeners.

But don't discard certain types of radio formats completely. You can custom-design your message to almost any format if you have the time. Several versions—for example, one for teenagers, one for young adults, and another for older adults—can help you target most radio formats. For instance, a Top 40 station with teenage listeners might not use a generic PSA that talks about the problems of adult heart disease. But a PSA targeted to teenagers could be very appropriate. Such an announcement might seek to make teenagers aware of possible future health problems and encourage preventive practices such as a proper diet and adequate exercise. Another approach would be a message to alert teenagers to the dangers of heart disease in their parents or older relatives. Family appeals would be very appropriate.

Radio PSA Formats

Scripts for radio PSAs are usually in single-voice format only. They can be read by the staff announcers and require no production expense. You can use music, sound effects, and multiple voices, but do so only if you know you can get the spot produced. Because stations prefer PSAs that are easy to use, a single-voice script is the best bet.

Radio stations also prefer to use a standard length. Many use only ten-second PSAs, while others use twenty-second, thirty-second, and occasionally, sixty-second announcements.

Brevity is especially important in publicizing events of limited appeal that don't have to be sold to the public. Announcements of class reunions, bake sales, and health-care classes are examples. Because radio stations target their audience or community, they like to broadcast announcements of local interest. However, brevity is important because such announcements are often broadcast in bulletin boards—a series of brief announcements broadcast over a musical background or in simplified PSAs that a disc jockey reads, asking listeners to call the station for complete information.

The five *W*'s (who, what, when, where, and why) should be clear in a standard informational PSA. That basic information alone will suffice for a ten- to thirty-second announcement. The following script illustrates how easily a ten-second PSA can be written by using the five *W*'s as a guide.

Who: Ourtown Little League

What: is sponsoring a car wash

When: this Saturday from 10 to 3

Where: at the Burger Boy on Main Street.

Why: Proceeds will be used to buy new uniforms.

The addition of a few words, probably in the "why" section, will provide enough length for a twenty- or thirty-second message.

A wise practice is to prepare three versions of a public-service announcement, as illustrated in Figure 11.11. Stations can then choose the length that best fits their time requirements. When preparing a PSA with multiple lengths, start with the shortest length. That version must contain the most important information you wish to convey to your audience. Add additional, but less crucial details, to the longer versions.

Television PSAs

Since television stations appeal to a broader audience than radio stations and are fewer in number, they tend to receive many requests from nonprofit groups for public-service announcements. Further, the majority of commercial TV stations successfully sell advertising and have only limited availabilities for PSAs—and very few in prime time. Add to this the fact that a TV PSA is more costly to produce than a radio PSA, and the result is that television stations are highly selective in accepting requests for PSAs. They are more likely to give time to those causes they judge to have the greatest worth to their viewers.

While the production budget for most PSAs is low, TV stations are concerned about the visual appearance of the message. They don't want to send the audience to the kitchen while an announcer or spokesperson (known in television as a talking head) delivers the message. That's dull TV, whether the spot is a PSA or a commercial. Your greatest challenge may be in writing a television PSA, since your goal is to produce an announcement that is of professional quality, interesting to watch, and low in cost.

The script that follows illustrates the emotional appeal a television writer was able to capture in a PSA for rape prevention. With no budget, the writer was able to use a volunteer for talent. As is common in local television production, the director had considerable flexibility to turn a brief description of the visual concept into a finished product.

VIDEO	AUDIO
USING DRAMATIC BACK LIGHTING FOR CONTRAST, A WOMAN IN BLACK IS SITTING WITH A WHITE BLINDFOLD. THE FIGURE TURNS TO THE CAMERA AS THE COPY READS ". . . RAPE IS A CRIME OF VIOLENCE, NOT SEX," AND BEGINS TO LOOSEN THE BLINDFOLD AS PREVENTION TIPS ARE HEARD. THEN JUST BEFORE THE BLINDFOLD IS DROPPED, THE PICTURE IS FREEZE-FRAMED WITH THE FOLLOWING SUPER: GREATER ORLANDO CRIME PREVENTION ASSOCIATION (305) 422-8718	ANNOUNCER: (SFX HEARTBEAT) It's easy to blind yourself to the facts of rape if it doesn't happen to you. But the fact is rape is a crime of violence (not sex), and it could happen to you or any man, woman, or child. Help protect yourself from rape . . . be aware and avoid dangerous situations . . . use the buddy system, learn how to survive the rape, and report it. Call the Greater Orlando Crime Prevention Association for important information on rape prevention. Don't blind yourself to the facts.

Courtesy WOFL-TV, Orlando, Florida.

THE D÷V÷DENDS
SEMINOLE COUNTY SCHOOL VOLUNTEER PROGRAM

P.O. Box 703 ● Altamonte Springs, Florida 32715-0703

Phone
834-8211

10 SECOND OR 30 WORD PSA

Our Seminole County Public Schools need you! Call the D÷v÷dends School Volunteer Program - 834-8211 and learn how you can help a child.

20 SECOND

The Seminole County D÷v÷dends School Volunteer Program needs you! If you have
a few hours a week and an interest in children, the Seminole County schools could
use your help working with individual children in reading, math, science, art, music-
any area of education. We also need bi-lingual volunteers. Call the Seminole
County D÷v÷dends School Volunteer Program and help a child find success in school.
D÷v÷dends - 834-8211.

30 SECOND

The Seminole County D÷v÷dends School Volunteer Program needs you! If you have
as little as two hours a week and interest in children -- we want you.

The Seminole County schools are in need of volunteers to help individual children in all areas of education, including reading, math, science, art or music.
Your volunteer work can be as simple as listening to a child read aloud or using
flash cards to go over simple math facts. We also need bi-lingual volunteers.
Call the Seminole County D÷v÷dends School Volunteer Program - 834-8211. You <u>can</u>
make a difference.

GAIN ASSETS - BE A D÷V÷DENd

FIGURE 11·11   PSAs of differing lengths. *(Courtesy Dividends School
Volunteer Program)*

The voice-over technique is one of the most common types of production used for local
PSAs. A staff announcer or a spokesperson for the charity may read the script. Slides, video-
tape, graphic work, or production effects can be used to provide the visual portion of the
PSA. The script that follows is a typical example of a PSA using these techniques.

VIDEO	AUDIO
SLIDE 1, PIC OF SCIENCE CENTER	Beginning in April, the Orlando Science Center presents Celebration '84.
SLIDE 2, PIC OF MR. WIZARD. SUPER APRIL 14, 15 LOWER 1/3 OF SCREEN SLIDE 3, PIC OF MR. WIZARD SLIDE 4, PIC OF NODDY.	Headlining the series on April 14 and 15 is television's Mr. Wizard, Don Herbert.
SUPER MAY 5, 6, LOWER 1/3 OF SCREEN SLIDE 5, PIC OF NODDY SLIDE 1, PIC OF SCIENCE CENTER. SUPER PHONE NUMBER	Then on May 5 and 6, Tom Noddy will appear with his fascinating bubble magic. Call the Orlando Science Center at 896-7151 to make your reservations.

Courtesy SFN Communications of Florida, Inc.

Stations will sometimes send a photographer or a production crew to produce a local PSA. The decision will depend on the availability of station personnel and the value of the cause.

Television stations keep their public-service announcements brief in order to accommodate more organizations. Thirty seconds, twenty seconds, and ten seconds are the most common lengths. Some sixty-second announcements are used, mainly late at night or on weekends. Some stations use 3–4-second station ID PSAs.

Like radio stations, television stations use bulletin boards to present informational items that don't require selling the ideas. These items are brief, limited to who, what, when, and where. They are usually presented as a roundup and often appear on TV as words superimposed over a background tape accompanied by music. Information that requires advocacy is usually presented in longer public-service announcements.

Television stations won't often write more than one variation of a PSA, but a writer for a nonprofit organization might. The reason is to use the announcement flexibly. Some scripts are produced so the complete PSA can be shown on TV and the audio track alone can be used as a radio PSA. Varying lengths may also be written to meet the requirements of each station that uses prepared scripts. The scripts that follow are television PSAs of differing lengths for a single organization.

Client: Council for Florida Libraries
Project: 1984 Library Public Awareness Campaign
Title: "Phone"
Cut 1: 10 Seconds

VIDEO	AUDIO
SLOW ZOOM FROM MEDIUM SHOT OF PHONE TO CLOSE UP.	Narrator: Who gets 15,000 business calls a day and answers every one?
CLOSE UP ON PHONE AS HAND REACHES INTO FRAME AND PICKS UP RECEIVER.	SFX: Ringing phone
	V.O.: Public library
FREEZE FRAME. SPECIAL EFFECT OF PAGE TURNING TO ART CARD OF LOGO "WE	Narrator: We do more than keep the books . . . at your library.

DO MORE THAN KEEP THE BOOKS—AT
YOUR LIBRARY."

Courtesy Barratt Wilkins, Florida State Librarian.

Client: Council for Florida Libraries

Project: 1984 Library Public Awareness Campaign

Cut 3: 30 Seconds

VIDEO	AUDIO
CLOSE UP OF A BUSINESSMAN SITTING BEHIND DESK.	Businessman: (TONE OF INCREDULITY) Now, let me get this straight.
SLOW ZOOM OUT THROUGHOUT SPEECH	You have 330 service centers around Florida. You get 15,000 business calls a day and you answer every one. And you have over eleven million resources available to my staff. And most of your services are free. Just who are you, anyway?
EXHIBITS SURPRISE	V.O.: (BOOMING VOICE) We're your public library. We offer all this and more.
SPECIAL EFFECT OF PAGE TURNING TO ART CARD OF LOGO: "WE DO MORE THAN KEEP THE BOOKS AT YOUR LIBRARY"	Narrator: We do more than keep the books at your library.

Courtesy Barratt Wilkins, Florida State Librarian.

Opportunities Writing PSAs

Local organizations often can't afford to hire a writer or an advertising agency. As a result, many requests from local groups consist of a press release or a letter written by someone from the organization. The organizations hope that the stations will write the PSA for them. Because stations are deluged with PSAs, they are not able to honor all of these requests.

This situation has some important implications for the beginning copywriter. Local non-profit organizations are often looking for someone to write public-service announcements for them. It's a good opportunity to break into writing for radio and TV. Here are some specific pointers for the volunteer PSA writer.

1. If you're writing radio PSAs for a nonprofit organization, analyze the stations in your area. Determine what audience each station is trying to reach and send your PSAs to the stations most likely to broadcast them.

2. The PSA script you write should include certain noncopy data in the same manner as a commercial. What is the name of the organization? What is its address and telephone number? Who is the contact person? What is the length of the message(s)? If your organization frequently sends out PSAs, they'll likely have prepared copy paper that will include much of the foregoing information in the letterhead. If prepared copy paper isn't available,

follow the rules in Chapter 3. Specifically, type the copy double-spaced on standard 8½-×-11-inch paper that won't rattle on the air. Put the noncopy data on the top one-third of the page as follows:

YOURTOWN HUMANE SOCIETY

123 East Park Street, Yourtown, Neb. 60000

PUBLIC-SERVICE ANNOUNCEMENT

CONTACT: A. Writer   START: July 1, 1986

PHONE: 123-4567   STOP: September 1, 1986

SUBJECT: "Traveling with Pets" (a pamphlet)

---

10 seconds   The Humane Society of Yourtown has a free pamphlet
                                  describing tips on traveling with pets . . .

Note that the preceding illustration includes the dates to start and stop airing the PSA. That's crucial information for the station no matter what the length of the activity. Since broadcasters will air those PSAs they can handle easily, they look for the information that's important to them. Unlike commercials, PSAs don't come with a traffic order. Instead, the data are often a part of the script.

While knowing when to begin broadcasting a PSA is important, knowing when to stop broadcasting it is even more important. The PSA script may be put in a copy book as received, or the copy may be retyped on 3-×-5-inch cards with only minimal identification data. Radio PSAs often aren't scheduled on the program log. Instead, they're often rotated in order.

The date the PSA should stop running is crucial, especially for events that end on a specific date. That's one item that will be retyped on cards or circled on the script. DJs often read scripts cold, so it's important that they be able to see the end date easily. It's embarrassing to the DJ and your organization if the announcer gets halfway through a PSA and then says, "Oops, that was yesterday." If the subject of the PSA is less topical, it's permissible to indicate that the copy can begin "immediately" and run "year round."

3. Acquaint yourself with the policies of the TV stations in your area. Most won't want a completed script. They'll prefer a press release and professional-quality visual material that station writers can use to adapt to the station's specifications. If you're working for the local chapter of a national charity, you may receive videotapes of completed spots. These can be supplied to stations along with sufficient data for a local tag.

4. TV stations will accept slides from local organizations, but they expect them to be 35-mm color slides of professional quality. In addition, pictures in slides must be horizontal images.

5. Photographs can be used on TV if they're 8-×-10-inch matte (dull) finish in horizontal images. If your organization is prominent enough to get on TV regularly, supply each station with a photo or artwork of your logo so that the station has it available.

POINTS TO REMEMBER

- Promotion tells a broadcast audience about upcoming programs and keeps them interested in regularly scheduled programs.

- Cable promotion is designed to attract new subscribers and keep current subscribers.

- Promos are used to reach a station's established audience, the people most interested in the message.

- Specific promos ask viewers or listeners to make up their minds, and then to do something.

- Generic promos are used to promote the image of the station, its programs, or its personalities.

- A teaser announcement is designed to stimulate interest in an upcoming program.

- A logo is often used to position a station's sound or appearance.

- Public-service announcements are messages broadcast (or cablecast) free of charge for nonprofit organizations.

- If a PSA deals with the fears of the audience, it should impart a feeling of hope.

- PSAs written for radio stations should consider the station's target audience.

- A television PSA should have a strong visual quality even if its production budget is low.

EXERCISE 1

Prepare a thirty-second public-service announcement in which you urge teenagers not to drink while driving. Appeal to the teenagers' need for self-preservation. Emphasize that while drinking may seem like a grown-up thing to do, drinking and driving can lead to crippling injuries or death.

Don't use any slogans from previous public-service announcements on this topic. Be as original as you can.

EXERCISE 2

This is an exercise in writing radio PSAs of differing lengths.

Visit a service office on your campus (campus police, legal assistance office, placement center, a religious organization, and so forth) or the offices of a club. Gather as much information as you can: brochures, handouts, pamphlets. If need be, interview the person in charge.

Prepare three informational PSAs for radio—ten-, twenty-, and thirty-second spots for the same service or organization. Make certain the PSAs are airworthy.

EXERCISE 3

You're employed to write commercial and promotional copy for W___ AM and FM, Yourtown. The stations have used these call letters for many years, and management doesn't want to change them. But station management does want the two stations to have a stronger identity, especially the FM station. The FM station programs hit country music and operates on 100.2 mhz. The AM station, an old, established station in Yourtown, programs a blend of country hits and oldies, plus news and sports. In the past, the FM station was simply identified as "FM-100, W___." Now station management wants to call it Hit Country 100. Your job is to write two promos for Hit Country 100.

1. Write a thirty-second generic promo that establishes an image for Hit Country 100.
2. Write a thirty-second specific promo that calls attention to the change in logos and asks people to listen to Hit Country 100.

You've been hired to write promotional and commercial copy for a new television station in Yourtown, K _____-TV, Channel 38. This new station is an independent not affiliated with a network. It programs movies, sports, and syndicated reruns. The station wants to serve the needs of its community by presenting live local news. The station is broadcasting a half-hour local newscast at 10 P.M., and it has two minutes of local headlines each hour at 7 P.M., 8 P.M., and 9 P.M. The headlines and the newscast are anchored by Fred Cannon, a veteran newsman in Yourtown. Betty Brown does the weather on the 10 P.M. newscast and Steve Frasier the sports. Frasier formerly played for the Yourtown Jackrabbits. The logo for the news presentations is Channel 38 Newsline.

Write two thirty-second on-air promos for the station's news programming (both the newscasts and headlines).

1. Write a thirty-second specific promo urging viewers to watch the news on Channel 38.

2. Write a thirty-second generic promo that establishes an image for Channel 38's news services.

Write two thirty-second PSAs for Yourtown's Summer Youth Employment Program. Emphasize that Yourtown will be hiring high-school age youth to work on city projects—landscaping parks, cleaning roadways, doing maintenance, and so on. The jobs will pay the minimum wage. Also, Yourtown is sponsoring a job placement service with local employers. Its goal is to bring employers and teenagers together to aid in filling summer jobs.

1. Your first PSA should target an adult-oriented radio station. Write an announcement that informs adults about the program so that they can tell their children.

2. Your second PSA should be written for a Top-40 station. Aim this PSA at the teenagers in the program's target age group.

Student Name _____   Advertiser _____

Date Submitted _____   Commercial Length _____

Student Name _____   Advertiser _____

Date Submitted _____   Commercial Length _____

Student Name _____   Advertiser _____

Date Submitted _____   Commercial Length _____

Student Name _____   Advertiser _____

Date Submitted _____   Commercial Length _____

Student Name _____   Advertiser _____

Date Submitted _____   Commercial Length _____

VIDEO   **AUDIO**

Student Name _____   Advertiser _____

Date Submitted _____   Commercial Length _____

VIDEO   **AUDIO**

Student Name _____   Advertiser _____

Date Submitted _____   Commercial Length _____

Student Name _____   Advertiser _____

Date Submitted _____   Commercial Length _____

12 The Legal Implications of Writing Copy

Federal Regulation

The Federal Communications Commission

Sponsorship Identification

Payola and Plugola

Lotteries

Station-Conducted Contests

Political Advertisements

Political Sponsorship Identification

Federal Trade Commission

Rigged Demonstrations

Testimonials and Endorsements

Comparative Advertising

Research Data

State Regulation

Self-Regulation

Points to Remember

Exercises

A ll of the commercial, public-service, and promotional copy that you write must comply with the laws and regulations that govern it. Both federal and state laws apply to broadcast copy, and stations must also be concerned with copy that, while not illegal, raises questions of taste. However, few legal restrictions apply to copy for cablecasting.

When copy might violate state or federal laws, your foremost concern should be the impact of possible violations on the station's license. Your copy can actually jeopardize the station's license to broadcast, so you must be aware of the laws and regulations that apply and be cautious about copy that might violate them. This chapter examines the various types of government regulation of advertising and their implications for commercial, promotional, and public-service copy.

Federal Regulation

At the federal level, broadcast advertising comes under two jurisdictions. The Federal Communications Commission regulates radio and television broadcasting, and the Federal Trade Commission regulates the content of advertising.

The Federal Communications Commission

The Federal Communications Commission is the principal government agency with which broadcasters must be concerned. The FCC was established by the Communications Act of 1934. It is directly responsible to Congress for regulating interstate and foreign communication by radio, television, cable, and wire.

Radio and television stations are licensed to private investors and nonprofit groups, but they are regulated by the FCC since they use public airwaves. While the Communications Act prohibits direct FCC involvement in programming matters, the act does require the commission to regulate radio and television stations in "the public interest." As a result, the FCC must evaluate the commercial broadcaster's service to the public, including its programming and advertising, at license renewal time. This process enables the FCC to examine such practices as unfair political broadcasting and fraudulent billing. The FCC also enforces stipulations in the Communications Act that have a direct bearing on the commercial, promotional, and public-service copy aired by a broadcast station. The following section covers the provisions of most importance to the broadcast copywriter.

Sponsorship Identification
The first FCC requirement we'll cover is one that may seem obvious. It's a provision of the Communications Act that requires stations to make a sponsorship identification announcement during commercial announcements or sponsored broadcasts. In the majority of cases this requirement does not pose a problem since advertisers want their name or product name mentioned frequently.

Nevertheless, stations might not want to identify a sponsor in some situations. For example, teasers designed to attract the audience's attention are sometimes run without revealing the sponsor's identity until later in the advertising schedule. Here's an example of an illegal teaser that might start such a campaign:

ANNCR 1	Save money on food for your family.
ANNCR 2	Where at?
ANNCR 1	Can't tell you till Friday.
ANNCR 2	Why not?
ANNCR 1	'Cause it's a surprise. One you'll like!
ANNCR 2	But I have to wait till Friday?
ANNCR 1	Yes, but the wait will be worth it. Listen Friday for details about the greatest food-buying plan ever to come to Yourtown.

This announcement looks and sounds like any other commercial, but it's strictly a teaser. No sponsor is mentioned, and the FCC considers that to be a serious offense. A station and its advertisers can attract attention and build interest, but they must mention the advertiser's name at least once in each announcement.

Payola and Plugola   Another identification problem that violates the Communications Act is a failure to disclose payments that involve programming. This may occur in *payola,* an illegal payment for promoting a record or other product on the air. A record promoter, for instance, might make under-the-table payments to a disc jockey to play a record. Since the payment is not disclosed, payola violates the Communications Act and carries a penalty of a $10,000 fine and a year in jail.

Plugola is a variation of payola in which a commercial product is gratuitously mentioned during an entertainment program. For example, a disc jockey might urge listeners to go to a rock concert that the station is not advertising without mentioning that he has been given free tickets to the event.

Items promoted through payola or plugola can generally be advertised legally if the promoter is willing to buy advertising on the station and the station identifies the payment on the air. Events such as concert promotions, which are often joint promotions between stations and advertisers, can lead to identification difficulties. A station violates FCC rules if it coproduces a local concert and promotes it on the air without identifying the station as a cosponsor. In the same manner, a station can accept free concert tickets in return for promoting a local concert, but it must identify the arrangement in its on-air promotional announcements. As a rule, this requirement poses no problem, and many stations have joint campaigns with advertisers to give away concert tickets, tour jackets, record albums, T-shirts, and other souvenirs. In fact, cooperative promotions are generally advantageous to stations because the advertiser usually provides the giveaway items and pays additional costs such as direct mail and newspaper advertising.

Lotteries   Federal law prohibits the broadcasting of lottery promotions or advertisements as well as information pertaining to a lottery. This rule places a heavy burden on the station, especially on the copywriter, who must determine if promotional data constitute a lottery. Failure to observe federal lottery laws can result in penalties against the station ranging from fines to loss of license.

Lotteries cannot be part of giveaway promotions by the station or the advertiser, nor can bingo games be publicized in public-service announcements. Only state-operated lotteries are exempt from the laws prohibiting broadcast promotion of lotteries. Promotions for a state-run lottery can be broadcast if the station is located in the state conducting the lottery, or if the station is located in a city adjacent to the state that conducts the lottery.

According to FCC rules, a promotion legally constitutes a lottery if three elements are present. Note that the contest or promotion is *not* a lottery if only two of the elements are present. These elements are:

1. *Prize.* Is a prize, which can be anything of value, offered to participants?

2. *Chance.* Is the winner selected by chance, rather than by a test of the participant's skill or other factors within his or her control? Is the amount of the prize determined by chance?

3. *Consideration.* Must the contestant spend money or substantial time or effort to qualify for the contest?

Suppose that an advertiser wanted you to include the following material in a commercial. A local sporting goods store wants to promote the start of Little League baseball season. With each purchase, contestants can try to guess the correct number of baseballs in a large container. The winner, who will receive a new baseball glove, will be drawn from the entrants guessing the correct number. Could you safely include the material in a commercial?

The answer is no; this contest would legally be a lottery. A prize, the baseball glove, will be awarded. Consideration is present, since participants must make a purchase to enter. An element of chance exists, since participants must guess at the correct number, with the winner being drawn at random from the correct entrants. All three elements exist, making the contest a lottery. Since FCC licensees bear the ultimate responsibility to see that contests are not operated as lotteries, the contest could not be broadcast as structured.

The promotion could easily be made legal by removing the consideration—the requirement that only those making purchases can enter. If anyone going to the store could fill out an entry blank without a purchase, only two elements would exist and the contest would not be a lottery.

Remember also that a lottery can exist in a public-service announcement as easily as in a commercial. Suppose a local church group wants to promote its weekly bingo night in a public-service announcement. There is a $2 admission fee and all proceeds go to a nonprofit, aid-to-the-elderly fund. Would this PSA violate the law?

Yes, bingo and similar games are considered lotteries if participants are required to pay in order to participate. It does not matter that the proceeds go to charity. Information about this game of bingo cannot legally be broadcast. The promotion would be legal if participants were not required to pay an admission fee. Many cable television systems also program games of bingo, but they are not considered to be lotteries since there is no consideration—that is, viewers are not required to pay to play the game.

Lotteries can be complex, and it is is often difficult to determine whether a promotion is legal or not. The most you can do is to be alert to suspect material and seek clarification from the station manager or program director when difficult questions arise. If the promotion is especially complex, it may be necessary for station management to seek the advice of an attorney.

Station-Conducted Contests Contests conducted by stations have become a successful promotional device for many broadcasters, especially in highly competitive markets. Both radio and television stations conduct contests to increase commercial sponsorship and audiences. Contests such as "The Lucky Bumper Sticker" and "Dialing for Dollars" have become familiar in many cities. To protect the public from deceptive contests, the FCC has instituted guidelines that stations are expected to follow. Depending on the size of the station, the promotional copy for such contests may be written by the copywriter or the station's promotion director. In either case, it is important that the writer be familiar with the FCC's rules.

The FCC defines a contest as a plan in which a prize is offered or awarded to the public based upon chance, diligence, knowledge, or skill. While a lottery must consist of three elements—prize, chance, and consideration—a contest may contain only one or two of these elements. A contest promotion may be broadcast as long as it is not deceptive.

The FCC stipulates that a station must disclose the material terms of the contest. Although subject to some variation, the material terms of a contest generally refer to how to enter or participate: eligibility restrictions; entry deadline dates; whether prizes can be won and when they can be won; the nature, extent, and value of prizes; the basis for evaluating entries; time and means of selecting winners; and the method of breaking ties. The station is obligated to disclose the terms of the contest when the audience is first told how to enter, as well as periodically during the contest.

It is not likely that you will be designing contests. Station management will probably do that. But you may be asked to write promotional announcements for contests. Promotional copy for station-conducted contests may be recorded for broadcast, or it may be delivered live by station personalities. Television stations, for example, may have the host of a movie presentation ad-lib the copy for a contest promotion during the movie. Additional announcements for the contest may be recorded by the host for use at other points during the broadcast schedule. Radio stations may use live announcements, especially if they want their announcers to ad-lib the copy to add a personal touch. Recorded announcements may be used at some points in the contest, or all of them may be recorded if the radio station wants precise control over the wording of the contest announcements.

The following is a sample of the live copy used by radio station WBJW, "BJ 105," in a "Song of the Day" contest conducted by the station. You'll note that the copy was designed to give the DJs flexibility in ad-libbing the announcements on the air. Announcements for the contest began on a Friday and were delivered at least once an hour throughout the weekend by the DJs. The announcements said:

> BJ 105 . . . with a very special announcement, Monday morning at 7:15. Be here!!

Beginning the following Monday morning at 7:15, and throughout the contest, DJs were asked to ad-lib these facts:

> The biggest daily cash giveaway in the history of Orlando Radio. Listen each weekday morning at 7:15 for the song of the day. Later that day, sometime before 8 P.M., we'll play the song again. When you hear it the second time, simply be the tenth person to get through to BJ 105 at 424-4-105 . . . and you'll grab the thousand dollars!!
>
> Nothing to guess at or match up or keep track of . . . ya' just listen for song of the day and win a thousand bucks!!! A winner everyday!!!

The information for this contest was presented on an information sheet, rather than as a prepared announcement. DJs were encouraged to deliver the facts in their own personal style and to stress the ease of participating in the contest.

Once the contest began, DJs ad-libbed this and similar promos for the contest:

> BJ 105 . . . with well over (dollar amount) in daily winners! Our most recent thousand-dollar winner is:
> (Name of winner/city of winner)
>
> Add your name to the list of winners, and pick up an easy grand, simply by listening for the song of the day. We'll play it tomorrow (Monday) morning at 7:15, so you can hear what it sounds like. Then, when you hear it sometime

later that day (before 8:00 P.M.), simply be the tenth caller, when the song is over, at 424-4-105, and claim 'yer thousand bucks, from BJ 105.

Courtesy BJ105, Orlando, Florida.

As the contest proceeded, promos referred to the total dollar amount already given away. Some promos were recorded and included comments from previous winners.

Throughout the contest, the station informed its listeners of the material terms of the contest. Listeners could pick up a copy of the rules at the station, and the rules were broadcast over the air on a regular basis.

Promotional announcements are designed to stimulate interest in a contest and should be written with care. Several problems can arise.

One is misleading information. In one case, the FCC admonished a station for failing to make clear that the prizes in its contest—trips to vacation cities—did not include transportation. The promotional announcements for the contest implied that the prize included transportation, since the prize was described as a vacation and the distance to the vacation cities was substantial. Perhaps the contest was misleading. If not, the promotional copy was.

Promotional announcements that adversely affect the audience are another problem. An example is the broadcast of scare announcements or headlines that are either untrue or are worded in a way that misleads or frightens the public. For example, a radio contest could be promoted as follows:

SFX: TELETYPE

ANNCR (TO BE READ
IN SOMBER TONES)   Attention W_____ listeners. The most frightening event of your
life has happened. It's the arrival of the "Bat-Mobile" at Your-
town Mall. It's out of this world, and it's filled with prizes . . .

This promo would probably not frighten many listeners, especially after they had heard it several times. But the FCC wants to prohibit contest announcements that might be harmful to listeners under any circumstances. This example, at first hearing, could sound too much like a news bulletin.

Political Advertisements   It's not hard to tell when an important election is near, because you'll see and hear a lot of political advertisements. Candidates for office have found that radio and television advertising is an efficient way to reach the public. As a result, candidates spend huge amounts of money on political commercials. Many political candidates employ an advertising agency to handle their advertising, but in smaller markets you'll be asked to write political spots as part of your copywriting duties.

Note at the outset that a paid political message is a commercial. But instead of selling a product, store, or service, you're selling the virtues of the person running for office. Naturally, you'll have to rely on what the candidate wants said. That's likely to mean painting a favorable picture of the candidate you're writing for, and possibly discrediting the opposing candidate.

Writing a political commercial presents several difficulties. One is comparing candidates. The incumbent will claim to have done a "good" job, one deserving reelection. Opponents will claim the incumbent has done a "bad" job, and point out the reasons why they will do better. *Good* and *bad* are difficult terms to quantify. They really have meaning only in the eyes of each listener. No one knows whether a particular candidate really can do a better job with the city's garbage removal problem than the incumbent did. And you can only cite what the candidate says he or she *will* do. As a result, it's difficult for the public to make political comparisons.

Another problem is judging what political announcements can actually accomplish. Research has shown that most campaigns don't change people's minds. Most people have already decided which candidate and which political party they'll vote for before they hear the political commercials.

If political ads don't change minds, they do serve to reinforce existing beliefs and voting patterns. Thus, the most realistic goal in many political commercials is to keep the faithful committed and to encourage them to actually vote for the party or person they believe in.

The following are some of the specific goals you might seek to accomplish in political commercials:

1. *Introduce a new candidate.* New candidates for office don't have a record to run on and can only introduce themselves to the voters and explain their qualifications. If the candidate has held positions that qualify him or her for the office, that should be pointed out. Significant endorsements should also be noted. Of course, you should also stress the party affiliation. Those who vote a straight ticket may well vote for the candidate who represents their political party. They're even more likely to do so if they know the candidate has some reasonable qualifications.

2. *Present the candidate's record.* If the candidate is an incumbent, or is running for a new political office, stress his or her accomplishments. Candidates like to stand on their records, and well they should. If they have a significant list of achievements, they can point to their accomplishments and promise the voters that they'll do more of the same. This may be one of the easiest political commercials to write, especially if the record is strong.

3. *Argue the issues.* It's not always easy to tell voters where a candidate stands on the issues, since the issues are often complex. Still, candidates may want to use political announcements to tell the public their position on issues. This may occur when candidates have quite different positions on the issues and may be done in the form of a comparison. As with any commercial, it's best to address a single issue in each spot. The candidate's stand on an issue must be presented clearly and simply. If this is accomplished, the spot can reinforce the idea that the candidate is thoughtful, and, in the right situation, show him or her to be in line with majority opinion on the issue.

4. *Build an image.* A frequent criticism of political commercials is that they sell image and not substance. That may well be true, since radio and television aren't as effective at explaining complex issues as they are at dramatizing images. Candidates sometimes try to capitalize on this fact, since it's often easier for them to promote an image. A little show biz can work wonders. The governor of a southern state periodically held "work days" in which he "worked" for a day as a teacher, a farmer, a factory worker, and so forth. The work days not only made the news but provided material for his campaign commercials to show him in touch with the people. In another instance, a Florida candidate for the U.S. Senate walked from one point to another, meeting voters as he went. He, too, made news and generated material for his commercials, which depicted him as the hardworking "walking" candidate.

5. *Make political comparisons.* As noted before, it's hard for the public to make political comparisons, since they must judge what a candidate says he *will* do. Still, candidates may wish to compare their records, their background qualifications, or their stand on the issues in the hope that they'll look stronger than their opponents.

6. *Build credibility.* A political commercial may be used to enhance the credibility of a candidate. In fact, credibility may be a key ingredient in a campaign if there are questions about a candidate's honesty, voting record, or ethics. More than one incumbent has faced legal charges but has managed to get reelected. This type of spot must show the voters all the good things the candidate has done for them and discredit the negative factors.

As noted previously, the candidate will tell you what to say, and his or her concerns may be varied. The candidate may only want to build name recognition or to compare voting records. The possibilities are endless, and they'll usually be tied to the candidate's budget. If that budget is very small, it may only allow messages that say something like, I'm Joe Jones, Democratic candidate for mayor. Vote for me on election day!

Political Sponsorship Identification   The Federal Communications Commission requires that the sponsor of a political broadcast be clearly identified. Its goal is to make certain that listeners know they're hearing a political message and understand who paid for the broadcast time. To avoid confusing the public, the FCC requires that political commercials give two items of information:

1. that the matter broadcast was sponsored

2. the identity of the person or entity sponsoring the announcement

To accomplish this identification, it is not necessary for a station to broadcast a disclaimer such as "the preceding was a paid political announcement." Instead the station must:

1. announce that the message was sponsored (by use of the phrase *sponsored by* or the phrase *paid for*)

2. identify the sponsor in such a way as to reveal to the public the true sponsor's identity

Thus, it is sufficient that each political announcement conclude with a statement such as "Paid for by the Committee to Reelect Joe Jones County Commissioner." Note that in political TV spots, the sponsorship identification announcement can appear visually and need not be read on the air.

If a political broadcast is longer than five minutes, an announcement must be made both at the beginning and end of the broadcast. If the broadcast is five minutes long or less, a single announcement at the beginning or end of the broadcast is sufficient.

The two scripts that follow are typical of those written for candidates in local political races. The radio script was written for presentation by the candidate. Note the identification announcement at the conclusion of the spot. The television script does not include a sponsorship identification announcement in the audio portion of the script because this information was presented visually over the final shot.

Job No. <u>Radio / 60: Cut 1</u>　　　Date: <u>10/20/83</u>

Client: <u>Dick Batchelor</u>

THIS IS DICK BATCHELOR. OVER THE PAST EIGHT YEARS, YOU HAVE ELECTED ME TO FOUR TERMS. AS YOUR SENIOR REPRESENTATIVE, I'VE RECEIVED THE SUPPORT OF REPUBLICANS, DEMOCRATS, AND INDEPENDENTS IN PAST ELECTIONS. I'VE NEVER NEEDED YOUR VOTE MORE THAN ON THIS NOVEMBER SECOND. THE FIFTH CONGRESSIONAL SEAT IN WASHINGTON IS NOT GOING TO BE WON BY SPECIAL-INTEREST GROUPS, EXCESSIVE CAMPAIGN SPENDING. EVEN WITH ALMOST HALF A MILLION DOLLARS, MY OPPONENT CANNOT BUY THE FIFTH CONGRESSIONAL DISTRICT. IT'S GOING TO BE WON WITH YOUR VOTE FOR HONESTY . . . EXPERIENCE . . . AND MY PROMISE TO CONTINUE MY FIGHT FOR YOU IN WASHINGTON. THE CHOICE IS CLEARLY YOURS. VOTE DICK BATCHELOR NOVEMBER SECOND. Paid political announcement, Campaign Committee to Elect Dick Batchelor Fifth Congressional District.

Courtesy Kerns & Associates, Inc.

Job No. <u>M-676 / 60: TV</u>　　　Date: <u>8-5-82</u>

Client: <u>Batchelor for Congress</u>

MX: background instrumental/dramatic up and under sustain.

SFX: use b/w photographs with camera lens and photo taking sound effect with tape

CAM CARD: A New Congressman for a New District

From video tape: interior of Batchelor in office at desk. He answers phone has discussion.	(up music/sustain) V.O. . . . FOR THE LAST EIGHT YEARS, DICK BATCHELOR HAS HELPED WRITE A BALANCED BUDGET FOR FLORIDA. HE CHAIRED THE JOINT LEGISLATIVE AUDITING COMMITTEE TO RID FLORIDA OF WASTE AND FRAUD IN MEDICADE, FOOD STAMP AND OTHER FUNDING PROGRAMS.
ECU: black/white photo of auto accident Wipe on, go to black	SFX: photo lens
From video tape: Batchelor on highway with patrol officer, FHP car, blue flashing light. Shake hands.	DRUNK DRIVERS ON FLORIDA'S HIGHWAYS. DICK BATCHELOR WAS A PRIME SPONSOR OF THE NEW, GET-TOUGH DRUNK DRIVER LAW.
ECU: black/white photo of lake with pollution	SFX: photo lens
From video tape: Batchelor on lakefront deck with retired man fishing	CONVERSATION . . . HE SUPPORTED THE STOPPING OF THE CROSS FLORIDA BARGE CANAL, WROTE TOUGH HAZARDOUS WASTE LAWS, AND STEERED THE PASSAGE OF THE LAW CONTROLLING LOW-LEVEL NUCLEAR RADIOACTIVE WASTE.

Squeeze Zoom Lens Effect

Head of Batchelor in center screen, green background with BATCHELOR . . . A NEW CONGRESSMAN cam cards pan left and right stopping at top and bottom.	AS AN EIGHT-YEAR VETERAN, FULL-TIME LEGISLATOR, THE CLOSER YOU LOOK . . . THE CLEARER THE CHOICE. (fade)

Courtesy Kerns & Associates, Inc.

It is important to note that Section 315 of the Communications Act prohibits a broadcaster from censoring the political advertising of a legally qualified candidate. Thus, even though a station may judge a candidate's message to be vulgar, obscene, or in poor taste, the station cannot censor the content.

The Federal Trade Commission

The Federal Trade Commission is charged with protecting the public from unfair and deceptive business practices, including false and misleading advertising. Congress established the FTC in 1914 with the goal of protecting business from unfair competition. It subsequently broadened this mandate, giving the FTC considerable antitrust authority as well as extensive consumer protection powers.

A major source of the commission's power to regulate advertising comes from the Wheeler-Lea Amendment, which prohibits the false advertising of food, drugs, cosmetics, and therapeutic devices. The amendment also gave the FTC power to obtain temporary restraining orders against advertisements it believes to be false. A restraining order can prevent an allegedly false ad from being run until a court hears the case.

The FTC generally brings suit against major advertisers, their practices, and/or claims. For example, the FCC brought suit against the Warner-Lambert Company, maker of Listerine. The FTC ruled that since 1921 the company had falsely claimed that Listerine could prevent or lessen the severity of a common cold. The commission ordered Warner-Lambert to spend more than $10 million in advertising to correct the false claims. The company appealed the ruling, but the U.S. Court of Appeals upheld the commission, and the U.S. Supreme Court refused to review the case.

Individual stations can also violate FTC rules by preparing advertising material that is not truthful or accurate. When this occurs, the FTC works closely with the FCC to resolve the problem. Thus, you should be familiar with several FTC rules when you write commercial copy. The following sections summarize some of the FTC policies most relevant for the commercial copywriter.

Rigged Demonstrations When a product is demonstrated on television, the advertiser wants it to look inviting. But because it may be difficult to keep the whipped cream from melting or to keep a good head on a glass of beer, producers may try visual deceptions to enhance the product's appearance. Shaving cream may be substituted for whipped cream. Viewers can't tell the difference on TV, and shaving cream won't melt under the hot lights. Fluffy soap suds make a great-looking head on a glass of beer, often looking better than the foam of the beer itself.

Is such doctoring of the product deceptive? The Federal Trade Commission believes it is, and expects advertisers, their agencies, and their television producers to show a product as it really is, not as it might appear under circumstances that are altered for effect.

Two cases illustrate the doctored presentations the FTC wishes to avoid. In the first case, the FTC in 1961 brought action against the Colgate-Palmolive Company for its Rapid Shave commercials. The commercials claimed that sandpaper could be shaved after being softened with Rapid Shave, and purported to show that happening. The actual production of the commercial, however, used plexiglas covered with sand rather than sandpaper. The FTC ordered Colgate-Palmolive to stop broadcasting the commercials. When the U.S. Supreme Court ruled on the case in 1965, it held that substitutions, mock-ups, and special props used in television commercial demonstrations must be acknowledged.

As a result, we're told, if briefly, when substitutions exist in television commercials. Commercials for television sets, for example, may include pictures on television screens with incredible colors and definitions. But we're usually told that the pictures are simulations.

In the second case, the Campbell Soup Company was cited by the FTC for putting clear glass marbles in the bottom of a bowl of vegetable soup used in a commercial. Campbell wanted the vegetables to be visible in the commercial, but they sank to the bottom. The marbles were placed in the bowl to make the vegetables, which were lighter in weight, rise to the top.

The FTC wants the public to see products in television commercials as they really are, not as doctoring will make them appear. Often, more time spent on arranging lighting and on staging the commercial will avoid the need for shortcuts.

Most television producers present legitimate demonstrations in TV commercials. But those who alter the product or setting, or who deliberately manipulate the visual presentation through deceptive tape or film editing, may feel the legal force of the FTC.

Testimonials and Endorsements   Testimonials can be a very effective form of advertising presentation, since they enable the audience to hear from someone who has actually used the product. A small amount of television viewing also tells us something else. Actors and celebrities endorse many products. We know they're paid for what they say, and we aren't certain that they have even used the product.

This factor might appear to diminish the effectiveness of the endorsement, but usually it doesn't. The public seems fascinated with celebrities, whether they are athletes, models, actors, or in some cases, well-known business executives. In fact, celebrities seem to provide something that ordinary consumers do not—credibility. Professional talent makes for a good presentation, something ordinary consumers sometimes aren't able to achieve. Because actors are trained to appear before the public, they convey warmth and sincerity. Ordinary people can tell you what an effective job the product did, but their comments may be flat and colorless.

As a result, advertisers generally choose professionals for endorsements. Actors and celebrities usually don't pretend to be experts; they simply lend their credibility to the presentation of the product. Usually this practice is harmless, but it certainly isn't when the spokesperson seems to have special expertise. Specialized knowledge in science, medicine, and engineering should be presented only by people who are actually qualified.

There is, of course, no way for the average listener or viewer to know whether a person delivering a testimonial actually uses the product. The person in the commercial may really be Mrs. Smith from Omaha who regularly uses Brand X to remove the stains from her laundry. But the person may also be an actress paid to tell you that Brand X will do the job. To ensure that testimonials and endorsements are reasonably genuine, the FTC has issued several sets of guidelines. They have been summarized below.

1. *General considerations.* Endorsements must reflect the honest views of the endorser. That person must be a bona fide user of the product at the time

the endorsement is given and must make only claims that can be supported if made by the advertiser rather than the endorser. The endorser may be paraphrased but not used out of context. The advertiser may use the endorsement only for as long as there is good reason to believe that the endorser, if a celebrity or expert (ordinary consumer endorsements are exempted), continues to subscribe to the presented opinion.

2. *Nonexpert consumer endorsements.* The advertiser must be able to prove that the average person can expect comparable performance. The ad must clearly and conspicuously disclose what performance can be expected or disclose that the endorsement has limited applicability. The endorsement of nonprescription drugs by consumers must be consistent with any determination about the product by the U.S. Food and Drug Administration.

3. *Expert endorsements.* Whenever an advertisement represents, directly or by implication, that the endorser is an expert with respect to the endorsement message, then the endorser's qualifications must in fact qualify him or her as a true expert. If the net impression in the advertisement is that the advertised product is superior to other products, then the expert must in fact have found such superiority.

4. *Endorsements by organizations.* Organizational endorsements, especially expert ones, are viewed as representing the judgment of a group whose collective experience exceeds that of any individual member, and whose judgments are generally free of the subjective opinions that vary among individuals. Therefore, the endorsement must be reached by a process sufficient to ensure that the statements fairly reflect the collective judgment of the organization. Such organizations might be comprised of engineers, scientists, or other specially trained experts.

5. *Disclosure of material connections.* When there is a connection between an advertiser and an endorser that might materially affect the weight or credibility of the endorsement, it must be fully disclosed. In the case of experts or celebrities, payment is not considered a material connection unless the advertising implies that the endorser is *not* being paid. Only compensation provided in exchange for endorsement need be disclosed. In addition, if an endorser owns stock or has some similar financial stake in the success of the advertiser, that connection must be disclosed.[1]

Comparative Advertising   Advertisers have always compared their products or services with those of their competitors. Often the comparison is implied rather than direct. An automobile dealer, for instance, who says, "We sell cars for less," implies that all other dealers charge more. An appliance dealer who advertises, "See us last," invites consumers to compare prices.

Comparative advertising is not always indirect. Advertisers today frequently identify their competitors by name and make a direct comparison in their commercials. Anacin claims more

---

1. Summary of FTC Guidelines, 1975, 1980, in Elizabeth J. Heighton and Don R. Cunningham, *Advertising in the Broadcast and Cable Media,* 2d ed. (Belmont, Calif.: Wadsworth, 1984), 108–9. Used with permission.

headache-killing power than other leading brands of pain relievers and names them. Sprite claims that it beats Seven-Up in a taste test.

Comparative advertising that directly names competitors is relatively new. Before 1970, some broadcast networks would not accept commercials involving a direct comparison, and many advertisers felt it was confusing to identify more than one brand in a commercial, even for comparison. The FTC urged broadcasters to accept comparative ads, arguing that they would better inform consumers about competing products.

Comparative advertising is now acceptable. But comparative ads can present problems if the claims are misleading or the comparisons rigged. Comparative ads can be effective if they are properly developed. Some suggestions will guide you in the preparation of a comparative advertisement. A comparative ad is most effective when one brand is clearly stronger than others, and its strong points can be demonstrated. Pepsi Cola used taste tests to show that many people preferred the taste of Pepsi to Coke. The taste tests were included in Pepsi commercials. However, comparative ads should not disparage or unfairly attack competitors. Consumers may react negatively to a comparison that belittles a competitor and decide not to use the product as a result.

Finally, consumers should be able to verify the claim made for the product. This might be difficult, since they may not make the same comparison made in the commercial. Still, if consumers use the product claiming to do the best job, they should see the results that are promised.

Research Data   Advertisers commonly run tests on their products to show the public that the product will produce better results than a competitor's. Since consumers like to feel they're spending money wisely, advertisers find research data to be effective in convincing people to buy a product. Advertisers have used research data to sell a variety of products. Household cleaning products, gasolines, tires, cars, and a variety of cold and headache remedies have been presented with the help of scientific information.

Tests conducted by a laboratory may involve complex methods that yield equally complicated results. As a copywriter for an advertising agency, you may be asked to translate these data into a message that is meaningful to the public. If you have difficulty understanding the research, it will probably be difficult to put the results into language that consumers can understand.

The FTC frequently asks advertisers to substantiate claims based on research studies. When this happens, the FTC also asks another group of scientists to review the data. If there is evidence that the claim isn't valid, the FTC may ask the advertiser to stop using it.

Claims based on research data can be used as long as they're not false or misleading. Only when data are presented recklessly does the FTC act to protect the public. Copywriters can present research data in several ways. Comparisons are often used, and they require the care previously mentioned. Dramatizations can also be used, but abuses have led to a set of guidelines. Commercials using actors to play doctors, dentists, or pharmacists are unacceptable. So are commercials with statements such as "Doctors recommend . . . ," "Doctors at a leading hospital have found . . . ," or presentations by a third party—for example, an actor who says, "My pharmacist told me . . ."

Research material can also be presented by couching it in qualified language. One pain reliever, for instance, claims its ingredients give no stomach upset for millions. The commercial doesn't state what percentage of users might experience stomach upsets. Other products claim they "can be effective" or "can help relieve" certain problems. While legal, such wording does not tell the full truth and may infer results that the product doesn't deliver.

State Regulation

Even though federal agencies are primarily responsible for regulating broadcast advertising, most states also have some form of regulation. For example, most states have laws prohibiting or regulating broadcast advertising of lotteries and alcoholic beverages.

Of more specific concern to the copywriter are state consumer protection laws. Practically all states have laws that discourage false and misleading advertising. In addition, each state has its own laws that regulate the advertising of professional services. Physicians, dentists, opticians, chiropractors, attorneys, and health-care facilities may be permitted to advertise on radio and television. Since state laws vary widely, you must be familiar with the statutes of your state and those of adjacent states if your station's signal reaches them and if advertising time is sold to businesses in those states.

State laws regulate two aspects of advertising professional services. First, each state determines whether a given service can be advertised. If it can, state statutes typically spell out guidelines.

While it is impossible to describe the relevant laws of all states, some generalizations illustrate the concerns with which you should be familiar. State laws typically stipulate that advertising of professional services cannot be false, deceptive, or misleading. This means that advertising copy cannot create false or unjustified expectations of beneficial assistance or successful cures. A law firm, for example, cannot guarantee that it will win a client's case, and a chiropractor cannot promise that treatment will eliminate all aches and pains. Advertising rules for physicians and dentists often state that advertising copy cannot appeal to a layperson's fears, ignorance, or anxieties regarding his or her health or well-being.

Another problem pertains to professional specialties. If a dentist or a physician has the required academic education to practice a specialty, state laws usually permit the specialty to be advertised. Thus, a dentist with the required training to practice orthodontics may advertise that specialty. In the event that a dental clinic has one orthodontist as part of its dental team, however, the clinic would not be permitted to advertise itself as an orthodontic clinic.

Some state laws also prohibit celebrity or authority figures from narrating advertisements on television. Where these laws apply, they stipulate that only the advertising professional may appear and speak on camera. If the professional does not want to use the spokesperson approach, the station can use a staff announcer to deliver the commercial.

As a result of such rules, commercials for professional services often appear as straightforward, institutional-style announcements. The script that follows is an example. The commercial identifies the law firm and explains what it will do for its clients. There is no attempt to dramatize the situation. The result is a low-key, soft sell approach for an advertiser that wishes to appear serious and responsible.

> IS THERE A POINT OF MARITAL OR FAMILY LAW ABOUT WHICH YOU NEED SOLID LEGAL ADVICE? CALL THE FAMILY LAW CENTER AT 894-2671.
>
> THE FAMILY LAW CENTER SPECIALIZES IN MARITAL AND FAMILY LAW. THEY ARE LAWYERS WHO WILL EXPLAIN WHAT YOUR LEGAL RIGHTS ARE IN CASES INVOLVING DIVORCE, SEPARATION, CHILD SUPPORT AND CUSTODY, AND ALL OTHER AREAS INVOLVING MARITAL OR FAMILY LAW. ALL MATTERS ARE HANDLED WITH UNDERSTANDING AND CONCERN FOR YOU. THE LAWYERS AT THE FAMILY LAW CENTER WILL FIGHT HARD TO PROTECT YOUR RIGHTS. CALL THE FAMILY LAW CENTER AT 894-2671.
>
> OUTSIDE THE ORLANDO AREA PHONE 1-800-223-1804 AND FIND OUT WHAT YOUR LEGAL RIGHTS ARE.

LET HANDLIN, HEFFERAN, AND LANIGAN AT THE FAMILY LAW CENTER FIGHT FOR YOU.

PHONE 894-2671. OUT OF TOWN, CALL 1-800-223-1804.

Courtesy Family Law Center and JOY 108, Orlando, Florida.

Commercials for medical clinics have also been written in an institutional style. They often feature a tip on preventive medicine along with an announcement for a particular health service available at the clinic. The spot in Figure 12.1 takes a bolder approach. It advertises a clinic for alcohol and drug rehabilitation. This is a sensitive topic for both the client and the public. Clinics and hospitals don't wish to seem crass in their attempt to fill rooms and beds. And the public may not be receptive to a commercial that is not in good taste. Still, clinics and hospitals compete for patients, and each facility hopes to convince those who need specialized treatment to use their facilities. Good taste and sensitivity are essential in such commercials. That point is illustrated again in the following script dedicated to the problem of cocaine abuse.

SFX	ROLL OF GUN BARREL, COCK AND CLICK OF HAMMER
ANNCR	A lot of people are playing a deadly game these days. It's called cocaine.
SFX	ROLL OF GUN BARREL, COCK AND CLICK OF HAMMER
ANNCR	Maybe they think cocaine isn't addictive. That's just not true. Cocaine can make life unmanageable. Unbearable. Unlivable.
SFX	ROLL OF GUN BARREL, COCK AND CLICK OF HAMMER
ANNCR	If someone you love is dependent on cocaine or other drugs, get help. Now. By calling Brookwood Recovery Centers' 24-Hour Crisis Line. Qualified, caring counselors are ready to listen. And ready to help you help someone beat this deadly game. So call now. Brookwood Recovery Centers' 24-Hour Crisis Line is open. Because if they don't win . . .
SFX	ROLL OF GUN BARREL, COCK OF HAMMER, SHOT
ANNCR	Sooner or later, cocaine will.
TAG	Brookwood Recovery Centers. (APPROPRIATE TAG INFORMATION) Someone you love needs you to call.

Courtesy Brookwood Recovery Centers. Not to be reprinted without the expressed written permission of Brookwood Recovery Centers.

Remember, each state has its own laws regarding the advertising of professional services. If a professional service can be advertised in your state, check the appropriate regulations. They will usually be available at a good library. You can also check with the state attorney general's office, the local Better Business Bureau, and the Chamber of Commerce. The professional firm that wishes to advertise on your station may also have a copy of your state's rules. Ask the salesperson to check for you or call the client yourself. Legal action can be brought against the station if a commercial for a professional service violates state guidelines. It is your responsibility to familiarize yourself with the rules that exist in your state and to follow them.

BROOKWOOD
RECOVERY CENTERS
Adolescent Services

"Crying Out" :30 TV

Your child may be crying out for your help...

and you may not even know it. Because the warning signs of alcohol and drug dependency

are so very hard to recognize.

A drop in grades, a change of friends

an irrational change of mood. They're your child's cries for help.

If you're listening, call Brookwood Recovery Centers Adolescent Services.

Now at Chocolate Bayou.

We're a unique treatment center in the Houston area dedicated solely to Adolescent chemical dependency probelms.

And we can help.

FIGURE 12·1   A professional services ad. *(Courtesy Brookwood Recovery Centers. Not to be reprinted without the express written permission of Brookwood Recovery Centers.)*

Self-Regulation

For many years, self-regulation of broadcast advertising operated primarily through the radio and television codes of the industry trade association, the National Association of Broadcasters (NAB). Both stations and networks subscribed to the codes. Subscribing stations were provided with code requirements for a number of advertising problems. Although subscribing stations (about half of the commercial radio stations and sixty percent of the television stations) were expected to follow these requirements and observe their prohibitions, many stations followed the code requirements even though they never subscribed.

In 1982, the NAB Code Authority, which implemented the codes, was terminated as a result of a detrimental court ruling that stemmed from antitrust charges. The U.S. Department of Justice brought the charges, maintaining that commercial time standards within the television code constituted an unjustified restriction on the rights of advertisers. A U.S. District Court ruled for the Justice Department and the NAB agreed to abolish the commercial time provisions. Eventually, the NAB shut down the Code Authority, and the government dropped its antitrust suit.

The guidelines within the NAB codes provided standards for advertisers to follow in preparing acceptable commercials. These guidelines identified problem areas and presented suggested solutions. The codes, for example, completely banned the advertising of hard liquor, contraceptives, fortune telling, palm reading, occultism, and phrenology. Publications used for giving odds or promoting betting were also prohibited. Guides for sensitive products were developed. They included nonprescription medications, beer and wine, weight reduction products, foundation garments, and personal hygiene products. Presentation guidelines, including testimonials, safety portrayals, and product demonstrations, were also developed.

In addition, the Code Authority screened commercials for products that were controversial when advertised on the air. This included commercials for feminine hygiene products, premium offers aimed at children, children's toys, and food products with cholesterol claims. Since the Code Authority evaluated commercials for these products, the networks and stations accepted the results, alleviating the need to evaluate each commercial.

The dismantling of the Code Authority means that stations and networks must assume a stronger role in reviewing commercials. Each network and each station must determine what they will accept or reject. This is a difficult task for smaller stations, since they often lack the staff to systematically evaluate commercials with questionable content. Nevertheless, broadcasters, not the NAB, now do the evaluating.

Many broadcasters still follow the general guidelines of the NAB codes. The codes are reasonable guides for determining good taste, and can be useful when no other standard is available for evaluating the acceptability of a spot.

Broadcast commercials, like other forms of communication, are subject to laws and regulations that seek to protect the public from material that is false or misleading. Advertising is a highly competitive business, and companies have gone to great lengths to convince the public that their product or service is best.

The more blatant excesses in commercials are covered by existing regulations, but there are some approaches that are not illegal but nevertheless offensive. Some commercials are too loud, some promote products of questionable value, and some use techniques that raise questions of good taste. For instance, the Frito-Lay Company once used an animated cartoon character called the Frito Bandito. Many found the character amusing, but some Hispanics found the character offensive. The character is no longer used.

Such questions of taste can only be regulated by advertisers, networks, stations, and advertising agencies. Standards of acceptance constantly change, so it is imperative that those who write and prepare broadcast commercials be alert to words, slogans, and presentational techniques that might offend the audience. It may be tempting to gain attention by using a double entendre as a slogan, for example, but if people find it offensive, they probably won't buy the sponsor's product. When that happens, you've wasted the advertiser's money no matter how clever or funny the commercial may have seemed.

The Legal Implications of Cable Advertising

While broadcast stations are heavily regulated by the Federal Communications Commission, cable systems are not. Local franchising authorities determine a cable operator's legal, character, financial, and other qualifications. Cable is considered a nonbroadcast facility that is much more in touch with local franchise stipulations than with federal regulation.

As a result of their status, cable operators have much more flexibility in dealing with advertising matters than do broadcast stations. This enables cablecasters to engage in several types of advertising practices that differ from those used in broadcasting.

Cablecasting program-length infomercials is one unique form of cable content. As noted in Chapter 10, an infomercial is a full-length program in which the advertiser's message is subtly presented. The FCC once prohibited such programs on commercial television in the belief that purportedly noncommercial content might be interwoven with the sponsor's advertising, so that the program constituted a single commercial promotion for the sponsor. Thus, a program sponsored by a real estate firm, with commercials for the firm's services, and with agents of the firm introducing their latest listings could be a program-length commercial. A TV station could not broadcast it, but a cable system could, since it is a nonbroadcast entity regulated by a local franchise authority.

Another area of difference relates to political candidate access. Commercial broadcast stations are limited in the amount of time they can give to candidates for political office. It is economically unwise to turn all the station's advertising over to politicians, but that is what could happen under the FCC's lowest unit rule. It requires that political advertising be sold at the lowest rate the station charges to an advertiser. That rule can benefit candidates, but stations do not like selling advertising at their lowest rate. They may choose to give a certain amount of free time to candidates and dispense with selling political advertising.

Cablecasters must provide all candidates for a given office with equal opportunity, but cable systems have a number of options that broadcast stations do not have. Most local access rates for cable are low, much lower than the lowest rates of the smallest TV stations. This gives even the poorest funded candidate the opportunity to campaign on a local cable channel. Second, most cable systems allow any member of the public the right to appear on a cable channel. Thus, if the candidate is not able to appear on a commercial channel, it may be possible to appear on the public-access channel. Third, cable systems operate in many small communities that do not have television stations. The presence of the cable system enables candidates to campaign via TV. Fourth, cable systems seek highly specialized audiences by narrowcasting. This permits political candidates to seek the specific audience they desire, not the broad audience desired by television stations. Finally, cable systems are not bound by the equal-time requirements of the Communications Act. Broadcasters argue that this requirement (that they give equal opportunity to all candidates for a given office once they have given time to one candidate for that office) interferes with their ability to broadcast political material. No doubt cable operators will display fairness in putting candidates on their channels, but they need not seek out all candidates for a given office and give them time.

As noted earlier, cablecasters must observe the FCC's prohibition against putting lotteries on their channels. Some cable systems do televise games of bingo; however, they are careful not to require a payment or consideration for playing, so the games do not constitute a lottery.

Cable advertising must adhere to requirements from two quarters. As we noted earlier, the Federal Trade Commission is empowered to review false and misleading advertising of any sort, including that on cable channels. Cable operators also must adhere to state laws against false and misleading advertising, and laws that regulate the advertising of professional services. In fact, the very absence of FCC regulation leaves state and local governments free to oversee cable operating practices, including advertising.

POINTS TO REMEMBER

- The Federal Communications Commission is empowered to consider a station's advertising practices at license renewal time.

- Broadcast commercials must include a sponsorship identification.

- Broadcasting of lottery promotions or advertisements is illegal except for state lotteries.

- A contest or promotion is a lottery if the following three elements are present: (1) prize, (2) chance, and (3) consideration.

- A station-conducted contest is illegal if the material terms are not broadcast.

- Promotional announcements for broadcast contests cannot include misleading information or material that might adversely affect the audience.

- The Federal Trade Commission is charged with protecting the public from false and misleading advertising.

- Products demonstrated in television commercials cannot be altered for effect but must be shown as they are.

- Testimonials and endorsements in commercials must be genuine.

- Comparative advertising or the use of research data in commercials is acceptable as long as claims aren't misleading and the comparisons aren't rigged.

- Most states have consumer laws that prohibit false and misleading advertising and laws that regulate the advertising of professional services.

- Each station and each network must review commercials to determine which they will accept and which they will reject.

- Commercials that are loud or otherwise offensive may not violate regulations but may still be in poor taste.

- Cablecasters are primarily accountable to local franchise authorities and not to the FCC.

You're asked to write a thirty-second radio spot for the following promotion:

Al's Auto Imports, 7803 West Federal Highway, wants to publicize the new RTE model auto. This new Japanese import gets 55 mpg and seats five comfortably. It's sporty. To interest people in the car, Al wants people to come in and take a test drive. Everyone who test-drives the car will become eligible to win one hundred free gallons of gasoline.

The station's account executive isn't familiar with all the legal restrictions that apply to such promotions, so it's your job to write a spot that is acceptable. This spot will go to Al for approval first, so you may change his requirements if you think doing so will solve any legal problems.

You're asked to write promotional copy for radio station XXXX-FM, a contemporary music station in Yourtown. The station is sponsoring a Halloween Fun House before Halloween. The Fun House is for children. When they go through the house they will encounter trap doors, trick mirrors, loud noises, ghosts and goblins, and so forth. It's supposed to be scary but fun.

Write a thirty-second promo that conveys the impression of the Fun House, but be certain it won't frighten young listeners.

Station XXXX, FM 104, wants to give away a RoughNeck four-wheel-drive pickup. Listeners can become eligible to win the pickup by filling out an entry blank at a RoughNeck dealer or at the station. The theme of the contest is "Win the Keys to a RoughNeck."

Write a thirty-second radio promo. Stress the contest theme prominently, but don't mislead the audience into thinking that the winner will win just the keys to the pickup. don't belabor the point, but make it clear that the winner will win the pickup.

Write a thirty-second television commercial in which you compare two products. Compare a new cold remedy, Kwikure, with an established product, Cold Eze. Both products eliminate nasal congestion from common colds. They stop runny nose, sneezing, and watery eyes. However, Kwikure is effective for up to fourteen hours. Cold Eze works four to six hours.

Prepare a straightforward demonstration in which you compare the features of the two products. Show that Kwikure is clearly superior.

Write a sixty-second radio commercial for Mary Brown, Independent Party candidate for mayor of Yourtown. Include appropriate sponsor identification. The fact sheet provided to you includes the following information:

> Resident of Yourtown for fourteen years.
>
> Married, three children.
>
> Attended public schools in Yourtown, graduate of Yourtown University.
>
> Lawyer. Partner, law firm of Henson, Earl and Brown.
>
> Member of Yourtown City Council for four years. Worked for improvement of streets and roads, sponsored bill that led to twelve percent pay increase for police and fire department personnel.
>
> Five years on Mayor's Task Force against Drunk Driving.
>
> The advertisement is paid for by the Citizens' Committee for Mary Brown.

Write a thirty-second television spot for Yourtown Treatment Center, a drug and alcoholism treatment facility. Focus this spot on the treatment of alcoholism. Stress that it is a disease, one that can be fatal. Appeal to the victim's family—children, husband, or wife. Use an emotional appeal but keep it in good taste. The Treatment Center has a twenty-four-hour crisis line. Its number is 123-3000.

Student Name _____   Advertiser _____

Date Submitted _____   Commercial Length _____

Student Name _____ Advertiser _____

Date Submitted _____ Commercial Length _____

Student Name _____   Advertiser _____

Date Submitted _____   Commercial Length _____

Student Name _____   Advertiser _____

Date Submitted _____   Commercial Length _____

VIDEO   **AUDIO**

Student Name _____   Advertiser _____

Date Submitted _____   Commercial Length _____

Student Name _____   Advertiser _____

Date Submitted _____   Commercial Length _____

VIDEO   **AUDIO**

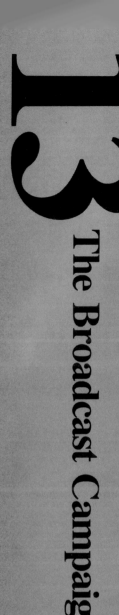

13 The Broadcast Campaign

So far in this text we've looked at the basic activity of a broadcast copywriter—writing individual radio and television messages. However, broadcast announcements are not always independently written and scheduled. Announcements of all types—commercial, public service, and promotional—are often written and scheduled as part of a broadcast campaign. A campaign multiplies the effort of an individual order, which includes one or more spots on a single station, and may involve writing both radio and television spots. Spots may be placed on selected stations in a given city, a region, or across the country. Since a broadcast campaign is complex, strategic planning is essential if the advertiser's message is to be properly conceived, written, and scheduled.

Broadcast Campaign Structure

A broadcast campaign is a carefully prepared strategy to achieve a specific goal for the advertiser. The goal may be to introduce a new product, store, or service; to reinforce brand loyalty; to demonstrate a unique feature; or any other specific goal.

A broadcast campaign may schedule a commercial or commercials over a period of time—either over a long haul (with spots spread over a period of months) or in a concentrated blitz (with a heavy concentration of spots in a few days or weeks). Spots in broadcast campaigns are usually related to each other through slogans. Through repetition, they help build client recognition. They help the consumer to recognize the advertisements easily, and eventually to recognize the advertiser. The slogan "Have you driven a Ford . . . lately?" identifies the sponsor and is easy to remember. Unlike independently run spots, broadcast campaigns provide for planned promotion, which can have a strong cumulative effect.

Campaigns are used by major clients that can afford to pay for the planning, creative development, and production of spots beyond the placement of the spots themselves. Since the effort is more complex than preparing an independently run spot, campaigns are usually prepared by advertising agencies rather than stations or cable systems. An advertising agency has the resources to do the media and creative planning. It is rare for a copywriter at a broadcast station to develop a campaign. Exceptions may occur in small markets where a client might ask a station for an extra effort.

The Client and Competition Analysis

A broadcast campaign, perhaps more than independently run announcements, must be planned on the basis of the guidelines for creating a copy platform that we presented in Chapter 4. These guidelines include the determination of:

> Objectives
>
> Target audience
>
> Sales theme
>
> Bonus ideas
>
> Positioning
>
> Approach

Most of these items require little more mention than that presented in Chapter 4. However, our copy platform for independently run announcements did not include one item that is especially crucial to a broadcast campaign. That is an analysis of the client for whom you're preparing the campaign and its major competitors. While you might consider these items in preparing an independently run spot, you probably would not treat them with the depth that is necessary to prepare a campaign.

It's essential at the outset of a campaign that you have a good understanding of the client and its competitors. You must know the client's service, store, or product in depth if you're to promote it successfully. You should know far more about the client than you'll need simply to write the commercials. This insight will enable you to convince the client that you're knowledgeable enough about the product, store, or service to develop an effective campaign.

Clients generally supply a sizable amount of data about their business, but just as you can't rely completely on such data for an independently run spot, you should never rely on it for a campaign. It's important that you meet the client and see the business firsthand. Even if you're trapped in the office with a stack of copy orders, find (or make) a little time to visit the client. It's almost certain to be worth the effort.

There are several reasons why you can't completely rely on the data supplied by the client. One is that familiarity with the business may lead the client to overlook items that you can use to advantage in appealing to the public.

In one instance, a drugstore chain occasionally mentioned in its advertising that it would meet any other drugstore's prices. All the customer had to do was bring in the competitor's newspaper ad. If the competitor's price for an item was lower, the store would match it. Although this policy wasn't a major part of the chain's promotion, a copywriter from the agency handling the account noticed a customer bring a competitor's newspaper ad into the store she was visiting. She also noticed that the customer got the item at the competitor's price and that the clerk seemed pleased to see that people were aware of the policy. Rather than keeping this policy in the background, the copywriter focused a campaign on it. Because she visited the client for a firsthand look, her commercials emphasized an important selling point.

Another reason a copywriter can't rely only on information supplied by the client is that the client may be reluctant to disclose weaknesses of the product, store, or service. It's understandable that a client might not want to discuss product weaknesses, such as the fact that the chemicals used by a home pest-control service can't completely eliminate crawling insects. It is much easier to pretend that the product does the job, period!

But as a copywriter, you need to know both the good and the bad. If you don't know the shortcomings, both you and the client might be surprised by negative responses to your commercials once customers become aware of them. If sales go down, the client might cancel its contract with your station.

Client Strengths   Whether you visit the client or not, your first step in preparing a campaign is to determine the strengths of the client's business. What makes this product, store, or service superior? Is the store established or new, modern or quaint? Is the service convenient, inexpensive, or reliable? Whatever strengths exist, you need to identify them before you plan your campaign. These are the reasons why a consumer would want to buy a product, patronize a store, or use a service. The strengths are directly tied to the benefits that customers will receive. The advantages may be readily apparent, or you may have to conduct research to discover them.

Client Weaknesses

It's rare to find a product or business that doesn't have some short-comings, and you must be aware of them *before* you plan the campaign. The store may be inconveniently located, the service may cost more than that of competitors, or the product may not be available in all stores. Whatever weaknesses exist, you must know about them. If possible, try to turn the weakness in your favor. Curtis Mathes does this by acknowledging that its TV sets cost more, but its commercials emphasize, "They're worth it!" If you don't evaluate the shortcomings of the client's business, you may create expectations that the product cannot live up to.

Analyzing the Competition

Campaign planning requires more than analyzing your own client. You must also analyze the competition. If your client is a car dealership in a city of half a million people, for instance, it will have competition from a number of other dealers. You don't have to analyze all of them. The ones you must be concerned about are the primary competitors. You'll have to identify them.

You identify the primary competitors by looking at similarities. Which businesses have the same products as your client? Which businesses are seeking the same customers and serving the same geographic area as your client? If your client is a Ford dealer, a Buick dealer across town isn't a primary competitor. However, a Ford dealer across town is still a primary competitor, because it's selling the same product. A nearby Chevrolet dealer may also be a primary competitor, not because it sells the same product but because it seeks the same customers.

Once you've identified the primary competitors, you should work up a brief analysis of each of them. The analysis need not be as detailed as the one you do for your own client, but it should be thorough enough to describe each primary competitor's position relative to the strengths and weaknesses of your client. How does your client stack up against competitor A, competitor B, and so on?

Hopefully, your client will emerge stronger than its major competitors. If not, you must look for features that distinguish your client from its primary rivals. For example, if your client's service is priced the same as the competition and is as effective, you can't tout it as being superior. If your client is an established, family-operated company while the competitors are newcomers to town, you still have an edge to work with. Once you find such a feature or advantage, you can focus on your client as the firm customers should use.

An analysis of the competition should also include the type and amount of broadcast advertising that your client's major competitors have been using. This is an important element in assessing a competitor's strengths and weaknesses. If competitors are using radio and television, study their commercials and their schedules. Approximate their budgets and evaluate the approaches they are using in their commercials. Your decision to use radio and/or television will vary considerably depending on what the competition is doing. If your competition is spending a significant amount on a highly visible television campaign, you must decide whether you want to use television, and if so, in what way. It would be a reckless waste of your client's money to simply duplicate a competitor's broadcast efforts.

Objectives

Once you've analyzed your client and its major competitors, you're ready for the key question: What objective do you want this campaign to accomplish? This brings us back to the copy platform and the items we discussed in Chapter 4. For our purposes here, it's sufficient to say that advertising objectives should deal with specific communications activities and not with marketing goals. State your objectives specifically and thoroughly, as the following objectives do:

- Let business travelers know that Republic Airlines offers more service benefits than other airlines.[1]
- Convince women that Wrangler makes attractive nondenim apparel and not just jeans.[2]
- Persuade consumers that Pearle Vision Centers provide more convenient, cheaper, and faster eyecare than conventional eyecare specialists.[3]
- Inform business users that Pacific Bell provides a wide array of useful products, not just voice telephone service.[4]

Note that each of these statements describes a specific goal the advertiser wants to achieve. Further, they identify the primary benefit the advertiser wants the consumer to experience. Advertising objectives don't list marketing goals or describe commercial production techniques. They focus on the communications goals that the campaign hopes to achieve.

Target Audience

It's important that you target your campaign to a particular group. It's a waste of money not to delineate a specific audience, and the results could be disastrous if you target the wrong group. Go back to your initial analysis of the client. What is the client selling? What are its strengths and weaknesses? What is your objective? Weigh this information carefully. It should guide you in directing the campaign to the appropriate audience.

Remember that you'll typically define your audience on the basis of standard demographics—age, sex, education, income, and so on. You may supplement the demographic data with psychographic research describing the psychological characteristics of the audience. A standard demographic target might be adults aged twenty-five to fifty-four.

Sales Theme

The sales theme is the major selling point of your campaign. It consists of a major sales point tied to a strong consumer benefit. Initially, you should structure your sales theme as a simple declarative sentence that has broad and meaningful appeal to your target audience. Thus, the major selling point for Volkswagen might have been "A Volkswagen is more than just a car." When converted to a sales slogan, the line became "It's not a car. It's a Volkswagen."

Moreover, preparation of the sales theme forces you to concentrate on the client's greatest strengths. Since these strengths are probably the main points you'll want to emphasize anyway, the time you spend identifying the main strengths gives you more to work with in building a solid picture of your client. If you can build the major selling point into a sales slogan, you've developed an even stronger sales vehicle.

---

1. "Republic Perks Up Pitch," *Advertising Age,* 5 Aug. 1984, 4.
2. "Wrangler Campaign Soft-Pedals Denim," *Advertising Age,* 1 Nov. 1984, 3.
3. "Sentimental Spots Paying Off for Pearle," *Advertising Age,* 8 Oct. 1984, 4.
4. "Pacific Bell to Blitz Business Customers," *Advertising Age,* 26 July 1984, 3.

As we noted earlier, a slogan has the advantage of building client recognition. Through repetition, the client's sales theme can draw attention to the commercial and thus to the sales pitch. A slogan such as "Wouldn't you really rather have a Buick?" is ideal. It's brief, clever, and memorable. The product name is included for greater sales power. A slogan is a wonderful device to highlight your sales theme and gain exposure for your campaign.

Bonus Items

We noted in Chapter 4 that you may wish to consider using optional selling points in an individual commercial. The same is true for a campaign. It's best to stick to one main sales idea, but you can add an extra sales point or two if you can relate them to the main idea.

A campaign gives you additional flexibility in using bonus ideas that you may not have in an individual spot. A campaign may wish to stress more than one idea and may do so by building them around a common sales theme. For example, the Volkswagen sales theme "It's not a car. It's a Volkswagen" was used as the main selling point for a campaign promoting the Volkswagen Jetta and Golf.[5] The individual commercials, however, emphasized the features unique to each car and tied them to the sales theme.

Positioning

Positioning, you'll recall, is carving out a niche for your client's firm or product. You may not have the time or resources to position each client purchasing an independently run spot, but you'll probably want to position your client in a broadcast campaign. Positioning involves the creation of a separate identity for your client or product—an identity that helps the public distinguish your client from competitors. A planned promotion with a carefully defined objective means giving your client the highest possible visibility. Positioning is thus an essential part of a campaign.

One auto dealer may be described as "the volume leader," while another claims to be the dealer that "sells for less." If these claims have real substance—in other words, if one dealer offers good prices because it sells so many cars and the other for some reason really does offer lower prices—then both have a unique claim. Note that the position must be real. If the product or service doesn't deliver what is promised, the positioning won't work.

How do you position a product or service? You create the position through the analysis you've already done. Certainly, you need to know what claims your major competitors are making. Additionally, your sales theme indicates the stance you wish your client to take. If that claim is substantially the same as one or more of the major competitors, you have even more reason to position your client. You may not have a client with a unique product or business, but you can search for that unique aspect of your client's business that can be used to orient consumers' perception of your client's business. That's what positioning is all about.

Approach

Just as you want to use a suitable tone, mood, or style for an independently run spot, you also need a suitable approach for the commercials you prepare for a broadcast campaign. Will the

---

5. "VW Engineers Push for New Jetta, Golf," *Advertising Age,*
18 Oct. 1984, 3.

approach convey elegance, understatement, or an aggressive hard sell? Since the approach must match the objective and the target audience, you should refer to your initial planning. Look at what you want this campaign to accomplish (objectives), and who you want the message to reach (target audience). Those two items will guide you in determining a suitable approach.

Use of the copy platform can be a valuable aid in bringing order to campaign preparation. If the campaign is for a new client, the agency must work from scratch to analyze its strengths and weaknesses. Even if the campaign is a new effort for an established client, it's necessary to update the information on your client and its competition. The copy platform we've presented is a logical way to analyze these data. The platform begins with a broad overview of client strengths and weaknesses and narrows that information to a specific objective, target audience, sales theme, and market position. It's a system that helps bring order to a process that is often far from orderly.

Once you've completed your copy platform, you may write some sample scripts for the campaign. The spots may relate to a single objective or to several objectives that the campaign is to accomplish.

If the campaign is for television only, your initial efforts will probably be storyboards rather than scripts. Storyboards enable the clients to visualize the spots, while scripts do not. If the campaign uses radio, initial scripts may be shown to the client. Neither radio nor television spots will likely be produced until the client approves them. Production costs preclude the possibility of producing a spot purely on speculation.

Examples of Campaigns

Up to this point, we have discussed the process of planning a broadcast campaign. To help you appreciate the marketing and creative strategies that make up such a campaign, this section presents examples of campaigns that were conceived and implemented. Naturally, we cannot present every step of the planning process but when the cases are studied together they illustrate the interaction of marketing dynamics with the creative process.

Rent-a-Center

Rent-to-own businesses have experienced solid growth in recent years, with a number of companies now renting appliances and household goods. Many of the 4,000 stores are mom-and-pop businesses, but others, like Rent-a-Center, are sizable operations. Most rent-to-own businesses offer similar plans: A customer can either rent an item for a short time and return it, or rent it for a longer period, after which the customer owns it.

Publicly owned Rent-a-Center launched a campaign to differentiate its stores from those of its competitors. They did this with a national TV campaign aimed at convincing the audience that it's all right to rent rather than to own.

The agency for the account, Keller-Crescent/Southwest, conducted market research for Rent-a-Center. It found that even though rental customers are usually lower income workers with no opportunity to own in the traditional manner, these customers wanted to be treated with the respect and dignity afforded citizens who could buy items.

The campaign used the following sales slogan: "At Rent-a-Center, renting to own is the right thing to do." This campaign positioned Rent-a-Center as the industry leader, offering a "Customer Bill of Rights." This included a money-back guarantee, twenty-four-hour repair service, and loaners.

The spots for the campaign used humorous thirty-second spots to convince viewers of the respectability of renting. In one spot a young woman confessed to her traditional Italian mother, "Lately, I've been having these desires." To satisfy them, she told her worried mother, "I . . . rented a new sofa and love seat at Rent-a-Center." Another spot featured a football player confessing to his coach that he's "been getting these urges." In each situation, the person is told, "It's all right to rent."[6]

United Telephone System Yellow Pages

Like Rent-a-Center, the United Telephone System Yellow Pages had a number of competitors. United developed a new advertising campaign to protect its markets and to stop the erosion of its competitive position. The objective of the campaign was to "increase advertiser and consumer awareness of United Telephone System's Yellow Pages, their uses, their benefits, and their overall perceived value."[7]

The initial campaign involved two commercials, one business-oriented, the other consumer-oriented. Air time was split on a three-to-one business/consumer ratio. The sales theme "The biggest shopping center in town" was chosen to show the size and scope of the information contained in United's directories as well as their ease of use.

To measure the effect of the initial campaign, the firm measured customer awareness before and after the spots ran. The study showed that identification of United as the primary or only local provider of directory yellow pages increased 31.4 percent among residential customers and 20.9 percent among business customers. Identification of United as the local provider of telephone service (rather than other regional or competing telephone companies) increased 11.5 percent (residential) and 16.4 percent (business).

The measurements also showed which Yellow Page elements were most important to the target audiences. For business customers, it was frequency of use and broad distribution. For residential customers, it was ease of use and complete listings. Based on this information, two additional television commercials were produced. These two spots, "Hardware Store" (Figure 13.1) and "When I Shop," (Figure 13.2) continue to use the sales slogan "The biggest shopping center in town."

National Jewish Hospital/National Asthma Center

Nonprofit organizations also prepare broadcast campaigns, and they use much the same strategies as commercial advertisers. PSAs, of course, are run for free, but stations increasingly prefer professional spots that are not cluttered with disparate ideas and that do not run longer than thirty seconds. A PSA must thus be carefully prepared if it is to have any impact.

The National Jewish Hospital/National Asthma Center promotes the research and treatment of respiratory diseases. Public awareness, detection, and proper treatment are major goals of the hospital and center.

---

6. Extracted from Tom Bayer, "Rental Outlets Assure Folks Renting Is OK," *Advertising Age*, 25 October 1984.
7. Letter from Kenneth T. Cherry, manager, Advertising/ Promotion, United Telephone System, 20 March 1985.

1984 UTS YELLOW PAGES
Title: Business Oriented -- Hardware Store
Length: 30 seconds

My family's had this business for years now. It's been quite a success. Know why?

One reason is the United Telephone Yellow Pages.

The biggest shopping center in town!

92% of my customers use this directory. It's the only book they need. So I'm in it.

And this directory goes to all United Telephone customers. Guaranteed!

Take it from someone who knows.

It makes a difference when you're in the book everyone uses.

United Telephone
(Jingle Close)

FIGURE 13·1   Spot targetting business customers. *(Courtesy United Telephone System)*

1984 UTS YELLOW PAGES
Title: Consumer Oriented -- When I Shop
Length: 30 seconds

When I want to shop right, this is where I start.

The United Telephone Yellow Pages!

It's the biggest shopping center in town!

In it I can find everything from an airline ticket

to a zebra.

The United Telephone Yellow Pages has complete listings, too. And it's so easy to use! It's the only directory I need.

So shop the biggest shopping center in town first. The United Telephone Yellow Pages.

It makes a difference when you use the book everyone's in.

Wadsworth Publishing Company

FIGURE 13·2   Spot targetting consumers. *(Courtesy United Telephone System)*

The two PSAs illustrated in Figure 13.3 and Figure 13.4 have the following objectives: to promote public awareness of the seriousness of lung disease and the fact that it can be detected and treated if proper tests are given periodically.[8]

The "Living with Asthma" spot has a more specific subgoal; it emphasizes lifestyles and the fact that asthmatics can lead relatively normal and productive lives with proper medication and care. This spot targets people with asthma and informs them that they can enjoy exercise too.

In addition to these objects, the campaign has a secondary objective of gaining public recognition of the National Jewish Hospital and Research Center as the preeminent institution for research and treatment of respiratory diseases. A nonprofit organization, like a profit-oriented business, must promote its name and image, especially when fund-raising efforts are involved.

Radio Shack

Just as the National Jewish Hospital promoted several types of information about asthma treatment and care, Radio Shack used one campaign to promote several different computers. In the highly competitive world of computers, manufacturers must strive to maintain a competitive edge. As a result, the advertising objective in this campaign was to introduce three new models of the TRS-80 computer: the TRS-80 Pocket Computer, the TRS-80 Model Three personal computer, and the TRS-80 Color Computer.

Each new computer required positioning. The Pocket Computer (see Figure 13.5) was positioned as the smallest pocket computer available, the Model Three (see Figure 13.6) was positioned as a compact personal computer, and the TRS-80 Color Computer (Figure 13.7) was positioned as a low-cost computer that could be connected to any color TV set.

The sales theme was that each computer was a major computer breakthrough. This theme was tied to the idea that these models were brand new and used state-of-the-art technology. The sales theme was presented with animated graphics in the first three scenes of each spot. Spots for this campaign were placed on all three major television networks.[9]

WHOI-TV

Broadcast stations must always be concerned about the image they project to their listeners or viewers. Television station WRAU in Peoria, Illinois, found that it had an image problem. Over a period of time the station had experienced changes in its on-air staff and its ratings had slipped. Along with other changes, station management decided it wanted a new logo that tied in with the viewing area. The station had already changed call letters several times, but a new call letter combination seemed an important part of creating a new image.

The station decided to change its call letters to WHOI, with the letters *HOI* standing for *Heart of Illinois*. This reference was an important part of the new image because it identified the station's primary viewing area. Further, the Peoria area is commonly referred to as the Heart of Illinois, so the new call letters established a link between the station and its viewing area.

---

8. Letter from Don H. Blake, National Jewish Hospital/National Asthma Center, 27 March 1985.
9. Supplied by Mike Wood, Central Advertising Agency, Fort Worth, Texas.

LIVING WITH ASTHMA

A public service announcement from

National Jewish Hospital/National Asthma Center
3800 E. Colfax Avenue
Denver, Colorado 80206

30 SECONDS

STARTER: (on bullhorn) RUNNERS ON YOUR MARK....
GET SET....

VOICE OVER: IF YOU HAVE ASTHMA, YOU MIGHT HAVE
FELT LEFT OUT. EXERCISE CAN OFTEN TRIGGER AN
ATTACK.

BUT WITH PROPER DIAGNOSIS AND CARE, <u>YOU</u> CAN
EXERCISE TOO.

MAYBE NOT A MARATHON, BUT ALMOST <u>ANY</u> ACTIVITY
<u>ANYONE</u> ENJOYS. WE KNOW... AND WE CARE...
WE'RE THE NATIONAL JEWISH HOSPITAL/NATIONAL
ASTHMA CENTER.

CALL 800-222-LUNG FOR MORE INFORMATION...
BECAUSE ASTHMA IS SOMETHING YOU <u>CAN</u> LIVE WITH.

FIGURE 13·3   PSA targetting individuals with asthma. *(Courtesy National
Jewish Hospital/National Asthma Center)*

DID THE DOCTOR CHECK YOUR LUNGS?

A public service campaign by:

NATIONAL JEWISH HOSPITAL/
NATIONAL ASTHMA CENTER
3800 East Colfax Ave.
Denver, Colo. 80206

30 seconds

OFF-CAMERA VOICE:

GOOD CHECKUP?

A SIMPLE TEST IN YOUR
DOCTOR'S OFFICE WILL
HELP YOU BE SURE.

PRETTY GOOD SHAPE,
HUH?

DID YOU KNOW YOUR LUNGS
WON'T TELL YOU ANY-
THING'S WRONG WITH THEM
UNTIL IT'S TOO LATE...

CHECK EVERYTHING?

BUT THE SPIROMETER
TEST WILL...

HOW ABOUT YOUR LUNGS?

SO ASK YOUR DOCTOR...
NO, TELL HIM...

DID THE DOCTOR CHECK
YOUR LUNGS?

TELL HIM TO CHECK YOUR
LUNGS EVERY TIME YOU
HAVE A CHECKUP...

OH, I KNOW YOU FEEL
OKAY, BUT LOOK...

IT CAN GIVE YOU THE
BREATHING ROOM YOU
NEED.

FIGURE 13·4   PSA promoting public awareness of checkups for
respiratory disease. *(Courtesy National Jewish Hospital/*
National Asthma Center)

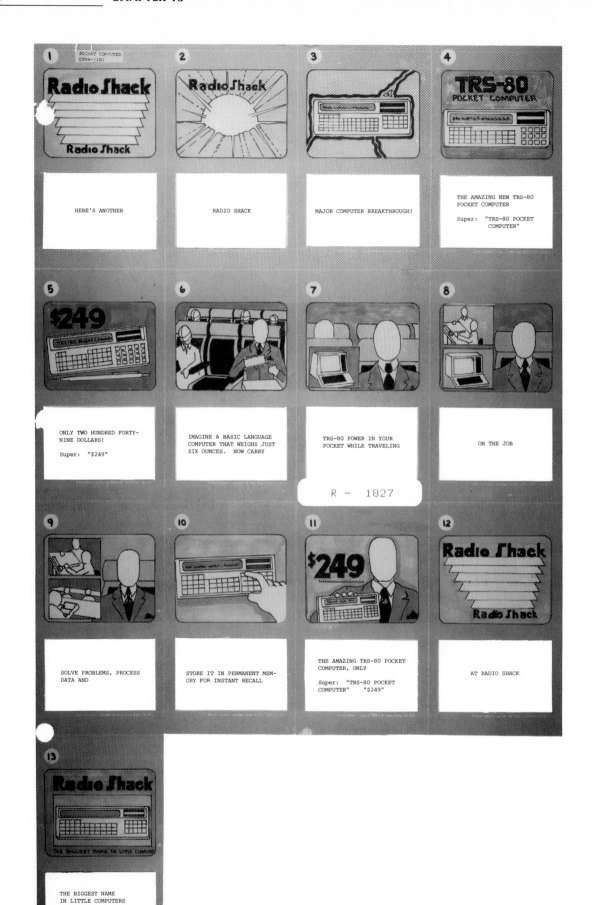

FIGURE 13·5   Part of Radio Shack's campaign: A spot for the TRS-80 pocket computer. *(Courtesy Mike Wood, Central Advertising Agency, Fort Worth, Texas)*

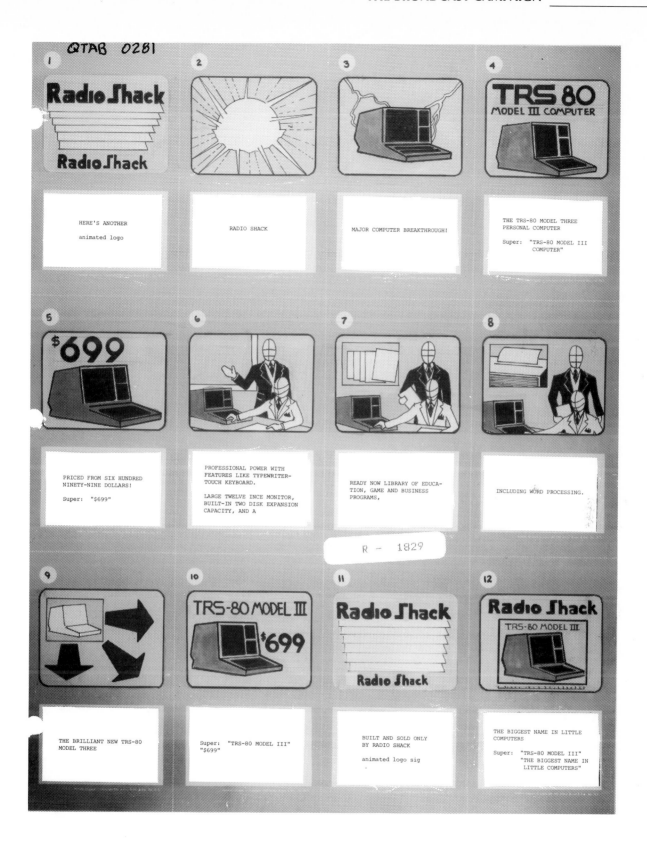

FIGURE 13·6   Part of Radio Shack's campaign: A spot for the TRS-80 Model III computer. *(Courtesy Mike Wood, Central Advertising Agency, Fort Worth, Texas)*

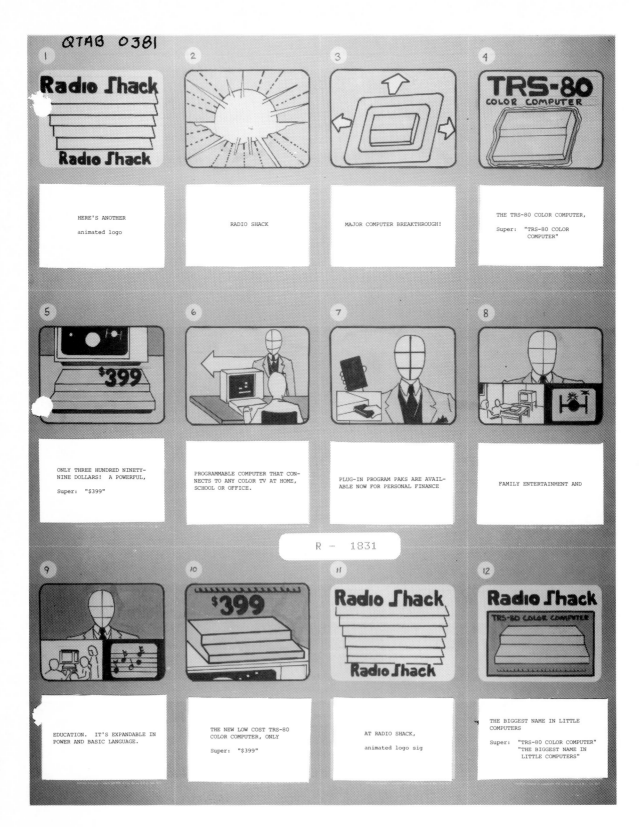

FIGURE 13·7 Part of Radio Shack's campaign: A spot for the TRS-80 color computer. *(Courtesy Mike Wood, Central Advertising Agency, Fort Worth, Texas)*

Radio, television, and newspaper advertising (Figure 13.8) were used to promote the new call letters. As you'll note in the television spot that follows, the video shows scenes of the Heart of Illinois.

VIDEO	AUDIO
FARM VIDEO FROM ¾″ (NOT HARVEST)	Illinois
WORKERS BY SULLY'S	You've got the best of it all.
LOW ANGLE OF CRANE AT ST. FRANCIS	
1) RAM AT ZOO	4 note answer
2) SMOKE STACKS	
3) TRUCK ON I-74	
4) BRADLEY FOOTAGE	
CUT MURRAY BAKER BRIDGE SHOT	Peoria, you're heart of it all.
DISSOLVE RACQUETBALL 1″ FROM YMCA	All the action
CUT EUREKA COLLEGE	the tradition
CUT RIVERMEN FOOTAGE	the excitement
DIS RICHWOODS WINNERS SLO-MO	the spirit is growing strong.
DIS SEPIA TONE TO NEW VIDEO OF COURTHOUSE SQUARE	Proud to be
DIS JULIA BELLE	such a part
DIS BARREL ROLLING PLANE	of the Heart of Illinois.
ANIMATION	19. A part of it all.

the new heart of Illinois

WHOI
PEORIA

TV-19 has changed to WHOI. Because we're proud to be part of the Heart of Illinois, we want our name to reflect that pride. So when you tune to 19 for news, entertainment and sports, remember, we're now WHOI. Bringing you the best of the Heart of Illinois.

We've got it all.

FIGURE 13·8   The newspaper part of an advertising campaign to change a station's image. *(Courtesy Chuck Sherman, WHOI-TV, Creve Coeur, Illinois)*

Radio spots were also developed. They used the audio jingle prepared as a part of the promotional campaign.

> JINGLE UP FULL FOR LYRIC . . . "19 WE'RE THE HEART OF IT ALL."
> (ANNOUNCER)
>
> Now we're the top-rated TV station in the Heart of Illinois.
> (JINGLE UP FOR FULL LYRIC) "AND YOU'RE A PART OF IT ALL"
> (ANNOUNCER)
>
> From the time the sun rises . . . until after the day is done . . . throughout the Heart of Illinois—19 means #1. Every day more men, more women, and more families turn to TV-19 than any other Peoria television station. Viewer surveys by both major rating services agree . . . from sign-on to sign-off, WHOI-TV 19 is far and away Peoria's top-rated TV station. Be part of the action, the adventure, and the excitement. We'll light your life up with the best news and entertainment in the Heart of Illinois.
> (JINGLE LYRICS UP FULL) "WE'RE 19—WE'VE GOT IT ALL."
>
> *Courtesy Chuck Sherman, WHOI-TV, Creve Coeur, Illinois.*

After the new call letters had been in use for four weeks, the station conducted a survey to measure community reaction to the campaign and to the change in call letters. The research showed that 68 percent of the respondents were aware of the campaign, 63 percent could identify that the new call letters were WHOI, and on a scale of 1 to 5, the campaign had a favorable 3.75 rating.[10]

Cross-Media Campaigns

It's not unusual for campaigns to be prepared for distribution on several media at once. Research and a large enough budget may make it possible, especially for an advertising agency, to disseminate the client's message on radio and TV, in newspaper or magazine ads, on billboards, and perhaps by direct mail. Naturally, this coordination requires the skills of a number of specialists, skills that a single copywriter probably won't have. Still, to have a full understanding of campaigns it's important to know how they work when more than one medium is used.

Even though several media are used in this approach, they must still be selected with care. The task is to get the most for the advertiser's dollar, and often radio or television alone won't do the job. Outdoor advertising is often used as a support medium for a campaign receiving heavy play in the major media. Over a concentrated period of time virtually everyone in town will see a billboard, even though they may not listen to radio or watch TV. Retail print advertising has advantages, too. Radio or television may tell people about a department store's special sale, but it can't list many sale items. Such lists can appear in a newspaper ad, and many readers seek out retail ads as much as they do news stories.

It makes sense to target the client's audience and then use the appropriate media to reach them. Several media, used jointly, can do an effective job of reaching all the audiences and demographic groups that the client wants to influence.

---

10. Letter from Chuck Sherman, president and general manager, WHOI-TV, 17 May 1985.

Using Other Types of Media

Much of the advertising used today comes from the four major media: newspapers, magazines, television, and radio. But other forms of advertising are important, too. Direct advertising (advertising transmitted directly to the consumer, such as direct mail), outdoor advertising (billboards or transportation advertising on buses), and point-of-purchase advertising (advertising located in the retail store) all do their part to spread advertising messages.

Even though this text focuses on writing broadcast and cable spots, a few basics of print layout will help you understand some essentials of nonbroadcast advertising. The key to print advertising is developing an effective graphic idea or visual. A visual idea is the starting point, whether you're preparing a magazine or a billboard ad.

Print Layout

An important first step in a print advertisement is layout. A layout helps you decide what is dominant in your ad and enables you to decide how the various parts will relate to one another. The layout gives your ad purpose and shows off the copy to optimum advantage.

Start a layout with a thumbnail sketch. Rough out a number of layouts, indicating their basic shapes, sizes, and relative proportions. Work in whatever size is comfortable for you. A number of thumbnail sketches, such as the sample in Figure 13.9, will help you direct your thoughts and focus on the purpose of the ad.

Once you've identified your purpose and approach, draw a rough layout. It should be drawn to the actual size of the proposed ad, with the primary elements (headline, art, copy)

FIGURE 13·9   Thumbnail sketch.

included. The rough should be legible, so that other people can understand how the layout works. Often the rough layout will be shown internally for comments and suggestions before a finished layout is prepared for the client.

Here are some key points about a layout. A layout should be conceived as a totality in which each point is related to the others. The layout should have an informal, three-point balance so that one dominant element is offset by two lesser ones. The advertisement in Figure 13.10 illustrates this point. The dominant element is the words *Good Cheap Food*. The two lesser elements are the hands holding the sandwich and the copy at the bottom. The dominant element in a print ad should attract people first, but the remaining elements should be constructed so that the reader's eye will follow them effortlessly until the entire message is absorbed. Look again at Figure 13.10. The words *Good Cheap Food* attract attention, and the dominant portion of the picture is completed with the hands holding the sandwich. The eye can easily move down the ad to read the copy and complete the message. A mix of large and small type, as used in this ad, can achieve the necessary contrast.

All print advertisements must have *white space*—an area without artwork or type around the outer limits or edge of the ad. White space draws attention to the ad's contents and sets it off from the surrounding material. However, the WFTV advertisement in Figure 13.10 reverses the composition, using white type on black space. In this case, the black background creates a more striking contrast with the adjacent layouts using black and white in the typical manner. This reversal of black and white is quite common; note that in practice the black space is still referred to by the term *white space*. Still, reversing body copy (white on black) can be tricky and must be done with care.

The advertisement in Figure 13.11 illustrates a more typical use of white space. This advertisement, a spot prepared by ABC, allows affiliates to promote their syndicated programming in the top third of the ad, the 7-P.M. slot, and to include the station logo in the bottom slot. In this advertisement, the dominant element is the words *Saturday Spectacular.* The lesser elements are the three program promotions and the "We're with You" logo at the bottom. This advertisement reads easily from the top down.

The Cross-Media Theme

Just as a single spot should have a sales theme and an individual print advertisement a dominant element, a full campaign also needs a theme or purpose. The theme should be used in all facets of the campaign, whether it uses several media or a single medium.

In a cross-media campaign, the theme should be consistent from spot to spot and from broadcast spot to print advertisement. Continuity of theme reinforces the message in all media and enhances the sales point. A Midwest auto dealer once purchased a shipment of foreign sports cars that had sat on a dock during a hurricane. Although the cars had suffered some water damage, they were otherwise sound and were offered for sale at reduced prices. An advertising campaign was devised around the theme "Once in a Blue Moon," referring to the infrequency of such foreign car prices. The song "Blue Moon" and the "Once in a Blue Moon" theme began each radio and television spot. These theme elements also appeared in each newspaper advertisement. Because the theme was clear and consistent in all media the campaign worked well and sales were brisk.

Let's look at the theme of another cross-media campaign, this time for a special news program aired by WFTV. Look closely at the radio and television scripts that follow and at the newspaper advertisement in Figure 13.12. The theme is "Deadly Convenience," a play on words to describe the dangers of working in a convenience store.

FIGURE 13·10 Print ad for a TV station. *(Courtesy SFN Communications of Florida, Inc.)*

FIGURE 13·11   Print ad prepared for ABC affiliates. *(Courtesy American Broadcasting Companies, Inc.)*

FIGURE 13·12   Newspaper ad from a cross-media campaign. *(Courtesy SFN communications of Florida, Inc.)*

30-SECOND RADIO SPOT FOR "DEADLY CONVENIENCE"

APPROACH	SERIOUS
MUSIC	SOMBER MUSIC UP AND UNDER THROUGHOUT
ANNCR	Wanted! People to work long hours at night . . . alone . . . for little pay. Must be willing to risk injury or death while on the job.
SFX	CASH REGISTER OPENS-SHOT IS HEARD

ANNCR   Last year in the state of Florida more convenience store clerks were killed in the line of duty than police. Watch "Deadly Convenience," a special report on a dangerous occupation, tonight at eleven on the Eyewitness Update on WFTV, Channel 9, Central Florida's news leader.

30-SECOND TV SPOT FOR "DEADLY CONVENIENCE"

VIDEO	AUDIO
UP ON LS OF NIGHTTIME VIEW OF CONVENIENCE STORE	It's one of the most dangerous jobs in America. . .
MCU OF SIGN FOR POLICE CRIME STAKEOUT	Consumer store clerks take maximum risks for minimum wage
REFLECTION SHOT OF STORE IN SECURITY MIRROR	and more of them are killed each year on duty than are police officers.
MS OF TRIGGS IN FRONT OF CONVENIENCE STORE	I'm Steve Triggs. Join me for "Deadly Convenience," an in-depth look at
MS OF COP INSIDE CRUISER DRIVING PAST STORE	convenience store crime . . . what law enforcement is doing to stop it
CU OF CONVENIENCE STORE SIGN. DISS TO SHOT OF EMPLOYEE	and what convenience store chains can do to better protect their employees.
CG: DEADLY CONVENIENCE, STARTING MONDAY 11PM, WFTV, CHANNEL 9	It starts Monday on the Eyewitness News Update.

Courtesy SFN Communications of Florida, Inc.

Note that the theme of the campaign is prominent in each advertisement. Use of the same theme not only achieves cross-media consistency but also means that each advertisement can stand alone. In other words, consumers did not have to see or hear all three ads to understand the message. Each spot or advertisement in a cross-media campaign should be able to communicate the message by itself. Each medium can then be targeted to a separate audience, and together all messages can deliver the total audience.

A good cross-media theme requires cooperation between the copywriter and the artist so that the theme will fit all media. For instance, a slogan like "The yellow pages that are really read" might look fine in print but translate poorly into a radio commercial. A cross-media theme that is strong visually and aurally can achieve high penetration, but it must be adaptable to all the media used in the campaign.

POINTS TO REMEMBER

- The schedule of a broadcast campaign may vary, with spots spread over a period of months or a heavy concentration of spots in a few days or weeks.
- An in-depth analysis of the client's business or service is necessary to develop a viable campaign. Identify the client's strengths and weaknesses. Your client's primary competitors must be evaluated relative to the strengths and weaknesses of your client.

▪ Positioning your client in a campaign allows you to create a separate identity for your client, an identity that helps the public distinguish your client from competitors.

▪ Spots and advertisements for a cross-media campaign should be able to stand on their own.

▪ A consistent sales slogan will reinforce the message across all the media used in a cross-media campaign and will enhance the sale point.

A new product is to be introduced and your advertising agency will compete to handle the account. Prepare a cross-media campaign for this new product. The product: A new tanning product that works anytime—sunshine is not required. It will not stain clothing. The product is appropriate for both men and women who want to maintain a good tan when it is not possible to be outdoors. It is an easy-to-use cream that will not irritate or harm skin and provides a darker tan with repeated usage. The product is packaged in an easy-to-use plastic container.

You are to:

1. Name the product.

2. Prepare a complete copy platform.

3. Create a sales slogan for the campaign.

4. Write two sixty-second radio commercials and two thirty-second television spots for the product. Each spot must be different from the others, although one radio and one TV spot should be aimed at winter users while the other two spots should be aimed at summer users. Prepare storyboards for both television spots. Use the sales slogan.

5. Prepare a rough layout of a newspaper ad for the product. Be certain that the ad uses the campaign sales slogan.

6. Write a strategy statement in which you analyze the selling situation and explain how the advertising for the product will be used to convince the target audience to try this product.

Prepare a cross-media campaign.

1. Obtain brochures or other literature on an existing product or service. Choose from such items as cameras, hair dryers, and health spas. Gather as much information as possible.

2. Prepare a complete copy platform for the product or service.

3. As possible, analyze the strengths and weaknesses of competitors.

4. Write two sixty-second radio commercials using dialog, sound effects, and/ or music. Aim one spot at Christmas shoppers, the other at shoppers for Mother's Day gifts.

5. Write two thirty-second television commercials. Aim one spot at Christmas shoppers and the other at people shopping for Mother's Day gifts. The TV spots must differ from the radio spots.

6. Prepare a rough layout for a Christmas ad and a Mother's Day ad.

7. Write a strategy statement in which you analyze the selling situation. Explain how the advertising will convince the target audience to use the product or service instead of a competing one.

Contact public-service offices on your campus or in your community. Find a nonprofit organization that has a message to communicate to the public but has no budget to prepare it. The health center, for instance, may have an alcohol awareness program, the police department may have a rape prevention program, and the library may have a number of informational programs. When you find a nonprofit organization that wants a public service campaign, gather as much information about the organization and its campaign as you can.

1. Once you've gathered the data, prepare a complete copy platform.
2. Write two radio and/or television PSAs that are appropriate for this campaign.
3. Write a strategy statement in which you analyze the selling situation. Explain how the announcements will be used to convince the target audience of your major objectives.

Prepare a cross-media campaign for Natural View Skylights. A copy information sheet provides you with the following information: Efficient way to lighten a dark room. Provides natural light for plant growth. Light beautifies a room and makes it seem bigger. Skylight uses natural light, not electricity. Skylight has double-layer construction. Reflects the greatest amount of heat out while allowing sunlight in. Insulation seal prevents outside air from seeping in. Skylight will not shatter. Both skylight and installation are guaranteed. Will not leak. Available in three models to fit all homes. Look for dealer in yellow pages.

1. Prepare a complete copy platform.
2. Create a campaign sales slogan to be used in each ad.
3. Write two sixty-second radio commercials for the product. Aim one at a Sunbelt audience, the other at a northern audience.
4. Write two thirty-second television spots. Use the demonstration approach for the Sunbelt audience. Use the problem-solution approach for the northern audience.
5. Prepare two rough layouts for print ads. Orient one ad to the Sunbelt audience and the other the northern audience.
6. Write a strategy statement analyzing the selling situation. Explain how the advertising will be used to convince the target audience to investigate this product.

Glossary

Account. A sponsor on a station or a client of an advertising agency; a buyer of air time.

Account executive. Advertising agency representative in charge of an advertiser's account. May also refer to a station or cable company representative.

Adjacencies. The program or time periods immediately preceding or following a program.

Ad-lib. Remarks not written into the script.

Advertiser. National, regional, or local purchaser of a commercial announcement or program.

Affiliate. A local station that is affiliated by contract with a network.

Agency. A business firm that gives advertising counsel by planning, preparing, and placing advertising for a client in the various communications media.

AM. Abbreviation of *amplitude modulation,* the older of the two technologies of radio broadcasting.

Announcement. Advertising message; also called *commercial* or *spot*.

ASCAP. American Society of Composers, Authors, and Publishers.

Audio. The sound portion of a TV program or announcement.

Availability. An unsold segment of broadcast time.

Bed. Music that is played behind a commercial.

Billing. Charges to advertisers from networks, stations, or cable companies for broadcasting time or services.

BMI. Broadcast Music, Inc.

Board fade. A decrease or increase in volume made at the audio control board. Could be either *board fade out* or *board fade in*. See also **mike fade.**

Break (or station break). Time allotted for local sale between or within programs. May also be used for station identification.

Client. An advertiser.

Cold. A program or commercial performed without rehearsal.

Commercial. An advertising *announcement* or *spot*.

Cross fade. To fade from one sound or music to another. Same as **segue**. This is to *audio* what a *lap dissolve* is to *video*.

Cutaway. Any TV shot that briefly switches attention from the main action to some related activity.

Director. Individual responsible for production of radio and TV announcement or programs.

Disc jockey (also **DJ, d.j., deejay**). The announcer who hosts a program of recorded music.

Double spotting. A station practice of placing two spot announcements back-to-back.

Echo. The effect you get when talking in a large, empty room with hard-surfaced walls and ceiling. The effect is best produced by putting a loud speaker at one end of an echo chamber and picking up up the sound with a microphone. The amount of echo can be controlled by changing the distance between speaker and microphone.

Editing. Revision of copy, or assembly of film or tape segments.

Establish. To bring sound effects or music to full volume, permitting the listener to hear enough to understand the sound or music.

Fact sheet. A list of facts given to an announcer to use in ad-libbing a commercial.

FM. Abbreviation for *frequency modulation,* a radio broadcasting technology that permits a better quality of audio than AM.

Format. The organization of each element within a program; a station's established program pattern. The physical arrangement of copy on paper.

Graphics. Any illustrative material.

Hold under. After establishing the sound effect or music, fading it to background and holding it (as in **bed**) behind the spoken message.

Hook. A strategic device used to involve the audience.

Idiot card. A cue card.

Independent station. A station not affiliated with a network.

Infommercial. A commercial, usually ninety or more seconds in length, that supplies information about a product or service, or about a topic relating to the advertiser's product or service, rather than presenting a specific sales message.

Institutional. A spot designed to promote image rather than product.

Live. Describes a commercial or program performed as it is being broadcast.

Log. The daily schedule of the station's program.

Logo. Symbol or slogan used to designate a program or an organization.

Mike fade. Performers move away from mike (*mike fade off*), or move to on-mike position (*mike fade on*) from off-mike position. Mike fade is a decidedly different effect from a **board fade.** In the mike fade, acoustical relationships change because of the performer's movement. In a **board fade,** only volume changes.

Mike filter. An electronic means for eliminating high and low frequencies. Often used to give the effect of speaking over an unequalized telephone line.

Montage. The *superimposing* of three or more shots to achieve an effect.

Narrowcast. To target programming, usually of a restricted type, to a defined demographic or ethnic group.

Network. A number of broadcast stations linked together by wire or microwave on a regional or national basis.

Package. A series of ready-for-broadcast programs or announcements bought by an advertiser that includes all components.

Production. The planning, preparation, and presentation of a commercial or program.

Promo. An on-air spot promoting one or more programs carried on the station.

Punch. To give special emphasis to a line or spot.

Rates. Charges established by a station for air time.

Reverb. Short for *reverberation*. An electronic device sometimes used in lieu of *echo*, but the effects are not the same.

ROS (run of schedule). Spots not ordered for a specific time period, and scheduled instead at the station's discretion.

Saturation. Intensive use of spot advertising by an advertiser on one or more stations for a specified amount of time.

Schedule. The station timetable.

Script. A broadcast program or announcement that is completely written.

Segue. Same as **cross fade.**

SESAC. Society of European Stage Authors and Composers.

SFX. An abbreviation for **sound effect.**

Sound effect. A reproduction of sounds, achieved by either actual recording of the original or recreation in the studio.

Sponsor. Advertiser who pays for commercials.

Spot. Generally, any commercial announcement; more specifically, commercial time sold independently of a program.

Sustaining. Any program that is not commercially sponsored.

Tag. Name and address of a local sales outlet *tagged* onto a recorded or filmed announcement furnished by a sponsor.

Talent. Actor or announcer who delivers a spot.

Talent fee. The production cost of a commercial for music, announcers, actors, and so on in addition to the time charge.

Traffic. The office that handles all programming and scheduling in a broadcast station.

TWX (pronounced "twix"). A *teletype* or *telex* message; used by television networks to notify affiliates of program changes and other information.

Video. The visual portion of a TV commercial or program.

Woodshed. To rehearse copy or script.

Bibliography

Chapter 1: The Broadcast Copywriter

Broadcasting Publications. *Broadcasting/Cablecasting Yearbook*. Washington, D.C.: Broadcasting Publications, 1986.

Broadcasting Publications. *Broadcasting Magazine*. Washington, D.C.: Broadcasting Publications, 1986.

Eastman, Susan T., Sydney W. Head, and Lewis Klein. "Cable Requirements." In *Broadcast/Cable Programming*. 2d ed., 213–217. Belmont, Calif.: Wadsworth, 1985.

Foster, Eugene S. Chapters 8–11 on broadcast advertising. In *Understanding Broadcasting*. 2d ed. New York: Random House, 1982.

Kleppner, Otto, Russell Thomas, and Glenn Verrill. "The Advertising Agency, Media Services, and Other Services." Chap. 20 in *Otto Kleppner's Advertising Procedure*. 8th ed. Englewood Cliffs, N.J.: Prentice-Hall, 1983.

Chapter 2: The Nature of Copywriting

Bunzel, Reed. "Defining the Creative Myth." In *Guidelines for Radio: Copywriting*. Washington, D.C.: National Association of Broadcasters, 1982.

Jeweler, A. Jerome. *Creative Strategy in Advertising*. 2d ed. Belmont, Calif.: Wadsworth, 1985.

Chapter 3: Copywriting Style— Basic Mechanics

Berner, R. Thomas. *Language Skills for Journalists*. 2d ed. Boston: Houghton Mifflin, 1984.

Kessler, Lauren, and Duncan McDonald. *When Words Collide*. Belmont, Calif.: Wadsworth, 1984.

Malickson, David L., and John W. Nason. "Basic Writing Style." Chap. 5 in *Advertising: How to Write the Kind That Works*, rev. ed. New York: Charles Scribner's, 1982.

Rodale, J. I. *The Synonym Finder.* Edited by L. Urdang and N. LaRoche. Emmaus, Pa.: Rodale Press, 1978.

Strunk, William, Jr., and E. B. White. *The Elements of Style*. 3d ed. New York: Macmillan, 1979.

Chapter 4: Broadcasting Copy Preparation

Ries, Al, and Jack Trout. *Positioning: The Battle for Your Mind*. New York: McGraw-Hill, 1981.

Chapter 5: Motivation

Bunzel, Reed. *Guidelines for Radio: Copywriting*. Washington, D.C.: National Association of Broadcasters, 1982.

Heighton, Elizabeth J., and Don R. Cunningham. *Advertising in the Broadcast and Cable Media*. 2d ed. Belmont, Calif.: Wadsworth, 1984.

Terrell, Neil. "Your Power to Persuade Listeners." In *The Power Technique of Radio-TV Copywriting*. Blue Ridge Summit, Pa.: TAB Books, 1971.

Chapter 6: The Anatomy of a Broadcast Commercial

Bunzel, Reed. *Guidelines for Radio: Copywriting*. Washington, D.C.: National Association of Broadcasters, 1982.

Peck, William A. *Anatomy of Local Radio-TV Copy.* 4th ed. Blue Ridge Summit, Pa.: TAB Books, 1976.

Chapter 9: The Television Commercial: The Mechanics

Barr, David Samuel. *Advertising On Cable*. Englewood Cliffs, N.J.: Prentice-Hall, 1985.

Kaatz, Ronald B. *Cable: An Advertiser's Guide to the New Electronic Media*. 2d ed. Chicago: Crain Books, 1985.

Orlik, Peter B. *Broadcast Copywriting*. 2d ed. Boston: Allyn & Bacon, 1982.

Zettl, Herbert. *Television Production Handbook*. 4th ed. Belmont, Calif.: Wadsworth, 1984.

Chapter 10: Types of Television Commercials

Baldwin, Huntley. *Creating Effective TV Commercials*. Chicago: Crain Books, 1982.

Book, Albert C., Norman D. Cary, and Stanley I. Tannenbaum. *The Radio and Television Commercial*. 2d ed. Chicago: Crain Books, 1984.

Coe, Michelle E. *How to Write for Television*. New York: Crown Publishers, 1980.

Nash, Edward L. *The Direct Marketing Handbook*. New York: McGraw-Hill, 1984.

Chapter 11: The Copywriter as Image Maker

Eastman, Susan T., and Robert A. Klein. *Strategies in Broadcasting and Cable Promotion*. Belmont, Calif.: Wadsworth, 1982.

Levey, Jane F. *If You Want Air Time*. Washington, D.C.: National Association of Broadcasters, 1983.

Chapter 12: The Legal Implications of Writing Copy

Gastfreund, Irving, and Erwin Krasnow. *Political Broadcast Handbook*. 2d ed. Washington, D.C.: National Association of Broadcasters, 1984.

Lotteries and Contests: A Broadcaster's Handbook. 2d ed. Washington, D.C.: National Association of Broadcasters, 1985.

National Association of Broadcasters. *Guidelines for Radio: Promotion*. Washington, D.C.: National Association of Broadcasters, 1981.

Chapter 13: The Broadcast Campaign

Quera, Leon. *Advertising Campaigns: Formulation and Tactics*. Columbus, Ohio: Grid, 1977.

Schultz, Don E., Dennis G. Martin, and William P. Brown. *Strategic Advertising Campaigns*. 2d ed. Chicago: Crain Books, 1984.

Index